ANGLO-RUSSIAN RIVALRY IN CENTRAL ASIA: 1810–1895

Anglo-Russian Rivalry in Central Asia: 1810–1895

GERALD MORGAN

With an Epilogue

by

GEOFFREY WHEELER

FRANK CASS

First published 1981 in Great Britain by
FRANK CASS AND COMPANY LIMITED
Gainsborough House, 11 Gainsborough Road,
London, E11 1RS, England

and in the United States of America by
FRANK CASS AND COMPANY LIMITED
c/o Biblio Distribution Centre
81 Adams Drive, P.O. Box 327, Totowa, N.J. 07511

British Library Cataloguing in Publication Data

Morgan, Gerald
    Anglo-Russian rivalry in Central Asia, 1810–1895
    1.   Eastern question
    2.   Great Britain – Foreign relations – Russia
    3.   Russia – Foreign relations – Great Britain
    I.   Title
    950   DA376.G7

ISBN 0-7146-3179-5

*Photoset in Times by Saildean Ltd and
Printed and Bound in Great Britain by
T. J. Press (Padstow) Ltd, Padstow, Cornwall*

To Geoffrey Wheeler without whom this book would never have been written; and to Anna Hunter for so cheerfully struggling with my early drafts.

Contents

Maps on pp. ix and xii reproduced by permission of Geoffrey Wheeler from his book *The Modern History of Soviet Central Asia.*

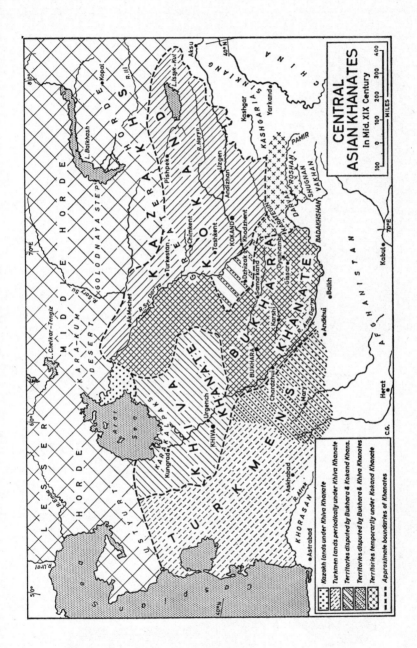

CENTRAL
ASIAN KHANATES
In Mid. XIX Century

MILES
100   0   100   200   300   400

Kazakh lands under Khiva Khanate
Turkmen lands periodically under Khiva Khanate
Territories disputed by Bukhara & Kokand Khans.
Territories disputed by Bukhara & Khiva Khanates
Territories temporarily under Kokand Khanate
Approximate boundaries of Khanates

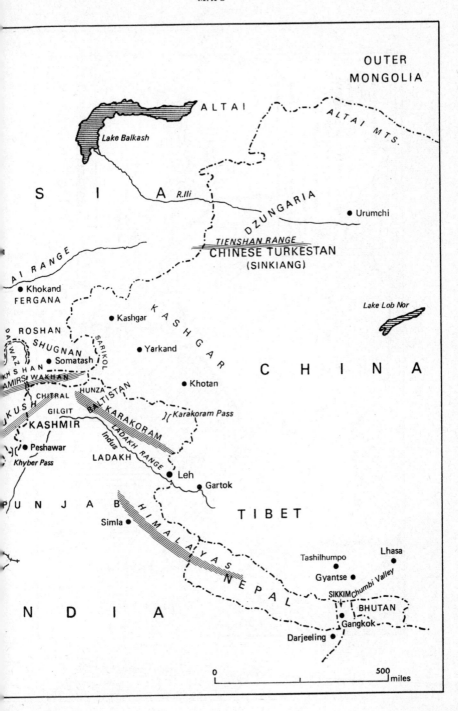

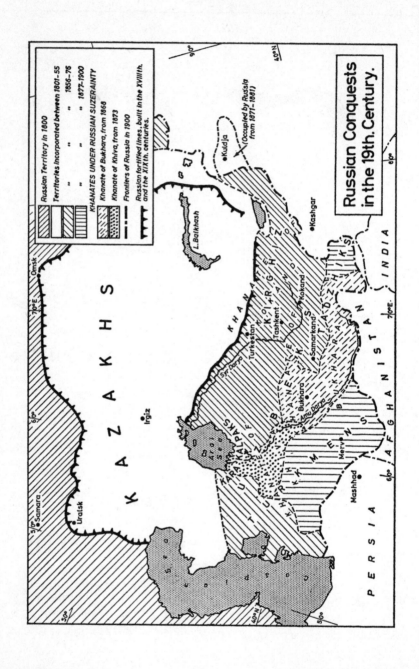

Russian Conquests in the 19th. Century.

Russian Territory in 1800
Territories incorporated between 1801-55
" " " 1856-76
" " " 1877-1900
KHANATES UNDER RUSSIAN SUZERAINTY
Khanate of Bukhara, from 1868
Khanate of Khiva, from 1873
Frontiers of Russia in 1900
Russian fortified lines, built in the XVIIIth. and the XIXth. centuries.

Preface and Acknowledgements

In the course of research for the life of Ney Elias, the remarkable nineteenth century explorer in Asia and for twenty odd years political agent on and beyond the frontier of British India, I came across much interesting material and food for thought which could not be included in the biography. One intriguing subject was the changing British policies dealing with the supposed threat of an invasion of India, and for that matter of Afghanistan, by Russia. Although he contributed so much to India's defences, Elias never believed Russia had any such intention. But many, perhaps a majority, did, including Governors-General, Viceroys and Tory publicists; and the belief still lingers. It was always called the Great Game.

It was Colonel Geoffrey Wheeler, founder of the Central Asian Research Centre, after wide experience in Iran and still a foremost authority on the region and on Russian history of the time, who pointed out to me that no comparative study of the century of rivalry for the control of Central Asia, in particular of Russia's intentions – in the well-known words of the Duke of Wellington 'guessing at the other side of the hill' – had ever been undertaken. He urged me to write a book dealing with these and other relevant issues. Here is the result, and I hope it will clear away a few misconceptions and put the whole of the period of the Great Game into better perspective. I had actually finished the final draft just before the revolutions in Afghanistan and Iran, but as this book is history not prophecy I have only thought fit to alter the very last sentence of the final chapter. Whether or not history repeats itself, this study may incidentally be of some help to those trying to follow and understand current events in this confused region where so much is at stake.

My first acknowledgement must be to Geoffrey Wheeler. Not only did he put me on to translated Russian works I should otherwise never have found but he edited every chapter, answered my innumerable questions – usually from his phenomenal memory – and finally contributed the important Epilogue which will still further enlighten readers, summarizing events from 1895 when this book ends, as far as is possible up to the beginning of 1981. I can never thank him enough. More formally once again I have to thank the staff of the India Office Library and Records (notably Martin Moir) for their invaluable and willing help. I am grateful to the Secretary and the Editor of the Royal Society for Asian Affairs (formerly the Royal Central Asian Society) for the use of the Society's archives and of material which has appeared in the Journal. Other material has also previously appeared in *History Today*. I am grateful to Dr G. J. Alder of Reading University for two of his lucid papers and for other help.

I have much enjoyed the frequent letters of encouragement from John Keay, author in particular of the delightfully written and informative book *The Gilgit Game* (1979). Finally my thanks are due to Mrs Barbara Fitness of the Foreign Office for her impeccable typing of the final draft, and to Peter Howard for reading the proofs.

G. M.

Introduction

Although the term is in general use, *Central Asia* has never been a clearly defined region. In the nineteenth century it was taken in Britain as stretching from the Caspian Sea in the west to the Kansu province of China in the east, and from Western Siberia in the north to the Himalayan approaches to British India in the south. In modern maps this area is shown as occupied by the Kazakh, Turkmen, Uzbek, Kirgiz and Tajik Soviet Socialist Republics, the Sinkiang-Uygur Autonomous Region of China and by the independent state of Afghanistan.

Physically, the western, now Soviet, part of Central Asia can be divided into four regions: the *steppes* of what is now the northern part of the Kazakh SSR; the *semi-desert* of the rest of the Kazakh SSR; the *desert region* lying to the south of the semi-desert; and the *mountain region* of which the main features are the Tien Shan and the Pamirs. Sinkiang consists of a large tableland with a high proportion of desert. From a military point of view the mountainous terrain of Afghanistan is the most difficult, while the Pamir constitutes a total barrier.

The region's climate is one of extremes, the temperature ranging from minus 60 degrees Fahrenheit in the north and in parts of Afghanistan to 120 degrees Fahrenheit in the Amu-Dar'ya (Oxus) basin. Throughout the whole region the population has always been sparse, and during the nineteenth century its total probably never exceeded 20 million. The indigenous population has always been Muslim, being made up of various Turkic and Iranian elements, of which only the Tekke Turkmens and the southern Afghans (Pathans) have shown themselves to be warlike in the past. During the whole of the nineteenth century communications were poor, living conditions primitive, and supplies for an invading army hard to come by.

Western travellers and explorers writing on Central Asia had good reason for giving their books high-flown titles such as Heart, Pulse, Cradle or Cockpit of Asia. Every major wave of migration or invasion inevitably passed through Central Asia, whilst internal conflicts were innumerable. The consequence was that Central Asia never knew peace for long. Its nomad tribes were born to fight and its settlers and town dwellers to be pillaged; it was part of their inescapable heritage; just as for example today Russia and China can never escape from the reality of their common frontier.

From whatever direction they emanated invasions were geographically confined to certain axes. That was because of the barriers of mountain ranges and deserts and the need to move through fertile grazing grounds. Thus the great Hun, Turkic and Mongol invasions from the east mainly followed the Silk Road passing through the fertile valley of the Ili. This was also a trade route and the original means of contact between China and the West. There were minor subsidiary routes crossing the mountains between the Ili River and the Pamir but all led to the fertile region of Western Turkestan beyond the Tien Shan. However no great invasion crossed in the reverse direction: Chinese Turkestan held no attractions for invaders from the west. They had other and richer objectives in view than relatively sparse grazing grounds and the few oases.

Invasions from the west, originating in more civilized countries, all had for their objective the fabulous riches of the Indian subcontinent and of the great oases in Western Turkestan. To reach India they followed two main routes. The first passed south of the Hindu Kush. The second crossed that range from Badakhshan to the north of it, but was confined to certain passes which led into the Himalayan hill states such as Chitral, Kashmir and Ladakh before debouching into the Indian plain. The main route was inevitably the former and the cities of Herat, in north-west Afghanistan, and Kandahar were the natural gateways in those days.

Western Turkestan was an objective common to invasions both from the east and from the west. The lands lying between the Amu Dar'ya and the Syr Dar'ya – the Greek Oxus and Jaxartes – are exceptionally well-watered and fertile and could sustain large armies. Besides lush grazing for horses and cattle they grew grain crops, lucerne and later cotton. There too lay the cities of Tashkent, Samarkand and Bukhara. Mongol and other nomad races from inner Asia had no economic need for the wealth of these cities. For them cities existed simply for plunder, wanton destruction and debauch. Aryan invaders from the west, on the other hand, though often ruthless were less destructive. They exploited the riches they found there. Western Turkestan had one other special advantage common to all invaders from whichever direction they came. The lands between the two great rivers supported a vast population of particularly fine horses combining both speed and stamina. Moreover the horsemen of these lands were notably tough fighting men. Their prowess and their fast horses made them of immense value either as allies or mercenaries to the commanders of all the great invasions, relying as much as they did on speed and mobility. These Turanian or Turkoman horses had been known in the West and to China at least since the first millennium BC and great numbers were exported. A particular breed imported by Emperor Wu from Fergana were called by him the Heavenly Horses. Ultimately they shared with their Arab cousins the foundation of the modern British Thoroughbred. To sum up, whilst Central Asia lay across certain axes to which all invading armies were confined, whoever possessed Western Turkestan gained not only particular economic advantages but great strategic advantages as well. It is no wonder therefore that it has had a turbulent history.

Mountains and deserts served to confine all invasions of India to the fertile regions. On the few occasions when campaigns were launched across mountain ranges they failed lamentably. Thus when Babur tried to invade Tibet from Kashmir his troops met disaster. His nephew Mirza Haidar Ali, author of the *Tarikh-i-Rashidi*, described how he set off with a force of 700 men and brought back only 70. Mountain sickness was only one ailment which took its toll. Invasions apart every nation has to take its inescapable geographical situation into account in its strategic plans. Consider for example the variety of the 2,400 miles of common frontier between Russia and China. In this book the Karakoram, the Muztagh and the Hindu Kush ranges, as well as the geopolitics of Afghanistan, will emerge as being of the utmost importance to India's northern and north-western defence plans. On the other hand, in Russia's southward expansion her problem will appear not as one of mountains but of the Kyzyl Kum and Kara Kum deserts. Matching the word geopolitics it is tempting to coin a word 'geostrategy' to describe such an important factor: readers may consider it is justified.

By the time we reach our period, Central Asia had long been in the trough of a wave. No great leaders had emerged since Babur, founder of the Moghul Dynasty of India, and Nadir Shah. In the nineteenth century possibly Abdur Rahman, Amir of Afghanistan, was potentially a great enough ruler to have filled such a role; but for reasons which will appear, he had no opportunity. Not unlike England in the twelfth century, most of the khans and amirs in the nineteenth century led an uneasy, insecure existence constantly in fear of usurpers, often younger brothers or sons, who would poison them or liquidate them by other equally unpleasant means if they did not administer similar treatment first. Otherwise they carried on desultory feuds with neighbouring khans. Intrigue, treachery and torture were the order of the day. The riches of the great khans such as the Emir of Bukhara living in the oases in more or less medieval style were still great. The riches of the lesser ones were sheep, cattle and horses. At the beginning of the nineteenth century the French traveller Pallas reckoned 'even a nomad of middle means owns 40 to 50 horses, besides huge flocks of sheep'. In 1895 the horse population of the Kazakh steppes was an estimated 4 million, mainly of the small Kirgiz breed. But with no great calls to arms, horse breeding must have been on the decrease, and some British observers from the middle of the nineteenth century were unimpressed with their quality. On the other hand, the American journalist, J. A. MacGahan, who accompanied the Russian expedition against Khiva in 1873, said the Cossacks on their Don horses were no match for the Yomud Turkoman horsemen.

Lacking greater appeals such as a Jehad, or Holy War, the tribesmen themselves, apart from indulging in inter-tribal and family feuds, spent a lot of their time robbing caravans, or crossing the indeterminate Russian and Iranian frontiers to plunder the oases. Russians, Heratis and Persians unlucky enough to be taken prisoner were sold as slaves in the markets of Khiva, Bukhara and Kokand which were the three great khanates in western Turkestan. They were also exported to Kashgar and Yarkand.

Matters in Chinese Turkestan were little different. Over this region, as over Dzungaria to the north of it, China exercised her traditional suzerainty. But the Manchu Dynasty was weakening and the Manchu Government, faced with civil wars, was hard put to it to maintain order in China proper; so Chinese Turkestan was being temporarily abandoned. China also claimed traditional suzerainty over some of the khanates in Western Turkestan, although these khanates had apparently already ceased to pay regular tribute. Only Kokand according to one source still had a Chinese garrison, probably a very nominal one, as late as 1840.

But even if a great leader had arisen in Central Asia he could never have hoped to emulate the illustrious conquerors of the past, such as Babur or his forebear Timur, both of whom were born and bred in Fergana. Times which had remained unchanged for centuries were changing fast elsewhere. Coincidentally with the slow decline of the Chinese Empire in the east, two new great empires, Russia and India, had emerged to the north and south.

CHAPTER ONE

Origins of Russian Expansion in Asia

For the past 50 years the core of Central Asia has formed an integral part of the Union of Soviet Socialist Republics. Its annexation and settlement had already been completed under Tsarist rule and recognized by Britain at the Pamirs Boundary Commission of 1895, followed by the more widely drawn Anglo-Russian Convention of 1907. But the final settlement only marked the end of the last stage of Russia's whole expansion in Asia. The expansion to the south had been preceded by a vast east-wards expansion, simply following the line of least resistance, which had carried Russia through Siberia to the Bering Sea. Like the British expansion in India, its primary incentive was trade.

The eastward expansion was a saga comparable only with all those earlier great waves which had swept westwards through Eurasia. There are several reasons why this cyclic element in Russia's expansion has been obscured. One is that compared with all earlier waves it was slow to gain momentum, although the final stage was accomplished with relative speed. Another reason is that, in strong contrast to earlier waves, the expansion was achieved without widespread warfare, and that was something unique for Asia. A third, and the most obvious one, is that Europe was too occupied elsewhere to realise what was going on till the last stage was nearly reached.

The Mongol wave had lasted nearly two and a half centuries before it exhausted itself with the end of Timur's rule. It was only in the sixteenth century that the hold of the Golden Horde was weakened enough to allow the first stirrings of Russian nationhood. Until then Russia had been a disparate miscellany of small independent states. The nucleus of the movement was in Muscovy, hitherto simply one of many unknown eastern European principalities. The movement itself was begun by merchant adventurers eager to extend their trade at whatever risk. It is surely no mere coincidence that the activities of these landbound Muscovite entrepreneurs began at about the same time as those of the maritime adventurers setting forth from Britain and Europe. The powerful Strogonov family based on Moscow had the same urge and the same drive as Columbus, the Cabots, Raleigh and the other great sailors of those days. The search for new lands and wealth was the same, only the prizes differed for the Strogonovs and their kind. The first great prize was furs, and the sable in particular. The sable, above all, was the fur for royalty and nobility: for instance the British Prince Regent paid £150 each for sable muffs for his favourite ladies. In due course these entrepreneurs brought back riches and were eagerly supported in their rough and ready methods by the rulers of Moscow who found themselves sharing in the new found wealth.

Hand in hand with the quest for furs and later gold and minerals, went colonization. The settlers, from all over eastern Europe, were peasants escaping taxes and army service, as well as land grabbers, criminals and other unscrupulous adventurers. By the end of the sixteenth century the Russians were becoming a nation and with their strongly Christian background, were beginning to be dimly conscious of a national destiny. We are in no position today to comment on the inhumanity and cruelty of those times from which the settlers, exiles and convicts suffered as much as the tribes they dispossessed. But even then there were missions and missionary priests who devoted their lives to alleviating the harsh lot of the convicts: for instance, a German doctor succeeded after years in having the weight of their shackles reduced by two pounds and their manacles lined with leather. The slowness of the advance was by no means due to opposition on the part of the tribes encountered; they were far too primitive to offer any resistance. Their trapping skills were exploited to bring in furs in return for vodka and tobacco which weakened their natural resistance at least as much as the diseases the settlers brought with them.

The main reason for the slow rate of progress was that it was unorganized. For instance, no corn was grown in these virgin lands and pioneers had to bring their own grain or starve: they had to drive their own roads through the forests and build their own bridges. But in spite of the slowness there were big changes during the seventeenth century. The Cossacks had become the first real settlers: they were already settled in the lower reaches of the Don, the Volga and the Dnieper, where they had been notable free-booters. Tough and hardy, they were not daunted by the hardships of Siberia and they were among the leaders in the great quest. When a Ministry of Siberia was set up they became police as well as settlers. By the middle of the century Russia was not only firmly established in Siberia but the first merchant adventurers had reached the Pacific, whither they were shortly followed by the first rush of settlers.

This astounding achievement which had gone largely unnoticed in the West now for the first time impinged on a civilized State. It was a long time before China realised what was happening and for the next hundred years she still had only a somewhat hazy perception. Indeed even when the Sino-Russian Convention was negotiated in 1792, she still regarded Russia as a vassal State. As the Middle Kingdom with the seas on one side and only primitive barbarian races on the other, all of whom she regarded as tributary, she was slow to conceive of any possible threat to her suzerainty other than the historical invasions by nomad races. In spite of the Manchu invasion from the north there simply could not be yet another threat to the existing order of things by a race she had never even heard of.

The Amur province and the great Amur river became the scene of the first clashes. In 1650 a small Russian force of Cossacks defeated the local tribes. There followed a clash with a small Chinese force and that too was ruthlessly defeated. That was just at the time when the weak Ming Dynasty was displaced by the Manchus. But under the first Manchu Emperor, K'ang-hsi, a Chinese force in turn defeated the Cossacks.

Moscow was at this time more concerned with fighting on her European front, and was badly in need of finances. Trade with Peking and hence the establishment of a mission there, was consequently more important than further fighting on the Amur. In 1685 Russian and Chinese delegates negotiated the Treaty of Nerchinsk, the first treaty ever negotiated by China with a Western nation. Both countries tried to define a border, but as they were both equally vague about the geography of the region it was an unsatisfactory treaty; particularly so to Russia because it left the Amur with China as well as giving her a free hand in Mongolia. This was the first of those treaties which today China still claims as 'unequal'. The subsequent Treaty of Kyakhta in 1723 was just as vague. Nevertheless there was peace between the two countries for nearly a century and a half.

The urge to press onwards did not expend itself when the Pacific was reached. The strategic advantage of ice-free ports may have been dimly appreciated, but the greater lure was commerce. On the other side of the Pacific lay Alaska and all the North American coast as far south as California, and thither the pioneers pressed on.

The whole story of the conquest of Siberia with all its dogged heroism, its administrative corruption and its obtuse inhumanity has been graphically and excitingly told by Yuri Semyonov. But at this stage we must leave the eastward expansion and cast back to consider the expansion in western Siberia during the same period. In the light of history this can now be seen in perspective as a rolling back of the previous Mongol wave.

Towards the south and south west the problems facing Russia differed greatly from those which confronted her in eastern Siberia. The break-up of the Golden Horde still left the Muslim Turkic tribes offering a formidable menace to Russian unification and frontier making. These tribes were of Mongoloid origin, and originally hailed from east of Lake Baikal. When Chingis Khan drove into the Near East and Europe they joined in under his banner and they remained there when the Mongols withdrew. That they were only pushed back by slow degrees was partly because they were still formidable and partly because Russia's limited military resources were constantly engaged in Europe from the Baltic, through Poland and the Ukraine to the Black Sea; and there was internal strife as well. Meanwhile the Russians marked each step of their progress by establishing a line of elementary fortifications; a system which they continued to use into the nineteenth century.

The last bulwark of the Turkic tribes was in the Crimea, where their khanates were captured by Turkey at the end of the fifteenth century. That did not prevent them from carrying out frequent raids into Russia with quite large armies which, however, included temporary allies. They were greatly feared for they were as ruthless as their Mongol cousins before them. Ultimately in 1783 Russia, under Catherine II, annexed the Crimea although even then they still retained a considerable amount of autonomy.

The Turkic states of Kazan and Astrakhan were conquered and incorporated in 1552 and 1554 respectively; but only after many uprisings did Catherine II end religious persecution and allow some cultural independence. The result was 100 years of prosperity, which lasted till the conquests in Central Asia in the nineteenth century.

The Kazakh steppes of southern Siberia were acquired gradually from the eighteenth century onwards, with loose protectorates over the khans. The process of constructing fortresses and fortified lines was continued into the heart of the region. The Kazakhs were excused military service and retained their own laws and self-government at local level.

All these annexations were bedevilled from the end of the nineteenth century onwards by the uncontrolled influx of settlers, initially Cossacks and later Russian and Ukrainian peasants. An important effect of their colonization was that there were many revolts against the settlers. Naturally enough the tribes strongly disapproved of their ancestral lands being seized by immigrants whether Christian or Muslim. The nomad Kazakh tribes still remained a formidable nuisance, for they refused to settle, and their activities of slave-raiding and caravan robbery constituted one of Russia's lasting and extremely important frontier problems in the south.

Leaving for the moment Russia's early contacts with Turkey it is appropriate to make an initial survey of her relations with foreign countries to the south; all of them, be it noted, a great deal nearer the motherland than either China in the Far East, or India. Antagonism towards the Turkish Empire had begun very early in Russia's history. A decadent Muslim state as Turkey was already becoming, could not possibly be a good neighbour. Furthermore she blocked what Russia came to regard as her legitimate aspiration to control the Black Sea littoral. Later on, Turkish control of the Black Sea exits of the Bosphorus and the Dardanelles, which effectively blocked Russian access to the Mediterranean, led to wars. It was this conflict which embroiled Britain and France in bolstering up Turkey, and which had important repercussions for India and Central Asia.

Seen in this light, the importance of control of the Caucasus in

Russian frontier strategy has been somewhat overlooked until recent years: it was certainly not recognised by Britain in the nineteenth century. Stretching between a decaying Turkish Empire and an equally effete Iran, it was essential for Russia to gain firm control of the isthmus between the Black Sea and the Caspian. When, in the nineteenth century, she finally achieved it she was in a much stronger strategic position not only towards Turkey, but towards Iran and eastwards beyond the Caspian as well.

In contrast with Christian Russia, a factor common to all the countries concerned was the religion of Islam. Historically Muslims had always tended towards militancy and to be intolerant of infidels. Trading relations with Iran had begun as early as the fifteenth century. By the seventeenth century there had been Russian embassies to Bukhara. Afghanistan lying mainly south of the Hindu Kush was part of the Indian Empire of the Moghuls; but Balkh, on the hither side of the range, was then an independent khanate, although rulers of Afghanistan had always claimed some degree of historical suzerainty and later it was to be recognised as part of Afghanistan.

Prince Lobanov-Rostovsky tells us that at this time Russia was full of travellers' tales of the marvels of India; but as they were based mainly on Marco Polo's descriptions they were out of date by the better part of two centuries. In fact in 1675 the Moghuls rejected Russian overtures on the grounds that the two countries were far apart, that they had never quarrelled, and perhaps most importantly, that they could not become friends because they were of different faiths.

Peter the Great, the first modernizing Tsar, turned his attention towards Central Asia early in the eighteenth century. With K'ang-hsi asserting firm Chinese suzerainty over the whole region of Turkestan, and with the Treaty of Nerchinsk in force, Peter could do nothing in that direction. So he began looking to the south with the objects of finding a route to India which would open up commerce, and of securing cotton from Central Asia for his new textile industries. But in 1717 the Khan of Khiva inflicted defeat on a Russian force and thereafter Peter began to look for a route through Iran. The consequence was two wars; the second of them nearly led to war with Turkey as well, but Peter was too prudent, and he had not the resources, to take on a country backed by Britain. Peter died with his vision of trade with Central Asia and India unfulfilled, but the vision did not die with him.

Nearly fifty years of weak rule elapsed before Catherine II took the throne in 1762. She was Prussian by birth, ambitious, far-seeing and determined to be an autocratic ruler. Her control over the Tatars has been noted and during her reign Georgia seceded from Turkey to Russia. In the south her ambitious designs led in the direction of the great cities of Samarkand and Bukhara. They lay 800 miles to the south of Orenburg, a fortified town which had already been built. Purely in terms of distance and taking no account of geographical obstacles, 800 miles was not far as distances go in Central Asia. By way of comparison the distance to those cities from India, let us say the Indus, was about the same. Under Catherine's rule the line of fortified posts designed to control the nomads of southern Siberia was further extended.

As a western European herself Catherine wanted her country to be accepted and recognised as a major European power. Turkey was her natural enemy on national, religious and economic grounds. Having in her first war succeeded in annexing the Crimea, her second gave Russia access to the Black Sea. When she died she had brought Russia face to face not only with Europe but with Asia, that is to say Iran in the Caucasus. She had further extended Russian controlled and settled territory in what is now Kazakhstan, although there was still no stable frontier in that direction.

Before she died Napoleon had appeared on the European scene. Part of his *folie de grandeur* was a descent on India which would follow after his conquest of Egypt. The idea of a combined Franco-Russian invasion of India appealed to Catherine's successor, the unstable Tsar Paul. But it was an impracticable idea, and although Paul actually assembled an army of 40,000 the project was little more than fanciful. Nelson's defeats of the French fleet at the Battles of the Nile and Trafalgar ended the fancy. But it had alarmed Britain and thus began the great obsession with the landward defence of India which was to last for the better part of a hundred years.

Following through this simple outline of Russia's expansion up to the beginning of the nineteenth century there are still a few more relevant factors to be noticed. There was no scope for democracy in Russia, whose rulers were only slowly knitting the country together. In these circumstances only autocratic rule could hope to prevail, and that was what the Romanovs, some good, some bad, but all with a belief in the greatness of Russia, provided for 300 years. And they provided it against an uneasy background of possible assassination, frequent rebellions and much corrupt administration. Autocratic rule had the great advantage over the Western democratic variety that swings of policy were less frequent. Curiously enough, so far as foreign relations were concerned, the disadvantage that a disastrous policy might go uncorrected was never put to the final test. For all their eccentricities the Tsars nearly always selected sound foreign ministers; some indeed were brilliant. Nor were the key men in the government always from the Russian aristocracy; they numbered Poles and Baltic Germans amongst them.

A primary objective of all the Tsars was to catch up with Europe both in political power and in industry. Yet there is never a sign of any far-sighted Germanic policy of annexation. In the course of this book it will also appear that there is no real evidence, except for Tsar Paul's aberration, of any serious plans to invade India – which is not to say that no plans were ever considered. Up to this time the aim of expanding trade with Central Asia was certainly important, but much less urgent than the opening up of resources within Siberia and of developing trade with China. As the Russian Empire extended inexorably into Asia across Siberia it had found itself entering a region with an incalculable potential for trade and colonization. But towards the south, in the process of settling the Kazakh steppe region, an unexpected danger had begun to emerge. The great Uzbek khanates of the Central Asian oases appeared to be a menace to the settled steppe region. Either by treaty or by conquest and annexation they would have to be dealt with before fruitful trading relations could be developed.

So far there had nowhere been any stable population to be taken into serious account. Thus the lack of organisation which might have proved a weakness in other circumstances had never been put to the test either politically or militarily. Hence, when military campaigns came to be conducted the subsequent administration was naturally military too. Unopposed expansion could not continue indefinitely and we can now see where the checks would be. In the Far East the seeds of future frontier trouble with China had been sown. In the Near East her immediate neighbours were two ill-governed countries, Turkey and Iran (Persia), both of them in a chronic state of near collapse. Only in the south was there as yet no tangible frontier, but the same problem was about to arise there too. Unstable neighbours imply unstable frontiers and the establishment of settled peaceable frontiers was going to occupy Russian statesmen and soldiers throughout the nineteenth century. Rather surprisingly, until half-way through that century Russia believed that the Uzbek states of Kokand, Bukhara and Khiva were all three properly governed nation states, at any rate by Oriental standards, and could be dealt with as such when the time came. She did not discover the reality till she was already confronted beyond them with the political hostility of India and the warlike Afghans of uncertain allegiance sandwiched in between. It was a confrontation which she faced with pained surprise at the very idea that her desire for stable frontiers should be subject to challenge.

CHAPTER TWO

The Indian Background

The beginning of the nineteenth century coincided with the first symptoms of Britain's obsessive anxiety for the landward defence of India. Naturally enough it was in India itself that the anxiety first arose. The East India Company was responsible for the defence of its own territory, but until Napoleon's vain threat to invade the subcontinent, the Company had never had to guard against danger from without, nor even to think about it; now it had to look to its fences.

In spite of the great differences which faced Britain in her development of India compared with Russian expansion in Asia, there was nevertheless at least one common factor which will be discussed hereafter. But having shown the origins and development of Russia in Asia the object here is to discuss some particular influences which affected Indian defence policy in the making. These influences derived from previous experience and as the two nations drew nearer each other they continued to affect British thought and actions.

There was one fundamental difference from the beginning of the nineteenth century. Whereas Russia regarded her expansion in Asia as a logical extension of territory, Britain saw her role as a defensive one against what she regarded as a threat to India. There were of course always those soldiers who would argue that the best defence was to attack, but in the long run they were ignored. In spite of the statements of modern Soviet historians that British policy was ultimately to occupy Central Asia, and to extend what they claim was a system of slavery, no dispassionate reader of this study is likely to conclude that British policy was ever other than defensive or that the annexation of Central Asia was ever seriously entertained by successive British governments as an objective.

Nevertheless, that Britain and Russia were bound to regard each other as potential adversaries was an inevitable outcome of the way in which the two Empires had developed in Asia hitherto.

*　　*　　*　　*　　*

In an address to the Royal Central Asian Society, on 'British and Russian Imperial Attitudes in Asia',[1] Geoffrey Wheeler said 'Although the areas of the two regions are approximately the same, the indigenous population of India, at any rate during the past two or three centuries, has always been more than twenty times that of Central Asia. Climate ruled out the possibility of British colonization in India whereas in Central Asia, except in the extreme south, the climate is eminently suitable for Russian colonization'.

He continued 'Since ... the fourth century AD Hindu culture with its rich creations of literature and architecture had pervaded the whole subcontinent, and Islam began to have an important cultural effect from the eleventh century onwards. Central Asia on the other hand, had virtually no cultural heritage prior to that of Islam, which though firmly established in the south by the tenth century, did not reach the nomads of the Kazakh Steppe until the fifteenth century, and then took only superficial root there'.

Concerning the physical conquest of the two regions he said 'Britain was from the beginning confronted by such warlike peoples as the Marathas, Sikhs and later by the Pathans, and at times by armies trained and equipped by the French. The only warlike people of Central Asia were the Turkmens in the extreme south-west. The armies of the principalities of Bukhara, Khiva and Kokand were only undisciplined rabbles without any modern weapons'.

Wheeler's comparisons show clearly some initial differences of approach. Although it came to be overlooked during the conflict it has to be remembered that the original presence of both countries in Asia was for the purpose of trade; but trade can only flourish under peaceable conditions. Long before Russia met with the problem the East India Company had found itself having to raise an army to protect its stations against surrounding states that were hostile to the Company, to each other, and sometimes to both at the same time. What occupied the Company from its earliest days

---

[1] *Asian Affairs*, Vol 57 (New Series Vol 1), Pt 111. Oct 1970

was the establishment of *cordons sanitaires* within which trade could prosper. Sometimes these *cordons* were established peacefully by treaty, but often the Company had to fight first and negotiate afterwards. The successors of native rulers with whom the Company had negotiated treaties frequently did not live up to the undertakings of their predecessors. Some became openly hostile, others mismanaged their states. To guard against these eventualities all treaties stipulated that in either event the Company would take over the state. Much territory came under its direct rule in this manner. But even by the end of the British Raj over 500 Princely or Native States still remained under indirect rule. The consequences however were expansionist, in spite of the fact that it was very far from the Company's Charter or even its intentions that its territory in India should be extended. In fact the Board of Control consistently urged economy and caution on all its Governors and Governors General, although there were some few who did not observe the injunctions once they reached India. They were just those few whose policies had the greatest effect on the development of the subcontinent.

Pitt's India Act of 1784 specifically sought to prevent wars of aggression and placed the political conduct of the Company in subordination to the policy of the British Government; but it could not stop wars. One significant political factor was that the Moghul Empire was tottering to the point of collapse and every ruler of a native state was keen to seize the opportunity to extend his territory. Civil wars were as bad for the Company's trade as actual attacks on its territory. The political situation of India looked very different as seen by a remote Board of Control in London and by a Governor General five months away in Calcutta. The latter often had no option but to take military action without having time to await the Board's sanction. Thus the Company was somewhat reluctantly forced into the leadership of the Indian political world simply because the only ultimate alternative would have been to abandon trade and the subcontinent too.

The Marquess Wellesley, at the end of the eighteenth century, was the first Governor General to recognise that the interests of India and Britain were interlocked. In his far-sighted view peace and good administration were essential for the prosperity and welfare of India. In pursuit of these aims he nevertheless had to fight expensive wars; but in the end the means proved justified.

Another significant aspect of these interlocking interests was that it was the period of the Napoleonic wars. It was impossible to fight France in Europe whilst at the same time maintaining neutrality in the East, even if Napoleon had been willing, which he was not.

By 1818 the supremacy of the East India Company was assured, but the whole process of British expansion and consolidation only ended in 1849 with the annexation of the Punjab following the death of Ranjit Singh and the quarrels of his claimant successors. The result was a hundred years of peace within India such as its inhabitants had never known, and which was marred only by the Indian Mutiny of 1857.

How basically different therefore were the problems Britain had had to overcome compared with those of Russia by the time they came to face each other. On the one hand, Britain was concerned with defending a vast *overseas* territory acquired at great odds for commercial purposes. On the other hand, Russia was engaged in the logical extension of a vast land-locked Empire for which she had neither had to fight nor deploy any vast resources. She had met with no serious opposition till China checked her further progress in the Far East and Turkey, backed by Western allies, blocked her in the Near East. Not only did expansion in Asia seem to be logical but Russian idealism even saw it as her destiny.

Until the last two world wars the British have always affected to regard war as a game. In fact not only did soldiers discuss war in that light, but even British diplomats commonly used the word as well, whether in peace or war. Nowhere is this affectation more apparent than in India in the nineteenth century. So far as the army was concerned the romantic image helped to offset the daunting realities of active service in a hard climate. Mortality was high, nothing was known about hygiene, preventive medicine was equally unknown and surgery was primitive. Officers taking service in the Honourable East India Company did so without too much hope of ever seeing Britain again. Between campaigns there was only boring life in often unhealthy Cantonments with much drinking, although there was also the chance of sport – for example, pig-sticking, polo and tiger hunting.

But in every soldier's mind – and it applied as much to Russian as to British officers – there was the fantasy that campaigns offered hopes of glory, promotion and medals. In those days such ambitions were quite openly admitted. For example, we find General MacGregor writing in his diary that he might well have earned himself at least a knighthood for his work as Quarter Master General in the Second Afghan War. He even started to write the speech he would make when he returned to Britain. It began in the time-honoured style of being 'a simple soldier more accustomed to fighting than public speaking', at which point he wisely broke off his entry. As he was subsequently severely censured for writing a book *The Defence of India* in which he drew largely on confidential military documents, it is unlikely that he ever delivered his speech. That incidentally is just one example of how chary Viceroys and statesmen had to be of accepting the views of their fiery military advisers. It may have been lucky that British and Russian soldiers never got close enough to each other to start a war by mistake. Written in 1884 MacGregor's book showed where and in what strength the Indian and Russian armies might meet, but he virtually ignored the vital matter of logistics on either side, not only for the war but for any subsequent occupation force.

Simple Empire building patriotism played its part but there was another form of inspiration which was quite common in India at that time and that was Christian evangelism. Some of the early travellers beyond the Company's domains were actuated by the belief that they might spread Christianity amongst the savages. Even the higher ranks were sometimes under the same religious spell. The best-known to the public today was probably General 'Chinese' Gordon, though recent biographies have shown that it was not the only inspiration he had. Less well-known was General Sir William Lockhart who became Commander-in-Chief in India. In the report of his mission to Chitral in 1885/86 he suggested that the loyalty of the Kafiri tribe to India would be best assured by Christianising it – a task which somewhat oddly he recommended should be entrusted to German missionaries.

The romantic image of war as a game survived in India on the North West frontier until the 1920's. Up till then the frontier tribesmen against whom so many punitive expeditions were sent, were regarded rather as sportsmen who observed certain primitive rules and knew what to expect when they broke them. Whilst they behaved there was a considerable rapport between them and the Political Officers. When they transgressed they were punished by fines and, after due warning, the burning of their villages, by which time the inhabitants had taken to the hills. When aircraft with bombs replaced troops on the ground the tribesmen considered it unfair, whilst many British regarded it as unsporting and not playing the game; especially because the tribesmen had a sense of humour which appealed to them, even though they were capable of unprovoked murder. That attitude could not have been more different from the Russian approach to the same situation.

All this leads to a necessary explanation of how the expression 'The Great Game' came to be applied to the struggle for supremacy in Central Asia. Most people believe that it was coined by Kipling in his popular work of fiction *Kim*. His fertile imagination produced many happy inventions but the Great Game was not one of them for it has led to more than one current myth. In any case it was nearly played out when he published the book in 1901 but it had been in use long before then.

Kaye, the historian of the First Afghan War and the author of *Lives of Indian Officers,* himself frequently used the term and was at pains to trace its origin. He concluded that the first user of it was Captain Arthur Conolly of the Bengal Light Cavalry, to whose private correspondence he had access. After a period on sick leave in England and when still only 22 he got permission in 1829 to return to India through Russia and Iran, visiting Bukhara on the way. Back in England again after a successful journey he was in great demand by Members of Parliament to tell what he had seen, and even members of the Cabinet sought his views on Russian intentions. Conolly was deeply religious, and a disastrous love affair before he returned to India served, if anything, to strengthen his evangelistic leanings. In 1834 he became a member of the Political Service which had been formed by the East India Company in 1820. After an abortive attempt to reach Khiva in disguise in which he was captured by robbers but escaped, he was despatched to Bukhara in 1840 for a second time, largely at his own insistence.

Before he left he wrote to a colleague, Henry Rawlinson, then the Political Agent at Kandahar, 'You've a great game, a *noble* one, before you;' and a month later 'If only the British Government would play the grand game ...' It is clear from his correspondence, as well as fully in character, that he was not primarily concerned with the political rivalry between two Christian nations. In his view the game was a spiritual and anti-slavery crusade (at that time numbers of Russians were held in slavery in Bukhara and Khiva). He confirmed his viewpoint in another letter in which he wrote 'We should help Russia cordially to all she has a right to expect – unify Afghanistan, shake hands with Iran ... Thereafter we should civilize and Christianize the rest of the region'. His mission ended in tragedy. He joined Colonel Stoddart who was already in prison there and both men were finally executed in 1842.

It is debatable whether MacNaghten, whose ill advice to Lord Auckland, the Governor General, led greatly to the disastrous First Afghan War gave Conolly the idea of the Great Game. At any rate MacNaghten, who accompanied the army as envoy, wrote in 1840 of the 'beautiful game' to be played, which in his view was to get possession of Herat and coerce the Sikhs in the Punjab. He believed these actions would induce Russia to leave Khiva independent. It is possible that Conolly copied those words from MacNaghten's letter.

To judge by modern books with the Great Game as the title or the theme, the term has come to stay, although nowadays it does not seem to be a very felicitous one. It is misleading if readers new to the subject deduce from it that this whole period of Anglo-Russian rivalry really was a light-hearted affair. In fact nothing could be further from the truth; for nearly a century it was a deadly serious matter, as the participants whatever their affectations truly saw it, with war-clouds often looming menacingly on the horizon. But if it is to be accepted – and certainly the period is as much deserving of a title as the Seven or Thirty Year Wars in Europe – then let it be limited to this particular conflict and not used as it has been in a sub-title to a recent history of Sino-Russian relations, in any other context.

This discussion on the origins of the Great Game has led us rather far ahead of events. One of the earliest men in India to sound the alarm about a possible Russian threat to India was the somewhat eccentric adventurer in Central Asia, William Moorcroft. Moorcroft was a veterinary surgeon, nominally in charge of the Company's stud at Calcutta; but he had wide ranging ideas and a roving spirit. On a free-lance journey in 1812 to Kashmir, Ladakh and Little Tibet he conceived the idea of starting an Indian shawl wool industry. With no authority at all he concluded a treaty with the Maharaja of Ladakh, but the Company was not then interested in Ladakh and promptly disclaimed it. Whilst there he heard of a

Franco-Russian mission at Bukhara which he felt boded no good for India. In 1813 he begged to be allowed to send his agent, Izzat Ullah, and Captain Hearsey to Kashmir to see if the roads behind the 'Himackul' were suitable for artillery in the event of invasion, and thence to Balkh and Bukhara. The cautiously realistic reply of the Governor General, Lord Hastings, was that in his view 'the present situation in Europe differs from your own' and he saw no need to send a political mission to Bukhara or Kashmir. Ultimately in 1823 Moorcroft got permission to go to Bukhara to buy some of its famous horses to improve the Company's stud. But he was wisely refused an official letter of introduction on the practical political grounds that the Amir would expect support from India which it was impossible to give. Moorcroft went, only to be murdered on the way back. His career falls outside our main period but he may be accepted as possibly the first to voice suspicions of the Russian intention at any rate so far as India's northern flank was concerned.

Not all the later Governors General had the ability and judgment of Lord Hastings. Few connect Hastings the administrator and commander in the field with his *alter ego*, Lord Moira. As one of the Prince Regent's staunchest companions he was so extravagant that the Prince Regent had exercised his patronage to get him his Indian appointment to enable him to clear his debts. Unfortunately for him, though not for India, he lived in such state that at the end of his term of office he was still as much in debt as at the beginning.

Whether or not Moorcroft's own warning was later taken seriously, the fact remains that plans for the defence of India against invasion began to be seriously considered for the first time. By 1840 the much debated 'forward policy' had emerged. Hitherto it had only been discussed in imprecise terms, and in India there were many ideas as to how it should be carried out. Its origin lay not in the Russian threat, but in Napoleon's at the beginning of the century during the period of Lord Minto's Governor Generalship. It was then decided that Iran was the key to any French threat and from then on Britain tried to bring her within the British sphere of influence. The French threat evaporated, but whilst some progress was made in southern Iran, notably in controlling the ports which flanked the sea route to India, Russian influence developed in the north. Iran was between two fires. Liking neither Britain nor Russia and, because it was an ill-governed corrupt country, never receiving whole-hearted British support, she had perforce to look both ways. Not only British but Russian officers helped to train the Iranian army, with equally indifferent results.

The British Foreign Minister at the time was Lord Palmerston, as popular with the British people as he was disliked and distrusted abroad. Palmerston claimed 'We have no eternal allies and no perpetual enemies, our interests are eternal and those interests it is our duty to follow'. On the whole he was an improviser in foreign policy and at times was erratic. But though he always denied disliking Russia he certainly distrusted her, particularly with India in mind. He assumed office at a crucial period for British influence with Iran. By the Treaty of Tehran in 1814 Iran had undertaken to oppose the entry of European armies into Iran or India and to use her influence with the Khans of Khiva, Bukhara and Samarkand to the same end. But after Britain had failed to help Iran when Russia declared war against her and seized the greatly coveted Caucasus, such influence as Britain had in the country understandably waned; and with it any real hope of making Iran the outer zone of an Indian defence system. Palmerston tried to restore it through the strongly anti-Russian Sir John McNeill, appointed as Minister to Tehran. However, by that time Iran, to compensate for her territorial losses to Russia and feeling abandoned by an ally, had designs on Herat, formerly an Iranian province; later it was to become a province of Afghanistan but at that time it was virtually independent. McNeill having failed to dissuade Iran from her intentions, Palmerston abrogated the treaty and that was really the end of the policy of making her a buffer state under British influence, although McNeill never gave up trying. It was a policy which the Duke of Wellington never thought practicable and the Duke was undoubtedly right. Politically and economically it would have proved impossible to support such a chronically unstable country. Strategically Britain could only reach south Iran by the long sea route. Russia on the other hand was merely on the other side of the border. She was favoured geographically speaking, by possessing interior land lines of communication with short distances whereas the British Empire had to rely on long, costly and slow exterior sea lines.

Hitherto control of Britain's Iranian policy had shuttled between the Foreign Office and the East India Company, depending on whether first Canning and then Palmerston wanted to placate Russia, but always with the Company the principal supporter of the Iran buffer policy. The formation of a new policy was now relegated to the Company. So the power struggle began with the Company trying to establish a modified forward policy aimed at control over Afghanistan in some form but still hoping to maintain the independence of the Central Asian khanates. The establishment of a viable policy on these lines was made infinitely more difficult by British ignorance of the whole region and by the haphazard way in which the Company set about making good the deficiency.

It is a truism that policy and military plans must be based on the best information available; but in India there was virtually no reliable information at all, either about Central Asia or just as importantly about Russian intentions there. The fact that Khiva was 930 miles from Herat, which was about the same distance again from India, was ignored. So too were any possible Russian strategic difficulties. All that mattered was that Russia must be forestalled before she could reach Herat.

CHAPTER THREE

Britain's First Moves

By 1838 the momentum of events leading to the Great Game was gathering force. There were rumours that Russia was preparing an expedition against Khiva. In England anti-Russian feeling was very strong. Inevitably such a move was seen as evidence of an increasing threat to India. In Russian government circles British intentions in Afghanistan, Iran and Central Asia were all regarded with like suspicion. There was a belief, which had a readily understandable and indeed justifiable basis in Russian eyes, that Britain intended to absorb the khanates of Central Asia. That belief caused Russia to hasten her preparations for a campaign to capture Khiva. The early explorers, such as Conolly and others of whom more later, who were haphazardly trying to fill the void of ignorance of the region, were of course regarded as spies, just as Britain regarded their Russian counterparts. Afghanistan had had less experience of Western contacts than any other country in the Middle East and Central Asia, and was strongly averse to any more; but with the collapse of the British forward defence policy based on Iran, Afghanistan was now to become the object of a military campaign aimed at forestalling Russia, and its establishment as a buffer state. Just how Indian relations with that country should be developed was the subject of much argument in military and political circles. Military extremists wanted complete occupation, in other words to expand India still more. They argued that whoever held Herat, the traditional gateway through which the armies of Alexander and Babur had passed, held the key to India's defence. Others, more realistically, pointed to the problems of administering a country with such turbulent tribes, sparse resources and limited communications. They favoured the establishment of an independent unified Afghanistan under a weak ruler subservient to India.

There were some who argued that safety for India lay in having a frontier actually co-terminous with Russia which both countries would be bound to respect. They took the frontiers of Western Europe as their example – unreliable though it had so often proved. There was a third school, very influential in the early days, and always more intellectual, which held that because of all these difficulties, India's defence should be based on her natural strategic barriers: that is to say the sparse region of Baluchistan to the west and the great mountain ranges north-westward from the Hindu Kush to the Himalaya in the north. The rivers Indus and Sutlej, when made navigable, would be important as lateral lines of communication. The treaty with the Sind states was a step in that direction. A treaty with Ranjit Singh of the Punjab would help to protect the north-west still more. They believed Russia was too poor to sustain an attack on India. If she did she would become immersed in the Afghan morass, at the end moreover, of long lines of communication. This had actually been the policy of the Governor General Lord William Bentinck, which later came to be known rather loftily and loosely as that of 'masterly inactivity'. There was much to be said for it, politically as well as strategically; for example if Russia really had no designs on India as she professed, Indian activities in Afghanistan would be an expensive waste of effort. In India as events turned out the first and third schools of thought alternately had their day.

It was against a background of rumour, suspicion and ignorance that in 1835 Lord Auckland, a fervent Whig, took up his post as Governor General. He was a mild-mannered bachelor and even from his portrait he might be judged somewhat ineffectual – not at all the prototype of an Indian proconsul. He had previously held comfortable posts as President of the Board of Trade and subsequently at the Admiralty and was the personal choice of Melbourne and Lord Palmerston, the Whig Foreign Secretary, because of his amenability and his flair for administration. To help maintain his Viceregal state he took with him two unmarried sisters of whom the faithful, devoted Emily, who had once been courted by Lord Melbourne, was to keep house for him for twenty years. Although not a dominating type her face shows far more character than her brother's: in one of her many letters from India she wrote that she was his sole confidante. She never expressed her political views on paper but it would be surprising if in respect of Russia they differed from the popular one in Britain. The contemporary diarist Greville confirms that she had great influence over her brother, but that she was wrong-headed. One cannot help recalling that wayward indecisive Balkan king of more recent years who, it was said, always took the advice of the last person to offer it. As the last person at the end of the day was usually his mistress, a lady of great determination, he was the despair of his ministers.

From the start Auckland did not lack advice. He had received the usual caution against extravagant action from the Company's Board of Control before he left England. Its President at this time was the Whig politician, Sir John Cam Hobhouse, afterwards Lord Broughton. As President he was also *ex officio* a member of the Cabinet. Since their Cambridge days he had been the closest friend and travelling companion of the poet Lord Byron until Byron's death in 1824. Afterwards he had advised and helped the family in trying to sort out the poet's chaotic affairs.

As his gossipy diaries show, Hobhouse was a *bon vivant* who moved freely in that Whiggish social circle which was headed by Lady Holland and graced by Macaulay amongst other leading thinkers, politicians and socialites of the day, including for a time Lord Byron. He had once been an ardent radical and was committed to Newgate prison for contempt of Parliament. He was not particularly anti-Russian and among his many friends was Baron von Brunnow the Russian ambassador from 1840. He shows a clear preference for domestic politics over his duties as President of the Board of Control to which he was appointed in 1835, and as head of its Secret Committee which was mainly responsible for its policy. Indeed his correspondence and diaries concerning the First Afghan War and afterwards show that he played a distinctly ambivalent role in that affair. As a negotiator he showed a certain smoothness. For example Kaye tells us that von Brunnow said to him: 'If we go on at this rate, Sir John, the Cossack and the Sepoy will soon meet on the banks of the Oxus'. Hobhouse's cool reply was 'Very probably – much as I should regret the collision I should have no fear of the result'. Palmerston had already made much the same comment to Hobhouse in a letter in February 1840, adding, with his 'forward policy' in mind, 'It should be our business to take care that the meeting should be as far off from our Indian possessions as may be convenient and advantageous to us. But the meeting will not be avoided by our staying at home to receive the visit'.

Hitherto the Board of Control had believed Russia had designs on Bukhara and Khiva which might ultimately lead to an attempt on India; but its policy for some years had been one of non-intervention. In the short term its main fear was that the threat might lead to internal unrest in the subcontinent, and that was why she must not be allowed to advance into Central Asia. The Board hoped to frustrate Russia there by subsidising the khanates and increasing the Company's trade with them. Its optimistic view was that British influence would surely supplant Russian as the khans came to see where their more profitable interests lay. There was an important adjunct to this policy, which had the same end in view. It was that Britain should intercede with the khanates to free their many Russian captives. It had been the custom of Khiva for many years, to take prisoner Russians working on the shores of the Caspian and sell them as slaves to other khanates. The freeing of these slaves as well as others from Turkey, Iran and Herat, was the chief reason put forward by Russia for her increased activity in Central Asia – a worthy cause for a devoutly Christian country. Arthur Conolly thought fairly enough that Russia was under great provocation and that justice could not deny her the right to invade Turkestan.

In 1838 when British action in some form was contemplated in Afghanistan, Conolly was consulted by Hobhouse. He suggested that Russia might cease her pressure if the British could negotiate the release of the captives. It was an ingenuous view of Russian aims but Hobhouse and Palmerston, then Foreign Secretary, both thought the idea worth trying and it was actually put into action by Auckland to whom the idea also appealed. It was linked with the necessity for gathering information and thus became a diplomatic object of some of the early players. Laudable and idealistic as it was, it showed all too little understanding of Russian views on Central Asia.

Auckland's predecessor, Lord William Bentinck, had maintained Britain's policy of non-intervention in Afghan affairs. Confronted with the warlike rulers of Sind and the Punjab he had negotiated a treaty with Sind in 1834 and had regarded the opening up of the River Indus to navigation as a line of communication which could become important for India's defence. When Auckland first arrived in India he too was against intervention. Following the Board's briefing he did not then fear direct Russian aggression against

India, but he had not anticipated any interference with Herat on the part of Iran. His aim in Central Asia was to extend British influence there by commercial activity in accordance with the Board's policy. He rightly regarded Central Asia as the diplomatic responsibility of the Foreign Office. As usual however the view from India differed greatly from that of Westminster. In 1826 Shah Shuja had lost his throne at Kabul to Dost Muhammad who was faced with the difficult task of re-uniting Afghanistan. Dost Muhammad was a politician rather than a soldier: for instance one of his peace-making methods was to choose his wives from the families of powerful chiefs of the more troublesome regions, as well as from merchants and religious leaders. He was the first ruler of Afghanistan to seek European military advice though he was not always well served. Up to a point his re-unification policy was showing success, but Herat was independent and antagonistic and his claims to Peshawar were opposed by Ranjit Singh who held that it was part of his kingdom. Nevertheless, given the limitations of any ruler in Central Asia seeking to maintain his throne and his own life, and at the same time to extend his rule, here was a man with whom Britain might treat if she could decide on a policy: moreover Dost Muhammad had indicated his readiness to treat with Britain.

In India the allegiance of Herat to Afghanistan, in whatever form it might be achieved, was regarded by the majority of opinion as crucial. Soon after Auckland's arrival it became clear that Iran was intent on annexing Herat, which historically had once been an Iranian province, to compensate herself for her recent territorial losses to Russia. McNeill, the Minister at Tehran, had good grounds for alleging that Iran was being encouraged by Simonich the Russian Minister there. If Herat was lost to Iran, it was feared in India, more acutely than by the Board of Control, that the consequent unrest in Afghanistan would extend into India. That, said all the Russophobes, would create the opportunity for Russia to stir up further trouble for which her preparations for a campaign against Khiva were but a prelude.

There were still powerful advocates of a stationary policy, who refused to be stampeded by the Russian bogey. Foremost amongst them was Mountstuart Elphinstone who had visited Kabul in 1809 and had made a special study of Afghanistan thereafter. Not only was he the author, in 1815, of *An Account of the Kingdom of Cabool* which was still the standard work on the country, but from his post as Resident at Peshawar he was at pains to keep in touch with current events in Afghanistan. He interviewed returning travellers and traders and was the first to introduce the 'newswriter' service whereby Indian residents in the chief towns wrote him informative letters about tribal activities. What he established was a rudimentary local information service and he was indeed the first Company servant to appreciate the need for up-to-date information. Elphinstone was ahead of his time, for he and his equally intellectual contemporary, Sir Charles Metcalfe, both shared the opinion that Indians should be educated with the ultimate object of the independence of India in view. Unusually for their day neither of these men had evangelistic motives. Metcalfe had been acting Governor General between the departure of Bentinck and the arrival of Auckland, but in spite of his proved experience he was passed over for the appointment of Governor General simply because he was a permanent servant of the Company and the post was a political one. The story of the next fifty years would have been very different if he and Elphinstone had been heeded, for Metcalfe too saw the value of natural barriers and the dangers of becoming embroiled in Afghanistan.

Another influential servant who partly shared their views was Captain Claude Wade, the Resident at Ludhiana, appointed to watch over Shah Shuja whilst in exile there. He was strongly against active intervention in Afghan affairs and argued the case against uniting the tribes. But he advocated the installation of his protégé as a puppet ruler under firm British control. Auckland was inclined to accept his advice, which accorded equally with his briefing in London and his own natural inclinations. But he soon became so alarmed by the rumours about Khiva as to decide that some form of positive action in Afghanistan was essential. Unsuited by temperament to the situation which faced him and utterly unversed in strategy, he was from now on at the mercy of his advisers – and they were many.

Since Elphinstone the only officials to visit Afghanistan had been Henry Grant, Charles Christie and Henry Pottinger all of whom were in the Company's service. They were followed in 1829 by Edward Sterling who travelled from England to India through Khorasan and Afghanistan, only to be dismissed by the Company when he reached India. Now that up to date information was urgently needed, Alexander Burnes was instructed by Auckland to go there. He was chosen because of the success of his two previous missions, in 1828 to Ranjit Singh at Lahore, and in 1832 to Bukhara. On his way back from Bukhara he had been favourably received by Dost Muhammad in Kabul. He set out in 1836 with instructions which gave him scope to try and extend British commercial influence in Central Asia, whilst his other main task was to find out what was going on in Afghanistan, Herat and the small states north of the Afghan Hindu Kush.

Burnes's views and actions had a most disturbing effect on Auckland who complained to Hobhouse that he found him difficult. By the time he made his first report Herat was under siege by Iran and McNeill in Tehran had reiterated his view that if Herat fell it would destroy any chance of British influence in Afghanistan: furthermore it would put a major part of the country under Iran and hence ultimately of Russia. That too was how Burnes saw it, and on behalf of India he promised Dost Muhammad that all his expenses of a campaign of recovery would be paid if Herat did fall and Kandahar was menaced. In effect he was offering the Amir strong military aid. Burnes had made a considerable impression on Dost Muhammad who undoubtedly would have preferred to have British backing, but the Amir was a notable intriguer and an apt exponent of the art of keeping his options open. Whilst negotiating with Burnes he was negotiating with Iran too over Herat. He also had designs on Peshawar which he hoped to annex from the Sikh kingdom of the Punjab and which India strongly disapproved of. But even more importantly from the British point of view were his negotiations with Russia. That, in the anti-Russian climate of the day, was quite inadmissible to Britain.

The basis of Wade's recommended policy, which had at first appealed to Auckland, was that if Dost Muhammad's policy of consolidation was supported the result would be that others would rise up against him, with the consequence that India would certainly lose Herat; hence his preference for a British policy of *divide et impera* towards the disparate Afghan tribes with the defence of India based on the Indus line and a treaty with Ranjit Singh. He preferred a weak Shah Shuja and the renewal of his former treaty with Ranjit, to a potentially strong Dost Muhammad; but Burnes's forceful arguments for the policy of uniting Afghanistan, including Herat, under our control, swung Auckland in his direction and away from Wade.

Unfortunately, however, for Burnes and ultimately for Dost Muhammad too, he had promised a virtual military alliance which the Amir expected would enable him to annex Peshawar. That was well beyond Burnes's powers, which in fact had limited him to commercial backing for his protégé. When Dost Muhammad found he was not getting all the military backing he expected and that Burnes was little better than a commercial agent he lost faith in the British and continued his negotiations for a treaty with Russia. As soon as the news of this double-dealing became known it brought a sharp reaction. Burnes was ordered to withdraw his mission. In London it was decided that Dost Muhammad was not to be trusted or dealt with, and in India Auckland dropped Burnes as well as his protégé. In 1837 the news of a Russian mission to Kabul further strengthened Auckland's leaning towards urgent military intervention, and in this he was supported by Palmerston and Hobhouse. It also stimulated a wave of anti-Russian public feeling.

McNeill, in Tehran, was in frequent correspondence with both Palmerston and Auckland. He feared that if Iran captured Herat the Shah would be in a position to bargain with Britain. He believed that by threatening to create unrest in India and give passage to Russia, the Shah would hope to get British aid. McNeill also told Auckland that the countryside between Iran and India was more productive than was realised. He said it could support an army of 100,000 between the Caucasus and the Indus and consequently represented no security as a buffer for India. This, at best, was a wild surmise with no facts or reliable information to support it. But McNeill's fears played on Auckland's dilemma, and so too did the frequent reports of Russian preparations for the Khivan campaign. From London the Cabinet, advised by Palmerston, instructed him to take decisive action in Afghanistan but without specifying any form. Palmerston appears to have thought that Afghanistan was actually on the Indian frontier, and therefore not to have realised that at that time the Punjab, Sind and the Rajputana desert lay in between. In this situation, with the strongest protagonists of both the stationary and the extreme forward policies out of favour, Auckland resolved his indecision with a compromise which was approved in London, though not entirely unanimously. It was to establish a puppet state in Afghanistan to act as a buffer and thus to create a balance of power. Palmerston lent his support by threatening force against

Iran and instructing McNeill to break off relations with the Shah. At the same time he made strong protests to St. Petersburg against Russian activity both in Iran and in Central Asia. He also applied indirect pressure against Russia by giving support to Turkey just when it looked as though Russia might be seeking justification – as for instance the protection of Turkey's Christian subjects – for some form of control over the country.

Although McNeill played an important part, the man ultimately responsible for persuading Auckland to adopt the puppet state plan was Sir William MacNaghten, his Chief Secretary. Mac-Naghten, like other 'politicals' of his day, had a flair for languages though he had spent nearly all his service in Calcutta as an administrator. He had had a little practical experience of dealing with Indian States and even of the North West frontier, though not nearly enough to appreciate all the latter's multifarious tribal complications. But he had had no experience at all of working with the army in India and clearly had no knowledge of strategy. He was violently anti-Russian and in personality was both self-confident and over-optimistic. In fact he was just the kind of man to appeal to an indecisive Governor General: moreover he was always at his elbow.

The original plan was to persuade Ranjit Singh, the 'Lion of the Punjab', to send an army to defeat Dost Muhammad and to re-instate Shah Shuja-ul-Mulk whom Dost Muhammad had deposed. Shah Shuja was now an old man living comfortably at Ludhiana. To support him when re-instated it would be necessary to send an army from India. Part of the appeal to Ranjit Singh to launch a campaign was that Dost Muhammad had designs on Peshawar which Ranjit regarded as part of his Sikh kingdom. MacNaghten went to Lahore to negotiate the necessary agreement with him and to persuade Shah Shuja to accept the plan. In Afghanistan Shah Shuja had already proved himself a weak ruler. Now he did not much trust either Ranjit Singh or the British: it was only with considerable reluctance and the promise of generous rewards and support that he agreed to go back.

Meanwhile Lieut. Eldred Pottinger, a young Political Officer then in Afghanistan, had been sent on a single-handed mission to Herat to find out what was going on. There he took on himself without orders the task of encouraging a somewhat reluctant Amir of Herat not to give up the city to Iran, and furthermore to organise its defences. It was a big test for a young man, but he successfully carried out his self- appointed task to hold Herat, without receiving any further instructions from India. In view of Auckland's reputation for indecision it is worth pointing out that at least he firmly withstood Palmerston's urgings to send a force to Herat.

Apart from all the political and geographical ignorance concerning Afghanistan, little if any thought was given to the organization of a campaign on the scale envisaged, and the military and diplomatic arrangements were in different hands. The Commander-in-Chief in India, Sir Henry Fane, was an old man like all the other senior soldiers of his day, who had reached the top by rota and not by merit, by which time they were set in their ways and long past the ability to conduct a war. It is only fair to say that his acquiescence in the plan was reluctant. Tactics had not advanced since Britain fought Napoleon. The problems of administering a large army at the end of a long line of communication, through potentially hostile tribal territory and a sparsely cultivated country, were never faced. No wonder men of experience of Indian warfare like the Duke of Wellington and his elder brother the Marquess Wellesley at home, besides Elphinstone and Metcalfe in India, were against the Afghan campaign and foresaw disaster; Wellington said it would 'mean a perennial march on Afghanistan'. But they were all ignored. At home Hobhouse approved the principle but left the plan to Auckland. Palmerston, having written to Auckland of the excellent effect of making Afghanistan a British and not a Russian dependency, trusted the rest to the Governor General although not without later misgivings.

The initial plan was modified when Auckland was persuaded that if it was left to Ranjit Singh – a great warrior in his day, but then senile – to defeat Dost Muhammad, the operation would fail. Instead Auckland adopted Fane's plan, which was to send a 'Grand Army of the Indus', merely supported by some of Ranjit's and Shah Shuja's troops. The modified plan involved an advance through Sind, in complete contravention of Britain's recently negotiated treaty of independence for its Amirs. Kaye says that while many in India believed that a campaign to help Dost Muhammad to hold Herat would be justified, British opinion there was against a war with the object of replacing him. As it happened, thanks to Pottinger's energy on one side and McNeill's persuasive powers on the other, Iran had raised the siege of Herat before the army of the Indus set out. Moreover the Tsar had disowned the Vitkevich mission to Kabul, which will be referred to later, and Nesselrode his Foreign Minister assured Palmerston that no move against India was intended: the most immediate fears of a direct threat to India were thus removed. There would still have been time to call off the whole operation: but Palmerston did not suggest it, and apparently Auckland did not consider it. Even if he had, Emily Eden would perhaps have stiffened his resolve not to change his mind again. Besides, in his eyes and those of his now accepted advisers, the Russian bogey still loomed beyond.

So under Sir John Keane, a sick and feeble man, an army of 9,400 fighting men set out with a supply train of no fewer than 38,000 camp followers and 30,000 camels. MacNaghten – impulsive, enthusiastic, and inexperienced – appointed himself to accompany the army as Envoy to Shah Shuja. The army reached Kandahar in April 1839 and initially the operation succeeded. Dost Muhammad was exiled to India and Shah Shuja was installed at Kabul. But for the next two years the Company had to keep 4,500 troops in Afghanistan as an army of occupation. Soon there was increasing opposition to Shah Shuja from Afghan tribes. Burnes, now the Agent at Kabul, and Henry Rawlinson, the Agent at Kandahar, warned MacNaghten of trouble brewing, but he ignored them both. He made much use of bribes to tribal chiefs, and according to Kaye, continued to regard the campaign as 'a beautiful game' to frustrate Russia. By this time he was in open collision with the military authorities and complaining of their lack of support. The army was scattered in isolated detachments whose commanders were at loggerheads with the ineffectual occupation force commander, General Elphinstone at Kabul, and the troops behaved badly towards the tribesmen and their womenfolk. There was much corruption over the purchase of supplies, and the cost of living became a major factor of Afghan discontent. When the tribes rose in 1841, Burnes and Shah Shuja were assassinated in turn. Thereafter the only prudent course was to withdraw the army, but Elphinstone could not make up his mind, and MacNaghten continued to advise against withdrawal until he himself was assassinated. When Elphinstone finally ended his vacillations it was far too late in the year. The resultant winter retreat of 1842, harried throughout by savage tribesmen, was possibly the worst disaster in British military history. Only one man of the garrison at Kabul and a few subsequent stragglers reached Jalalabad. Elphinstone died in captivity; most, including wives and families and camp followers, suffered worse fates. The disaster shook the faith of the Company's Indian soldiers, and may have sown the first seeds of discontent which ultimately led to the Mutiny of 1857.

The Russian campaign against Khiva in November 1839 had also ended in a disastrous retreat; it is ironical that this campaign was really intended, even though not specifically stated, as a counter to the British expansion in Afghanistan. The Russian disaster, however, was caused by the climate. It happened after the raising of the siege of Herat had finally removed any immediate threat to India; but the implications of Russia's military weakness were lost on the ill-advised Governor General and apparently on Palmerston too. Thus the best chance to withdraw the army from Afghanistan just when it had achieved its immediate object was lost.

Auckland had swung from indecision to blind determination. In fact indecision, political ignorance, military incompetence and lack of coordination were the hallmarks of the First Afghan War and its aftermath; yet curiously enough there was no subsequent witch-hunt. Later, in conversation with Hobhouse, Auckland blamed his military authorities for 'the horror and disaster', but stood by his policy. He himself finished his term as Governor General and in 1846 was re-appointed to his old post as First Lord of the Admiralty. MacNaghten, who in India was perhaps the evil genius behind the whole enterprise, and who in Afghanistan tried to exercise too much authority over the army, was nevertheless appointed by Hobhouse to be Governor of Bombay. As it happened he was assassinated just as he was about to leave Kabul. Macaulay commented tartly that it was perhaps fortunate for him, for had he lived he would have had to bear all the responsibility of the recent disasters. At home the papers of the Secret Committee of the East India Company, describing the débacle, were alleged by Kaye to have been censored so as to minimise the extent of the disaster.

Following the lead of J. A. Morris in his book *The First Afghan War 1838–1842*, G. J. Alder has scrutinized all the evidence and considers Kaye's allegation to be without foundation: there was no wilful garbling of the 1839 Blue Books either by Hobhouse or Palmerston; it was solely a matter of editing the large number of lengthy despatches from India.[1] On the other hand, Michael Joyce in his book, *My Friend H.*, has pointed out that while the extracts themselves were marked as such in the books, there had been excisions in some of them which had not been marked. He quoted a letter of 1839 from Palmerston to Hobhouse which suggested that the former was responsible for them. The general effect of the Blue Books had been to show that Auckland had pursued the right policy in replacing Dost Muhammad by a puppet.[2] The omissions only appeared when the despatches were published in full in 1859. Hobhouse had successfully defeated critics of his and Auckland's policy (among whom was Disraeli), in 1842. Palmerston, however, was attacked on the subject at intervals for the next twenty years – finally by the Radical John Bright – and his reputation suffered thereby. The bone of contention centred round the omission of any reference to Burnes's despatches in which he disagreed with Auckland.

In 1841 the Tories ousted the Whigs, Palmerston and Hobhouse lost their offices and a Tory government under Sir Robert Peel appointed, as the next Governor General, Lord Ellenborough who had previously succeeded Hobhouse in the post of President. He sent an army to release the prisoners still held by the Afghans and to re-establish British prestige by exacting retribution on Kabul, by means which many considered inflamed Muslim opinion more than was necessary. Without orders he also annexed Sind. Having wrought vengeance on Kabul he then, at the end of 1842, issued the Simla Proclamation, which blamed his predecessor's policy for the disasters which had occurred. In it he said 'The British army.... will now be withdrawn to the Sutlej. The Governor-General will leave it to the Afghans themselves to create a government.... To force a sovereign upon a reluctant people would be as inconsistent with the policy as it is with the principle of the British government.... The Governor-General will willingly recognize any government approved by the Afghans themselves which shall appear desirous and capable of maintaining friendly relations with the neighbouring states'. The Proclamation continued, 'The rivers of the Panjab and the Indus and the mountainous passes and the barbarous tribes of Afghanistan will be placed between the

---

[1] G. J. Alder, *The Garbled Blue Books of 1839 – Myth or Reality? The Historical Journal* XV, 2. 1972.

[2] M. Joyce. *My Friend H.* John Murray. London. 1948.

British army and an enemy approaching from the west – if indeed any such enemy there can be – and no longer between the army and its supplies'. Because of this proclamation and the annexation of Sind, Ellenborough was recalled by the angry Court of Directors, against the Government's wishes. The cost of the whole Afghan affair had nearly ruined the Indian economy (a matter barely referred to by Hobhouse) and that was a further reason for Ellenborough's reversion to the Bentinck policy. In the event it gave the exiled Dost Muhammad his second chance. Readers will recall the Simla Proclamation when John Lawrence's policy falls to be discussed later in this study.

In spite of all the blame attaching to Auckland and to his advisers, it is fair to say that he did not receive the instructions and support that he was entitled to expect, either from the British government or from the Secret Committee of the Board of Control of the Company in London. Palmerston's foreign policy was pragmatic. He had never given as much thought to Russia's threat to India as to her designs on the Dardanelles and the Eastern Mediterranean. Earlier he had been disposed to be friendly towards Russia, under the benign influence of Princess Lieven, the wife of the Russian ambassador in London; though when she departed and Russia negotiated the Treaty of Unkiar-Skelessi with Turkey in 1833, his views were modified considerably and permanently.

Turkey, in Palmerston's view, must be supported not only to keep Russia out of the Mediterranean, but also to protect the land route to India. He had been very concerned to avoid an open war with Iran, but that was because it might lead to war with Russia, which it was even more important to avoid, especially in Europe. So when his plan to build up Iran failed, he decided that Afghanistan ought to be the buffer. It was as far as possible from Europe as well as from India, and an added attraction, since Whig governments disliked extravagance, may have been that the expense would fall on India. Palmerston only took the situation seriously as a result of pressure by McNeill and Burnes, and when he heard of the Vitkevich mission to Kandahar and of preparations being made for the Khivan campaign. Up to that point his views and Auckland's had roughly coincided, but from then on he left all the preparations for the Afghan expedition to Auckland. He never studied the plans, nor heeded the advice of the Duke of Wellington and others with experience of India. He would still have had time to try to reach an understanding with Russia concerning respective spheres of influence both in Afghanistan and the rest of Central Asia, particularly when Iran raised the siege of Herat. But despite Nesselrode's reiteration that Russia had no designs on India, Palmerston's suspicions had become too strong for him to develop the opportunity.

Although Palmerston had chosen Auckland for the post and in general supported his plan for Afghanistan, yet in a letter to Hobhouse in July 1839 he expressed some misgivings about the outcome of the enterprise. In his reply Hobhouse wrote 'My own opinion also inclines to the belief that unless care is taken the Indian Government may enter into an engagement beyond the Indus which it may be impossible almost to maintain without a dangerous drain upon their resources'. That, of course, was precisely what happened. Yet in 1840 Palmerston was to tell Auckland 'Make fast what you have gained in Afghanistan, secure the kingdom of Kabul and make yourself sure of Herat'. On the other hand Hobhouse had written to Auckland in September 1839 '... We are exceedingly unwilling to sanction anything like an attempt to give a permanent character to your occupation of Afghanistan' and he continued 'I must express to you an earnest hope that you will not leave a decision on so significant a subject either to Mr MacNaghten, or Sir John Keane ... and above all remember that not only the Home Authorities but their parliamentary critics look with the utmost apprehension not to say jealousy, at any extension of British power beyond the Indus'.

Much has been written concerning this disastrous period and yet more remains to be said which is beyond the scope of this book. It is obvious that Palmerston had a good understanding of Russia's characteristic methods of diplomacy, but he saw her primarily through the eyes of the good European he was. On the tacit recognition that neither he nor Nesselrode wanted war, even though both feared it likely at some later stage, he handled St. Petersburg with skill if not always with tact. But although his perception of the Eastern Question was clear enough he never really understood either India or Central Asia. His judgment of strategic objectives there was variable and his choice of Lord Auckland as Governor General though based on his acknowledged administrative ability turned out to be lamentable when perceptive leadership was required. After Palmerston, Hobhouse was the man in the most crucial position to lay down the policy towards Afghanistan and to guide the Governor General. Hitherto his ambivalent attitude seems to have escaped notice. It becomes painfully obvious when his Diary and subsequent Recollections are compared with his memorandum to Palmerston and his despatch to Auckland quoted above. In the former he records that it was he who directed Auckland to go ahead with the expedition and that the Secret Committee approved the despatch with only one dissentient. When the disaster occurred in 1842 he told Lord Melbourne, the Prime Minister, 'that such reverses must always attend a small force occupying an extensive territory' and that 'I was only afraid of the authorities in India and England taking alarm and reversing the policy we had adopted'. Even in retrospect the nature and the extent of the tragedy seem not to have struck him.

Hobhouse had lost his post in 1841 when Peel formed a Tory Government. In his diary for 18 May 1843 is the following entry, 'The more I see of the conduct of Auckland and his Council, and his Commander in Chief immediately after the disasters in Afghanistan, the more convinced I am that the authorities in India were not equal to the occasion, and that Ellenborough found the question prejudged in regard to the occupation of Afghanistan when he arrived in Calcutta.... Ellenborough had to contend with great disadvantages, but after making all due allowance for these circumstances he still appears to me to have acted with lamentable want of courage and sagacity'.

Commenting in the same entry that Ellenborough's advance to Kabul and the victories that accompanied that triumphant enterprise were accomplished under every possible discouragement from the supreme Government Hobhouse said 'the real intention of the Governor General and his C-in-C were founded on the opinion that the speediest retreat from Afghanistan was the only safe policy'. And lastly 'I should stand almost alone in the House of Commons were I to advocate the maintaining of our positions in Afghanistan. Perhaps Palmerston would back me but I am sure no one else would'. In that judgment at any rate he was probably right. In an entry of the 3rd July 1843 referring to a confidential talk with Palmerston he wrote 'He condemned with me (Lord John) Russell's avowal in the House that the retreat from Afghanistan was inevitable.... He had exactly the same opinion of Auckland's lamentable panic at the close of his Government as I have'. The contrast between these entries of 1843 so clearly indicating the opinion that Afghanistan should have been held, and the earlier official exchanges of 1839 which express precisely the opposite intention is greatly to the discredit of Hobhouse. In spite of his private castigation of the unfortunate Auckland's conduct he was still able to visit and dine with him on friendly terms. Back in office once more in 1846 he was to change his view again, though this time with more sense. When Palmerston urged on him 'the necessity of preventing Persian, and in other words Russian, authority from establishing itself in Herat', Hobhouse advised him to leave India out of it. He considered that the annexation of Sind and the victories against the Sikhs put a different complexion on things. He did not think India should go beyond the Khyber Pass, still less the Hindu Kush, in search of adventures. Hobhouse continued in his post until 1852.

The First Afghan War, besides being a military disaster, had settled nothing; indeed it delayed for many years to come any settlement of India's north-west frontier and in the long run added greatly to Anglo-Russian rivalry. The rivalry was only temporarily subdued by its failure. Russia's immediate fear of a British invasion of Central Asia was also lessened by the fact that Herat still remained independent. This fear had been very real particularly after the failure of her own Khivan campaign.

Whilst military activity had been the key note of events in Afghanistan, British action in the rest of Central Asia was political. Auckland correctly regarded the Foreign Office as exercising the main responsibility for the region and for British policy there, and Palmerston certainly showed a more personal interest in it than in Afghanistan.

But before considering British activities there between the years 1837 and 1843 we must take one more look at Palmerston's role and at his relations with Nesselrode the Russian Foreign Minister. M. E. Yapp in his unpublished thesis *British Policy in Central Asia 1830–1843* (1959) says it was part of the tragedy of these relations that British and Russian interests in Central Asia were identical. Quite simply they were to preserve peace and to confine activity to commercial not political rivalry: as Nesselrode put it, to respect *'l'indépendance des pays intermédiares qui nous séparent'*. But

Palmerston could not overcome his suspicion, even though the cautious Nesselrode himself like many other able administrators and soldiers in Russia at that period, was not Russian but a Baltic German. So when Nesselrode made a proposal for mediation between Britain and Iran, Palmerston refused it. The facts were that neither country ever wanted war but that neither ever trusted each other's ultimate intentions. Kaye, writing in 1851, considered that it was 'six of one and half-a-dozen of the other'. He wrote 'True the Russian policy in the East had been distinguished by aggressive tendencies, but in the plenitude of national self-love we encouraged the conviction that Great Britain had conquered the entire continent of Hindustan by a series of purely defensive measures'. It was also Kaye's view that the Company's agents were less pacific than the Company itself. His history was based to a great extent on the private papers of individuals concerned. Yapp on the other hand was writing over a hundred years later and with access to Parliamentary Papers and the Company's secret files. Their opinions are complementary and equally acceptable so far as they concern the limited period with which they are both dealing. From Russia comes a modern Soviet viewpoint, 'It was not a case of Russia's attacking and of Britain's defending herself. Not a bit of it. Two opposite currents of expansion were in conflict in Central Asia. Both Russia and Britain were pursuing an offensive policy, and each was therefore apprehensive of the other'.[1]

To sum up it must be stressed that we are viewing the approach of two proud and expanding empires, with as yet no finally established frontiers, from opposite sides of a backward, uncivilized and undeveloped region. As Palmerston had put it in his blunt way in 1835: 'We are just as we were, snarling at each other, hating each other, but neither wishing for war'. And so it was to be for the next fifty years.

---

[1] *Istoriya Diplomatii,* Vol 2 1945 page 26.

CHAPTER FOUR

Russia in Central Asia Up Till 1842

For a comparison of Russia's situation in Central Asia from the beginning of the nineteenth century with the British position two paragraphs from *Aziatskaya Rossiya* (Asiatic Russia) (St. Petersburg 1914) afford a convenient starting point. This was the last official history of Russia in Asia to be published under the Tsarist régime. It describes Russia as holding a fortified line in Central Asia on three sides of a parallelogram, with the southern side still uncompleted. In particular the history said: 'Gradually the Kazakhs[1] became more and more bold. The Muslim world with every generation became more hostile to Russia. The Khans of Khiva, Bukhara and Kokand, believing that Russia was not in a position to get at them, constantly spurred the Kazakhs on to hostile action. Fortunately, however, there was constant internal dissension among the Kazakhs whose popular masses were hostile to the Khans. But the local Russian authorities were not able to take advantage of this dissension; usually they supported the Khans who with oriental cunning shifted the responsibility for keeping the people quiet onto the Russians and Russia. In addition the Russian government acted in such a way that the influence of Muslim organisation among the Kazakhs increased: from the time of Catherine II we tried to educate the Kazakhs in the belief that by this means they would be weaned away from their brigandish way of life. But for this purpose we sent into the Steppe Tatar Mullas from Kazan who merely preached hatred towards the Russians'.

---

[1] The Russians then called them Kirgiz, a misnomer which has been corrected here and elsewhere.

After discussing the reasons for the slow initial progress and commenting on the disappointing attitude taken by the European powers to every extension of Russian power, *Asiatic Russia* continued: 'Another fundamental aspect of our policy now became clear: the Kazakhs.... were under the strong influence exercised by the Khanates of Kokand, Khiva and Bukhara. Pacification of the Steppe was only possible by terrorizing or subduing these Khanates, who adopted a bold attitude towards Russia and not only considered themselves unassailable but encouraged others in the same belief'. From this followed the conclusion that it was necessary to deliver a decisive blow against the khanates.

The history was written as a *fait accompli* and that would account for the impression it gives of Russia following a long-term plan. In fact as we shall see such a plan did not exist. Certainly the ultimate fate of the Kazakhs was sealed, but the actual process of conquest was a matter of trial and error affected by many factors. Peter the Great's vision of trade with southern Asia (which included India) was still an abiding influence; but right up to the middle of the nineteenth century it was believed that the three southern khanates were properly constituted states which could be treated with as such and at whose frontiers the Russian advance might reasonably be expected to end. The facts about their decadence and their petty rivalries were slow to emerge and only when they did was the fate of the khanates sealed. Particularly as regards the khanates therefore the history is being wise after the event.

The importance of the paragraphs quoted above lies in their justification of the Russian advance as seen by historians of imperial Russia at the time: it is a justification which by no means coincides with that put forward by Soviet historians who now affirm that Russian rule was welcomed. Perhaps the only common ground they share is an immense pride of achievement.

The impression gaining currency in England by the 1830's that Russia was following some grand design in Asia was very far from correct. As in Siberia so now in Central Asia she was on the move and to that extent she was bringing Peter the Great's foresight to some reality, but nobody in Russia could visualize the ultimate result, still less was there any recognized plan. The extent and the rate of forward movement were largely dictated by practical considerations, in particular those of limited financial and military resources; more urgent needs in Eastern Europe and the Near East put Central Asia low in priority. The development of trade there was still the first aim, not only for its own sake but because the countries of Western Europe were ahead industrially. From Catherine onwards the Tsars wanted Russia to count as a leading European nation, but she was still poor and there were more opportunities for her to get rich in Asia than in Europe. However, good trading conditions needed stable frontiers and here again Russia was still at a disadvantage.

So when British fears for the security of India transferred themselves from France to Russia as a menace they were by no means justified by any action Russia had hitherto taken in Central Asia. That is not to say that Britain was wrong to make plans to counter any such possible menace, it would indeed have been short-sighted not to; it was simply that the immediacy was for various reasons exaggerated because Russia's aims and available resources were never properly assessed. Thus Poland in Eastern Europe and Turkey and Iran in the Near East all had prior claims. One of the principal aims of Russian diplomacy in Iran was to maintain disunity and to oppose any alliance between her and Turkey, whose ultimate collapse was both hoped for and fully expected. Hence the importance to Russia of control of the Caucasus. That was in itself a costly affair; even as late as the Crimean War she had to maintain an army of 200,000 in that cockpit alone. But stability and a firm frontier there were of the greatest importance to her both strategically and politically.

With Turkey controlling the Dardanelles and thus frustrating Russia's ambition of access to the Mediterranean, the Eastern Question, as it came to be called, was a great deal more urgent than control of the locally troublesome Kazakhs in Central Asia, or the southern khanates. For those reasons Count Nesselrode, who became Foreign Minister in 1816 and who held the post till 1856, was constantly more concerned with Europe than with Central Asian matters. He was a cautious far-seeing statesman and another example of those Baltic Germans who served their Tsars so well. They were loyal, hard-working and bureaucratically conservative, seeing themselves as servants of the Tsar rather than the Russian state. A consequence was that they tended to remain aloof from Russian society and rarely became russified, nor were they touched by the corruption which was so rife amongst Russian officials. It is significant that of nine ambassadors to London between 1812 and 1917 no less than four of them were Baltic German barons.

It is useful to describe briefly how Russian foreign and colonial affairs were conducted. Policy was decided by the Tsar and his Foreign Minister. At the Foreign Ministry there was an 'Asian table' or Department, which administered Asian affairs. Territories entirely under Russian rule were the responsibility of the Minister for Home Affairs, whilst the Minister for War managed the army including the military administration of conquered territories. The Minister of Finance was naturally an important and influential adviser to the Tsar. In the border regions of Central Asia which were under military administration the authority of all these ministries converged on the military governors-general. Although mainly obedient to Nesselrode's foreign policy in the early stages of his tenure of office, the governors-general became increasingly independent and autocratic as expansion gathered pace. They were entitled to appeal direct to the Tsar over the head of Nesselrode and his successors, whose instructions they ignored if they did not like them: thus to some extent they created their own policy. But their somewhat independent attitude also afforded the advantage of diplomatic finessing. When Britain sought an explanation or asked for re-assurance that some new Russian move in Central Asia did not mean a departure from previously stated policy, the Foreign Minister could reply that it had been unauthorized or would be forbidden, knowing that the governor-general would pay little or no attention. But Britain too could finesse likewise. Thus on one occasion Palmerston told von Brunnow that he could not control the Governor-General of India if Auckland decided to send an expedition to Khiva or the Oxus. That was in reply to an offer by the Ambassador to send a mission to Bukhara and Kokand to tell the Khans that Russia and Britain had reached an agreement concerning Central Asia; an exchange that some might call horse trading. Besides demonstrating Palmerston's suspicion of Russia this diplomatic exchange shows his preference for shuffling off responsibility for Central Asia onto India.

These reasons all help to explain why Russian expansion into Central Asia was only the last phase of the great forward surge. Although when it first began it was by no means in response to any suspicions of our intentions these suspicions when once they were aroused undoubtedly had the effect of speeding up the movement.

Initially however it is plain that the movement had quite different origins and that the response to them was no part of any coherent strategy. All the same Palmerston's perception was broadly sound when he wrote in 1838 that 'Russia is always pushing on as far and as fast as she can without going to war, but whenever she finds that perseverance or encroachment will lead to forcible resistance she will pull up'.

Until the early part of the nineteenth century the Orenburg-Siberia line of forts had sufficed to keep some sort of order in the northern Kazakh steppes and, for the past hundred years, it had reasonably satisfied the Russian instinct for a frontier. During that long period desultory trading with the southern khanates had been carried on, despite caravan raiding and slave stealing by Kazakhs in the unsettled parts of the steppes which were also extended into the northern settled part. The unfortunate merchants, who were all independent entrepreneurs, complained bitterly enough about their depredations, but military action to curb them was limited to very minor forays which resulted mainly in the acquisition of a few more kilometres of steppe and the setting up of another line of forts to keep order. These limited advances in response to the pressure of merchants were what British extremists mistook for a calculated plan. The lines of forts did not constitute a demarcated frontier in the European sense; they simply implied a tribute or nomad frontier and the limit of relatively stable settlement. True frontier demarcation did not begin till well on in the nineteenth century, when regularly effective government came to be established as the rate of expansion grew.

At this early stage Russian aims in Central Asia can be summarized as the checking of raids in newly acquired territory, ensuring to some extent the safety of caravans through nomad lands, and the release of prisoners kept as slaves. Somewhat later, as the advance gathered pace there was the additional aim of obtaining navigation rights for Russian vessels up the Amu Dar'ya; an aim no doubt inspired by the successful utilization of waterway communications in opening up Siberia.

Sporadic caravans, often with Cossack military escorts, were travelling to Afghanistan, Iran and Chinese Turkestan. Herat was another commercial objective. In 1808 a trade mission from Tiflis journeyed to Kashmir via Kashgar and returned with shawls and wool. That mission, which opened up prospects of a profitable new trade, was the one which first inspired William Moorcroft's belief that something more sinister than trade was in the offing. But the main objective was still to develop lucrative commercial relations with the three southern khanates. By the end of the second decade of the nineteenth century there had been no organized scientific Russian exploration in Central Asia and although there had been embassies of sorts in Bukhara since the seventeenth century, it is remarkable how little was known. Suspicion of British intentions had not yet been actively aroused, and rivalry with Britian was still in embryo. So far this rivalry extended no further east than Iran and Herat, and it was scarcely manifest in Afghanistan – a country of which Russia knew little enough.

During the next ten years Russia's attitude towards Central Asia underwent a change, which occurred for several reasons. With the final annexation and subjugation of the Caucasus no longer in doubt, there was no further risk of an alliance between Turkey and Iran against her. The Turkic tribes in the Crimea had already been subjugated and she had a footing on the Black Sea littoral. Thus her more immediate objectives in the Near East had been settled and she could spare some financial and military resources for an advance in Central Asia. This situation coincided with the appearance in the khanates of the first British travellers. First of all there was the inquisitive Moorcroft with his equally assiduous assistant, Izzat Ullah. Conolly's journey in 1829 from England through Russia, Iran and Afghanistan had not gone unnoticed, and no doubt news of his abortive attempt in 1830 to travel to Khiva reached Russian ears. Soon there were more British explorers in the field. It behoved Russia to set about establishing beyond all doubt her prior political claim. Action became the more important and urgent as rumours spread of British intentions. The most extreme theory was that, following precedent, Britain intended to swallow Afghanistan and then proceed to annex the khanates. The most moderate, and the one nearest the mark, was that she was seeking to develop trade with the khanates, with or without treaties, but in either case at Russia's expense.

The first Russian step was to send a series of missions to the khanates; the second was to initiate more military action against the Kazakhs in order to protect the caravan routes; the third was the erection of forts, notably Aleksandrovsk on the eastern shore of the Caspian, to protect fishermen there from being carried off as slaves. These quite unexceptionable steps precisely resembled the sequence whereby Britain had expanded in India. There the furtherance of trade had frequently led to military action, followed ultimately by the accession of more territory. Russia could see the same sequence being followed in Central Asia if she did not take action first. In fact there was the less risk of such a repetition if only because for India any worthwhile increase in trade was extremely doubtful. But as British doubts grew about where Russian action was leading her and diplomatic enquiries and protests became more frequent, Russia was able to quote Britain's own actions in India in justifiable reply. A further point of resemblance was that for Russia in Asia, as for Britain in India, once action was launched there could be no going back. Her prestige in Central Asia had to be maintained, and it was the more important to her because if she failed to establish herself Britain would move in, if not physically at any rate in that vital sphere of prestige which was so important in the East.

The pressure of colonization was yet to come but there was one other form of impetus behind the forward movement which had nothing to do with trade or politics and bore little or no resemblance to any factor in Indian expansion. Such control as there was over the Kazakh steppes was based simply on the lines of fortifications and was purely military. There was no attempt till the second half of the century to replace it or even supplement it with a civil administration. The Governor General at Orenburg was always a soldier and he deployed a relatively large number of troops under his command who had to be kept occupied. The Cossack soldiery who were the mainstay of these garrisons or frontier troops, were simple uneducated men accustomed to hard living in primitive conditions; they presented no great problem, at any rate so long as they got their daily liberal ration of vodka.

The problem for successive Governors General was their officers. Too many of those serving on the Orenburg line had been sent there either because they were not up to the standard of the army in Europe or because of misdemeanours such as debt and drunkenness. They were a restless lot and they needed to be kept occupied. The lure for these officers in their boring surroundings which drove them to drink, was the prospect of military action which would bring with it promotion, more pay and campaign medals. By comparison with campaigns in India which, against the fighting races of India were hard fought and bloody, Russian campaigns against the Kazakhs were no more than minor punitive sorties.

The Kazakh tribesmen, though aggressive and adept at raiding, were armed with primitive weapons which were of little use against Russian fire-arms and artillery. They rode only the small Kirgiz ponies which were ill-matched for speed and mobility against the Cossack cavalry mounted on the Don Cossack breed. Cossacks each had a spare horse and were armed with both lance and rifle. The consequence was that these sorties were one-sided affairs in which a score or so of tribesmen would be killed or wounded whilst there were rarely more than one or two Russian casualties. But medals were awarded, there were no restrictions on looting and so they were decidedly good for morale. Had the Kazakhs been able to organize themselves as an army under a good leader, operations against them would have been much more protracted. As it was only one Kazakh leader, Kenessary, in the 1840's, had ideas for unification and he proved really troublesome for some years till he fled to Chinese Turkestan.

The gradual settlement of the Kazakh steppes, which could not be described as complete till the turn of the century, offered no solution to the frontier problem either geographically or politically. There were no physical characteristics on which to base the former, whilst the disparate Kazakh tribes simply acknowledged Russian overlordship with the degree of advantage which that offered them. They still continued to give allegiance to the southern khanates as had always been their custom. So there was no immediate reward for Russia; indeed the settlement of the steppe region merely added to the financial burden. The first practical result was an influx of uncontrolled settlers with Cossacks, as always, leading the way.

Thus the further occupation and subjugation of the Kazakh steppe brought no solid gain in itself either in the form of trade or a stable frontier, in fact it was increasingly costly. But there could be no question of stopping or of consolidation at such an indeterminate stage.

In 1839 the first active move against the three major khanates was launched in the form of a campaign against Khiva. It was no chance that its timing coincided with the British campaign in Afghanistan. Tactically speaking its military objectives were feasible and unexceptionable: according to V. Potto in a lecture delivered to the Junker Cadet School at Orenburg in 1872, they were to cross the Ust Urt, to occupy the Khanate in order to liberate the slaves and to open up trade. Yet like the war in Afghanistan it too was a military disaster. Before describing what happened we must examine the background to the campaign and some important factors, which though they have not been precisely confirmed from the Russian side undoubtedly had bearings on it.

The Governor General at Orenburg was General Count V. A. Perovskiy. He is a significant figure in Russian Central Asian history, not only because he was the first Governor to ignore Nesselrode's policy of concentrating on the Near East and keeping action in Central Asia on a low priority. Whether he acted in open defiance of Nesselrode or whether the latter turned a blind eye because he was a personal friend of the Tsar we shall not know until some future Soviet historian turns up the archives. It is however possible that in this particular case Nesselrode was not altogether averse to Perovskiy's project. By that time there were a number of very important reasons why an active demonstration in Central Asia would not have been unwelcome to him.

The treaty of Turkmanchai in 1828 had legitimized Russia's gains at the expense of Turkey and Iran; but while the Western powers continued to block Russian aspirations towards the eastern Mediterranean, relations with Iran were more fluid and little less important in Russian eyes because here again there was that all-important factor of a stable frontier. The Shah of Iran was in a peculiarly awkward position. His country was weak, backward and by no means united in its loyalty. When he was attacked by Russia, Palmerston had decided not to fulfil Britain's treaty to support him against aggression, for the very practical reason in his pragmatic view, that it would have led her into war with Russia. He had been a Whig before he turned Tory and he may have retained some of the old Whig preference for non-intervention in risky foreign commitments. If so, in that respect he showed some consistency, though he did not mind letting India shoulder the burden. Now Britain was increasing her influence in south Iran with the view of protecting the sea route to India, whilst Russia was increasing her influence in the north partly in order to exploit trade, partly to offset Britain and partly to stabilize her Iranian frontier. Russia was determined not to let British influence extend to the north. That was why it suited her to keep Iran disunited, without going to the extent of any costly military action.

Just as McNeill was constantly sounding alarms to Palmerston about Russian intentions in Iran and Central Asia as constituting a threat to India, so Count Simonich, the Russian envoy in Tehran, was warning Nesselrode about British intentions in both countries. McNeill, as one of the chief exponents of an extreme forward policy in Iran and in Central Asia too, also saw the prospect of a Russian campaign against Khiva and Herat as part of a long-term plan. Simonich believed that the establishment of British control over Afghanistan would represent a step towards a hegemony over Central Asia and perhaps over Iran too. Thus suspicions and antagonism were nourished in London and St. Petersburg. It would have been delightful to observe the reactions of these two rivals when they met unavoidably at some official Iranian function. It is not difficult to guess what they were like: a hundred years later when the Bolsheviks had taken over, the successors to McNeill and Simonich were still trying to outdo each other in Iran. McNeill did not confine his warnings to London; naturally he directed them to the Company at Calcutta too. We do not know what communications passed between Simonich and Count Perovskiy but in the light of events it is a safe guess that they had their influence at Orenburg. Moreover Simonich, like McNeill, knew that Iran had long-standing ties with the khanates which might be useful to Russia.

Both men played an important part in seeking information about the region which would be valuable for any impending military operation, and both used envoys of their own to sound out political views and to intrigue for influence with local rulers. Whilst we know all about the men who went from India and Tehran, we only know in detail about one Russian – that was Vitkevich, who was sent by Simonich to Herat. In Afghanistan Britain fielded the greater numbers. Having decided that control of the country was essential in order to establish a balance of power, Britain went blazing into action before Russia had made any significant move.

It was a curious kind of transition whereby Britain and India, having begun with the perfectly sound decision that India's defences must be considered seriously, had become imbued with the notion that a threat from Russia was imminent, yet so far with little or no evidence to support it. Indeed more conceivable at that time was an Afghan invasion which certainly had to be taken seriously. On the other hand Russia, having seen how India had expanded, had as much, or even more, reason to expect the process to be continued into Afghanistan and even into Central Asia too. Thus she had every cause to mistrust Indian activities there and to take some positive steps of her own.

Of the British in Afghanistan two of the most active as well as the most vocal in expounding their views were the political officers Henry Rawlinson and Alexander Burnes. In 1836 Rawlinson had been posted to Kandahar, whilst Auckland had sent Burnes to Kabul with fairly wide powers. Besides these two there was Pottinger at Herat. Russia's response was to send Captain Vitkevich to Kabul in 1837: he had been a protégé of Simonich who recommended him to Perovskiy as an able young man. Vitkevich arrived in Kabul in answer to an appeal from Dost Muhammad, who by that time had been rejected by Auckland. Vitkevich carried papers said to have been signed by the Tsar, which authorised him to negotiate a treaty with Dost Muhammad. He might very well have brought off his coup, but Palmerston protested so vigorously against his mission that Nesselrode recalled both Simonich and Vitkevich – the latter to a fate which will be referred to later. Their recall might have been recognised, both in Britain and in India, as an indication of Russia's lack of any serious intentions either in Afghanistan or against India, but the point was missed. In fact Simonich's intrigues had been much more directed towards thwarting Britain in Iran. Their recall also shows how anxious the Tsar was not to offend Britain; but it had no effect on British policy. Concerning the affair, Palmerston wrote to Hobhouse '.... we want to carry our points without a rupture and as the Russians are disposed to quietly back out it is not for us to criticize their gait in so doing'. In the same letter of November 1839 he added '.... As to their purely commercial missions, of course we know what these missions really are'. Hobhouse in his reply agreed that Nesselrode ought to be let off as lightly as possible.

It is plain that quite apart from Perovskiy's stated tactical objects of his campaign against Khiva, there was no shortage of reasons for it on political grounds. If the timing of it in November 1839, perhaps by the Tsar's instructions, was influenced by the news of the British campaign in Afghanistan Perovskiy had a practical argument as well and that was the climate. The whole Kazakh steppe experiences severe contrasts in temperature with strong winds and little rain. The north and east favours good grazing and agriculture, but to the west, and southwards from Orenburg towards the Caspian and Khiva, there is much sandy waste with poor grazing and little water fit for drinking. So although the steppe there is everywhere passable it is very difficult campaigning country. By launching his campaign in the winter Perovskiy chose to avoid the great heat and drought. He expected to rely on snow for water which would also protect what grazing there was underneath. Unfortunately he had neglected, or else was given too little time, to carry out any previous reconnaissance, perhaps relying on Kazakh guides; at any rate the conditions he met were quite unforeseen and proved insurmountable. Khiva is 930 miles from Orenburg so the risk he was running should have been obvious on that score alone.

He set off with a sizeable force of 4500 men including Cossack cavalry, with 10,000 camels and 2000 Kazakh drivers for the carts and camels. The force soon ran into difficulties. It experienced severe frosts, gales and snowfalls, the men were badly clothed and equipped for winter and they suffered intense hardship and much sickness. The animals too suffered; frozen snow prevented them from getting at what grazing there was and too little fodder was carried. Before reaching Khiva and even before any serious clashes with the Khivans, Perovskiy had to order a retreat. By the time it returned to Orenburg his force had lost two thirds of its strength. It was a military disaster almost comparable with the British retreat from Kabul and likewise it had achieved nothing but suffering for the men and animals and a severe loss of prestige.

Tsar Nicholas immediately ordered another campaign. That again alarmed the Khivans who had already appealed to Herat for help which was not forthcoming. India had however sent the Political Officers Abbott and Shakespear to Khiva to negotiate a friendly and at least temporarily successful settlement between Russia and Khiva. At the same time Palmerston made another of his strong protests. The consequence was that the retributory campaign was cancelled by the Tsar; both Perovskiy and Nesselrode must have been glad of the excuse. The first campaign itself had cost £70,000 which Russia could ill afford and a second would have failed too; though the expense was small compared with the several million pounds which the First Afghan War had cost India for a fighting force only about twice the size. Ellenborough's subsequent punitive expedition to Kabul to restore British prestige itself necessitated the raising of a seven million pound loan in Britain. After these twin disasters both the rival powers retired to lick their wounds and they became relatively friendly. The Straits Convention of 1841 which ended Russia's privileged position in Turkey eased the tension and also India's fears.

The stationary policy for Indian defence received paradoxical endorsement by the conquest and annexation of the Punjab in 1847. Meanwhile Dost Muhammad returned to his throne in 1842 and continued with his task of unifying Afghanistan. Russia contented herself with several missions to the Central Asian khanates, and further extensions of her fortified lines in the Kazakh steppe. The Crimean War further delayed any important southward expansion in Asia.

By now, Russia had become fully aware of how sensitive Britain was to any threat to India through Central Asia, the only direction from which she was directly vulnerable. Hence to divert attention from the Crimea she initiated tentative plans for an invasion through Afghanistan. According to Lobanov-Rostovsky they were never intended to be more than diversionary, and they were dropped after the war. But in the years ahead Russia was to use the threat more than once as an effective diplomatic lever.

CHAPTER FIVE

Early British and Russian Reconnaissances and Missions

Some impressions will have been gleaned of the statesmen and diplomatists in London, St. Petersburg and Calcutta who were responsible for formulating policy in Central Asia. But it is impossible to assess Anglo-Russian relations during the Great Game without discussing the activities of the men in the field on either side.

The lamentable British ignorance of geographical, political and ethnological conditions in Central Asia during the period leading up to the First Afghan War was a direct product of the East India Company's cautious policy. It had always been reluctant to take on new commitments outside its commercial role and consequently tended to discourage exploration beyond its existing borders. The result was that such exploration as was carried out was mainly through the personal enterprise of restless young officers, and they had to press hard and persistently to get permission. When the need for it first arose the importance of up-to-date information in relation to a realistic defence policy never seems to have struck the Company's senior servants.

It was only in 1820 that the Company formed its Political Department. It was a misleading title, just as was the commercial term Agent which it applied to its staff. In fact the department was the Company's diplomatic corps and its members were really representatives of the Company as Residents at the capitals of the various States which comprised India and when they travelled on missions. In due course it was to become a *corps d'élite* but at this early stage that would have been a considerable overstatement. Its first members were a mixed collection of soldiers and civilians who were often misfits in their regiments or civilian departments. The only qualifications required of them were a facility for eastern languages, especially Persian, a thirst for adventure and a willingness to take risks. When going on independent missions they needed an elementary knowledge of topography, although very often they were accompanied by a surveyor who was either an Indian from the Topographical Department, or an officer of the Engineers. Once despatched on missions – often enough it was only because of their own persistence that they were allowed to go – the Company tended to neglect them. They frequently died lonely and violent deaths and their enterprise was rarely recognised; nor were their reports ever properly coordinated or evaluated. On the other hand, when they wrote books describing their adventures, as some did, they were widely read by an impressionable public at home eager to satisfy their romantic notions of Central Asia. Their views tended to be listened to with more attention by politicians at home than by the Company.

Broadly speaking it is possible to discern two categories of British traveller in Central Asia, the adventurers and the professional explorers. In some cases they overlap but in general the adventurers – who were usually free-lances and sometimes cranks too – were more apt to tell their stories and to expound their views to the public, whilst the professionals, especially latterly, were dedicated men who confined themselves to the job in hand and to official reports and memoranda. It is tempting to make a separate category of the evangelists. But that was a common characteristic in the Company as a whole, although later on the role was largely assumed by the missionaries: nevertheless it is a feature to be borne in mind, particularly in these early days.

The present study must necessarily be confined to the work of professionals and to an assessment of their contributions to Indian defence policy. Any such assessment must begin with Sir Alexander Burnes, not only because he was the most active of the earlier explorers, but because until he fell from favour his views carried the greatest weight. In character he was an adventurer, but his meteoric career showed that he had valuable professional talent as well, which historians have tended to overlook. Small, vital and fond of good living, he began his Indian career in a regiment of Indian infantry where he gambled and was often in debt. It was his facility for languages which brought him to the Governor General's notice, and in 1830 he was sent on a successful goodwill mission with presents, including some English Shire horses and a coach, to

Ranjit Singh with whom the Company wanted to conclude a treaty. Next year with the help of a naval officer and trained surveyor, Lieut. Wood, he carried out a survey of the River Indus. On these two missions he proved to be a remarkably good observer with a particular ability to get on well with eastern potentates and to adapt to their customs.

There was nothing reticent about Burnes: in 1831, as Kaye tells us, he wrote to his sister 'The Home Government have got frightened at the designs of Russia and desire some intelligent officer to be sent to get information from countries bordering on the Oxus and the Caspian'. He volunteered, 'hoping to pass through Bukhara and Khiva etc, if I can conceal my designs from Russian officers'. He set out in 1832 accompanied by a French surgeon, Dr. Gerard, an Indian surveyor and Mohun Lal, a well-educated Hindu trained at Delhi College. The mission was one of the first officially sponsored ones to Central Asia and its members carried passports.

Journeying through Afghanistan he was well received by Dost Muhammad, of whom he formed a high opinion. Crossing the Hindu Kush he reached Bukhara where, though he did not meet the Amir in person, he was again welcomed, not indeed entirely for himself, but more importantly as a possibly valuable representative of the Indian government. He noted during his visit to Bukhara, that Turkey and Afghanistan both had envoys there. So too had China, although the Amir had refused to help her against the Amir of Kokand in spite of China's historical claim to suzerainty over the latter. That was typical of the traditional intricacies of relationships in Central Asia. After his return to India through Iran Burnes went on leave to England. He wrote a vivid account of his travels which was widely read and he was lionized by London society. To have influential people hanging on his words was scarcely the best treatment for a young man of mercurial temperament still only twenty eight years old.

With his reputation and his self-confidence at their peak, he was despatched to Afghanistan once more in 1836, this time on what was intended to be a commercial mission. In 1838 he was still able to write that he was 'playing the boldest game that man ever dared', but as will already have been seen from the political results, his career had passed its zenith. His last act was a visit to Herat in a vain endeavour to bring the Khan under the rule of Kabul. He was then discarded by MacNaghten who was jealous of him (though they remained on friendly terms), and he found himself at Kabul practically without responsibility and attached, not to Dost Muhammad whose claims he had pressed, but to Shah Shuja of whom he strongly disapproved. Moreover MacNaghten ignored all his warnings of disaffection amongst the tribes. From that point Burnes, who had by then received a compensatory knighthood, created his own downfall; a disappointed and frustrated man, he gave himself over to fast living, solely for the moment. Now he was to write of giving a party 'with a rare Scotch breakfast of smoked fish, salmon grills, devils and jellies, the party puffing away at cigars'. But the man who boasted how well he understood the Afghans and how they trusted him pushed his confidence too far. He ignored the indications of trouble in the capital itself: when Kabul rose against Shah Shuja he and his brother were among the first to be murdered.

Yet in spite of his final fatal lapse this young Scot had more political wisdom and a greater appreciation of the strategical realities than those of his superiors whom Auckland chose to advise him. Burnes never wavered in his belief that a strong and unified Afghanistan, which must include Herat, was essential as a buffer for the defence of India. Thirty five years later that was achieved, not under Dost Muhammad, but under his nephew, Abdur Rahman. He was also adaptable enough to be able to modify his views on Russia in the light of his own experiences. Thus he had begun by asserting the necessity for the strongest possible relations with the Central Asian khanates so as to exclude Russian influence. But in 1840 he was able to write 'Nothing I see but to attach (to) ourselves just and deserved reproach for interfering with Russia in ground already occupied by her merchants – and far beyond our own line of operations'. In the same year he wrote clear-sightedly to MacNaghten, 'It must be at London or St. Petersburg, and not at Kokand, Bukhara or Khiva that we are to counteract Russia'.

Burnes also was among the first to realise the strategic possibilities of the northern route to India over the passes across the Hindu Kush. He believed that Russia had more justification for a campaign against Khiva to release Russian slaves than Britain had for her own aggression in Afghanistan: nevertheless he thought that if Russia occupied Khiva then India should occupy Balkh and thus cover the northern invasion route. (He meant of course the region, not the city sacked by Chingis Khan and still in ruins.)

Concern for this secondary possible invasion route led to journeys by two more explorers who made important contributions. It was Burnes who chose the two Political Officers, Lieut. Wood and Dr. Lord, to go to Kunduz and Balkh. In selecting these two men he showed that he was a good judge of character, for both men, at any rate by the standards of the day, were in the class of the best professional explorers. Wood had already worked with him on the Indus River survey whilst Lord was Wade's assistant at Ludhiana: a doctor who could treat the sick always had an advantage in the east and Lord made good political as well as medical use of his skill. Wood made an outstanding contribution to geographical knowledge when he reached the Zorkul Pamir and identified Lake Zorkul (which he named Lake Victoria) as the source of the Amu Dar'ya (Oxus). He subsequently surveyed the river, which along this stretch is now called the Ab-i-Panja, as far as Ishkashim. His visit to the Pamir and his survey were the first by any Englishman. The next British explorer there was to be another Political Officer, Ney Elias, who in 1886 carried his survey down the Amu Dar'ya to Waznud and beyond. Both surveys were ultimately accepted by the Anglo-Russian Pamirs Boundary Commission of 1895. The other task allotted to Wood and Lord was to sound out local political allegiances. These were very uncertain at the time, for whilst Afghanistan claimed historical suzerainty, Kunduz and Balkh and other small states in the region paid tribute to Bukhara, Badakhshan and some paid it to China too. At this time they preferred to regard themselves as independent of Afghanistan. Wood's recommendation was that both states should be brought under the rule of India. Such a solution would however have been ethnically unsound as well as strategically impossible.

Dr. Lord went even further in suggesting the annexation of Turkestan and an advance to Khulm to meet Russia and control Bukhara. MacNaghten with his far-fetched ideas of expanding Indian influence in the Cis-Oxus region, was probably the only senior official who took the latter proposals seriously. They did not appeal to Auckland, which partly explains why by this time MacNaghten was complaining of his lack of support. These wild ideas were examples of how too many Political Officers of the day made far-reaching recommendations which were beyond their capacity to assess. Through his control of Badakhshan, both Kunduz and Balkh were ultimately brought into a unified Afghan fold by Abdur Rahman: but in the meanwhile the best way of denying to Russia this northern route into India was to be hotly debated for the next forty years.

To digress from the actual work of these early 'Politicals', one of the practical problems which faced them all was what to wear. Some Central Asian travellers, especially those with a taste for fancy dress, favoured disguise, often as Afghan horse-dealers; others scorned it. Three extreme examples of the former who do not fall strictly within the period we are discussing were Pottinger, Christie and Lieut. Wyburd. In 1810 the first two travelled through Baluchistan to Iran in Muslim dress; Christie also visited Herat, worshipped in mosques and even indulged in religious discussions with learned Mullahs. Wyburd, who travelled to Bukhara between Conolly's first visit and Burnes's, was less successful. Despite his strong Christian beliefs he too posed as a Muslim, but his disguise was penetrated before he reached Bukhara. The Amir offered him the choice of service under him provided he renounced Christianity and adopted the Muslim religion – or death. Wyburd chose to die for his faith. At the opposite end of the scale some chose to travel openly as Europeans, either because they were too proud to wear a disguise or because they knew they could not carry it off successfully. Thus the illustrator of Burslem's book, *A Peep into Toorkesthan*, depicts him with his surveyor companion, Sturt, inspecting a cave, both men wearing incongruous frock coats and the immensely tall top hats of the day, as if they were in Piccadilly. Burnes's solution was to wear Indian dress not as a disguise but simply so as not to attract undue attention on the road. Sometimes friendly khans actually pressed him to wear their own dress as a mark of their respect for him. Stoddart on the other hand established a considerable local impression of British authority by wearing uniform with an imposing white plumed cocked hat. It was not his uniform but his unfortunate manner that let him down.

There are still a number of travellers of those days who must be considered for their political contributions to the tussle. Amongst them Henry Rawlinson was outstanding and his career lasted longer than any of the others; it was also the most diverse. By turns he was soldier, archaeologist, explorer and historian. He helped

Henry Layard in his excavations at Nimrud and Nineveh, both near modern Mosul, and explored the region. He also deciphered the Persian and Babylonian cuneiform script. As an officer in the Company's army he was recalled to the Political Service for the First Afghan War and was Agent at Kandahar, later returning to help Layard once more. After the Mutiny he joined the India Council set up to advise the new India Office in London and was later its chairman. As a geographer and also an historian of Central Asia he was President of the Royal Geographical Society, a post of which he made political use even when he was a Conservative member of Parliament. As an archaeologist he found time to be actively concerned with the British Museum's Middle Eastern antiquities.

Above all Rawlinson was a publicist with a tendency to extreme views. Thus he believed that Russia had long term plans for Central Asia, and that she was advancing by calculated stages on India: therefore she must be told she would be met with armed resistance even if it resulted in war, if she overlapped certain limits. That, he said, was not a warlike policy but in the interests of peace. He did not precisely define the limits, except to name Herat as the key. As for the khanates he thought Britain had a right to some influence there and a fair access to trade, equally with Russia. He prophesied forcefully after the First Afghan War that 'if we did not re-assert ourselves Herat and Kandahar would go to Persia, with the prospect of a Russian fleet at Astrabad (on the Caspian) and a Persian army at Merv'. His argument against the Indus defence line was that it suggested passivity which was bad for Indian morale. In the aftermath of the war his extreme forward policy views put him in the political wilderness, but he did not cease to expound them. He was also among the first to point out the dangers of a Russian invasion from the north, through Badakhshan, and hence the need for it to be brought under a unified Afghanistan under British control.

In later years he was inclined to modify some of these extreme views without apparently realising that he had done so. Thus in 1868 he was no longer fearing a Russian invasion. What he then saw as the main risk was that Russian subversion in Afghanistan would in turn lead to disruptive effects in India. Here he must have had in mind the Muslim unrest which led to the Indian Mutiny ten years earlier and was still fresh in many minds. Finally when in

1875 he published his book *England and Russia in the East* he wrote in the last part, which was based on a speech he had been unable to deliver in Parliament, that he had never subscribed to the view that Russia intended to invade India. Yet in the earlier part that was just what he had expounded. The book appeared at the end of Northbrook's period as Viceroy when the previous policy of non-intervention in Afghan affairs was giving way to a more positive one in the light of Russian activities, but the discrepancy in his views evidently did not occur to Rawlinson.

In 1873 when Britain and Russia were nearing an agreement on their respective spheres of influence in Central Asia and Afghanistan and Russia had recognised Afghanistan's right to Badakhshan, Rawlinson was instructed to define Afghanistan's northern frontier. That, he decided, on the incomplete information then available, was the line of the Amu Dar'ya from its source at Lake Zorkul. Unfortunately he did not scrutinize, or perhaps even receive, his final draft for checking and in the version sent to Russia some important clarifying words were omitted. Neither government noticed the error at the time, but it caused considerable confusion later and Rawlinson's subsequent attempt to minimize the mistake by the manipulation of commas only made matters worse.

In his biography, *Layard of Nineveh*, Gordon Waterfield quotes a letter by Layard concerning Rawlinson's archaeological work: '....He is much too eager at snatching at a theory, propounding a paradox and pooh-poohing at once anyone who disagrees with him. This is a great pity as his analysis is generally excellent...' That could equally well apply to his views on Central Asia. Russian historians are inclined to overrate his political influence, but his forward policy did come into its own for a short period when the Conservatives took power under Disraeli and Lord Lytton became Viceroy.

All the men discussed so far made their various contributions, of whom Burnes, Rawlinson and Wood were the most important. But there were several others whose qualifications and contributions have yet to be discussed. A point to be noted about those which follow is that they were all primarily concerned with the khanates of Central Asia, whereas of the previous ones, except for Wood, Afghanistan was the focus of their work and only Burnes had been to Bukhara. As their dealings were with those khanates which were ultimately annexed by Russia and now form part of the USSR most of them have received a good deal of attention from pre-Revolutionary and Soviet historians.

The first to claim attention is Colonel Charles Stoddart who was sent from India to Iran in 1835 as McNeill's military assistant at Tehran. In that capacity McNeill sent him to watch the siege of Herat and to use his influence towards raising it. He was a deeply religious man of little imagination and every inch the soldier accustomed to obeying and giving orders. So far as giving orders was concerned he could have had little difficulty in persuading the Iranian soldiery to lay down their arms. They were not keen on fighting and their pay was always in arrears – as it was for at least the next fifty years to come. The regiment of Russian mercenaries that took part in the siege seems not to have been very effective either. After playing his part in raising the siege McNeill selected Stoddart to go to Bukhara in 1838. McNeill saw the khanates partly from the particular angle of their relationships with Iran which were historically continuous and in the current situation were therefore politically important.

Unfortunately Stoddart's shortcomings soon became apparent. As a British officer he could not demean himself to conform to any eastern prejudices and customs. His particular mission, like that of his successors, was to try to placate Russia by effecting the release of Russian captives. But he gave immediate offence to the Amir, who was a man of a suspicious nature, by refusing to conform to local and Muslim customs. The consequence was that he was quickly imprisoned, where he remained on and off for the next two years, including two months in the hideous Dark Well where those incarcerated were eaten alive by rats and tormented by snakes and vermin, as well as starved. At one point he obtained release from prison by affecting to have turned Muslim and offering his service to the Amir, but he was still held captive. His treatment depended largely on British fortunes in Afghanistan. When at first they waxed the Amir prudently released him; when they waned he threw him back into prison. The Amir said he wanted a letter from the Queen of England, and Stoddart wrote to Palmerston, from whom he actually received a reply but without a letter from the Queen.

During a part of his imprisonment a Russian mission under Colonel Butenov, which had been sent to forestall Stoddart, was also in Bukhara. Being on relatively good terms with the Amir its leader offered to negotiate his release. But Stoddart was too proud to accept help from a potential enemy and said he could not leave Bukhara without an order from India. Unfortunately no such order was ever sent. Instead MacNaghten even contemplated sending a brigade to effect his release. This was at a time shortly before the final collapse of MacNaghten's Afghan venture when as Dr. Yapp tells us, he was still contemplating the release of all Cis-Amu Dar'ya territory from Bukhara and handing it over to Afghanistan before Russia could annex it. It is not difficult to imagine how Russia would have reacted: either action would have confirmed her fears about British intentions in Central Asia. But they were typical of MacNaghten's ignorance of strategy, for even if affairs in Afghanistan had prospered such a military operation would have been impossible to mount. Nor would any British government have given its approval.

At this point Arthur Conolly re-appears. He had been in Afghanistan throughout the military occupation and had been urging MacNaghten to send him to Bukhara. Not only did he want to effect the release of the Russian slaves but he wanted to bring spiritual comfort to Stoddart, particularly when he heard that Stoddart had professed conversion to Islam. Burnes opposed his departure. Rightly enough he considered Conolly was too unstable a character for the job and that moreover, as signs of unrest in Afghanistan were increasing, he would achieve nothing in Bukhara; if indeed he did not make matters worse. However Burnes's views were ignored as usual and Conolly happened to be Mac-Naghten's cousin. So he finally got his way and set out in September 1840. His instructions were to establish an impression of British strength, to reach an amicable understanding with the Uzbek tribes, and to effect the release of Russian slaves. So much really represented the extent of Auckland's policy, as against MacNaghten's at that time. His last instruction was to gain the release of Stoddart who had now been held for two years.

Conolly travelled first to Khiva where he was treated with some scorn by the Khan. The latter could afford to spurn British offers of friendship, for the threat from Russia had receded with the failure of Perovskiy's campaign and the events which followed it. For the same reason Conolly fared no better with the Khan of Kokand who was also pre-occupied at the time with a desultory war against Bukhara. The Amir of Bukhara, having likewise seen the threat to his future independence disappear, and having a shrewd idea that things were not going well with the British in Afghanistan regarded Conolly's appearance in the light of his own suspicious nature. He was veering once more towards Russia.

The Amir still expected a letter from his fellow-sovereign Queen Victoria. But the letter which Conolly brought was only from MacNaghten which the Amir regarded as a snub to his prestige. So he consigned Conolly to joining Stoddart in prison whilst he continued to watch events in Afghanistan.

The collapse of Shah Shuja's short-lived régime and the disaster to British arms set the seal on the fate of the two men. Obviously the British could provide no help against any future Russian threat and the prisoners therefore had no bargaining value. The Amir continued to torture them with spells in the Dark Well and severe privation, during which the two men gave each other Christian comfort and support. At last in 1842 he executed them. They were out-dated crusaders and, like Lieutenant Wyburd, they died bravely for their ideals, but the plain fact was that neither of them was temperamentally suitable for a task for which they should never have been chosen. Even if they had been fitted they could have achieved nothing politically useful. In fact the inability to rescue them severely damaged British prestige in Central Asia.

They were not the only envoys to be sent to the khanates during this period. When Burnes withdrew from Herat three Political Officers who had gone with him were left behind, of whom Major D'Arcy Todd was instructed by MacNaghten to act as envoy there. Todd was another devoutly religious man and he made himself unpopular locally by his efforts to put down slavery. At the end of 1839 the Khan of Khiva sent a messenger to Herat demanding urgent help against the expected Russian onslaught. Todd could offer no help, only moral support, but he saw the approach as an opportunity. If only he could persuade the Khan to release his Russian slaves that would achieve the purpose, without bloodshed, of General Perovskiy's principal stated objective. More important still he thought it would indirectly relieve the supposed threat to India.

So he decided to send a Political Officer, Captain James Abbott, to conduct the negotiations at Khiva. At the same time he was to find out whether Russia really was preparing a campaign as was rumoured, and also to discuss the means of releasing Stoddart through any influence the Khan might have with Bukhara. Abbott's passport was no more than a letter from Todd. It said nothing about negotiations with Russia which were beyond his powers to authorise but he asked MacNaghten for such authority. Abbott was another imaginative romantic type. He too was a devout evangelist and saw his mission as a wonderful chance to free Central Asia from slavery.

He left on the 24th December 1839. When he reached Khiva the Khan at first suspected him of being a Russian spy. He professed not to know the difference between the British and the Russians and it took Abbott several audiences to allay his suspicions. The Khan, of course, wanted help against the Russians who he believed were only a few days' march away, but Abbott persuaded him that if he would release their prisoners and slaves he would not be attacked. The Khan said he was ready to release them provided the Russians would release his caravans. Hitherto it had not been known in India that they held any of the latter. Abbott also discussed means of releasing Stoddart, indicating that unless his release could be negotiated the British might send an army to do so. That was not at all to the Khan's liking, even though for years he had been waging a desultory war with Bukhara. His own suggestion was to send a party to kidnap Stoddart whilst he was at exercise, but nothing came of it.

As for the Russian slaves, the Khan gave Abbott a promise to release them if St. Petersburg would reciprocate and he gave Abbott a letter to take personally to the Tsar. Furthermore he issued a Rescript, a copy of which exists in the archives of the Royal Society for Asian Affairs,[1] forbidding his subjects to take any more Russian prisoners on pain of punishment. Without further orders but armed with the Khan's written promise and a copy of the Rescript, and without telling the Indian government, Abbott set off for Orenburg in a rare state of excitement at his success, with a small escort provided by the Khan. Up till his departure his main trouble had been a shortage of funds, so much so that he had had to sell some of his horses and even borrow money at an extravagant rate of discount in Khiva. He had sent only one despatch which was delayed for three weeks before the messenger could get away. After his departure he learned that the Khan had intercepted

---

[1] See Appendix 1.

messages for him from Herat. A later despatch date-lined in April from the Caspian only reached Herat in July: it described his misfortunes after leaving Khiva and only added that he had no authentic news of Russian troop movements. (In fact he did not hear of the failure of the Khivan campaign till he reached Orenburg.) Probably deliberately he said nothing about his further intention.

His misfortunes were indeed severe. Before he reached the Mangyshlak Peninsula on the Caspian he and his escort were set upon by 'cuzzack'[1] brigands; several of his party were wounded and he himself lost a finger. Rival Kazakhs held him prisoner for a fortnight and his life was in the greatest danger till an Afghan messenger arrived from Todd with a supply of 'ducats' and negotiated his release. He reached the Caspian in a sorry state; even so being the emotional man he was, he celebrated his arrival there in April by composing a lengthy paean in painful doggerel in praise of Queen Victoria, with the refrain:

> Queen of the Isles
> Queen of the Deep
> Of Freedom, Valour, Beauty, Queen.

Although in uniform he was at first refused entry to the Russian fort. It transpired that rumour, preceding him, had reported that he was leading an army of 10,000 to attack the fort. When the discrepancy between his ragged escort of 10 Khivan soldiers and the 10,000 had been cleared up, he was received as a guest, had his wounds dressed (another finger had to be amputated later) and altogether received a generous welcome. Travelling on to Orenburg he was accorded a remarkable reception by the Governor General, General Perovskiy. The General was a most cultured man. He dined and wined Abbott and even gave him presents from his art collection and lent him a watch. He also lent him his carriage to drive round the district. Much to his delight Abbott, who had an eye for feminine beauty, attended his first European ball, where he fell in love with a colonel's daughter and wrote a love sonnet to her. Everywhere he went he was accorded traditional Russian

---

1 The variously spelt term 'Cuzzak, 'Cuzzack', or 'Kuzzauk' (Abbott and Shakespear both spell it each way) sometimes implied Cossack and sometimes Kazakh. In this context Kazakh was intended: when Abbott meant the former he spelt it Cossaq.

hospitality. He was presumably under some surveillance by the aide whom Perovskiy attached to him, but he had given his word not to speak to 'Tartars' and he and the aide became firm friends. They met again in St. Petersburg and the aide showed him round the capital. Meanwhile having welcomed Abbott and ensured his comfort Perovskiy departed for St. Petersburg.

He had exercised caution in two other respects: he refused to accept Abbott's credentials (the letter from Todd) and treated him solely as a private traveller, and he would not give him permission to write an account of his experiences. It may be guessed that he saw several advantages in summoning him on to St. Petersburg rather than returning him to Khiva. So having undertaken to deliver the Khan's letter to the Tsar himself, Abbott set off for the capital as soon as he had recovered. He was shown the sights of Moscow on the way and had an even greater reception at the capital. There he delivered the Khan's letter to the Foreign Minister, Count Nesselrode, whom he described as a cautious man asking many questions; in particular he asked whether the Khan of Khiva's word could be trusted. An additional reason for his caution was that he knew Perovskiy, like other Governors General, could go over his head to the Tsar.

With his credentials established by the British ambassador the Tsar invited Abbott to a grand review of the Imperial Guard and personally addressed him – a rare honour, especially for a mere Captain in the East India Company's Bengal Artillery. Perovskiy had mounted him well on one of his own chargers. There was probably a more significant reason than the mere desire to impress a British officer, which would account for Abbott's unusually warm reception. Perovskiy was using him as a means of influencing the Tsar to cancel a second campaign against Khiva. Back in England he was interviewed by Palmerston and Hobhouse. The latter described this strange man as ceremonious, grave and almost obsequious.

By June 1840 Todd had received no word from Abbott since the despatch announcing his safe arrival at Khiva. Meanwhile Mac-Naghten had given permission for the latter to negotiate with the Russian authorities if desirable. Thereupon Todd sent another Political Officer, Lieutenant Richmond Shakespear, to Khiva with this further authority. There was no evangelistic idealism about Shakespear. Concerning his mission he wrote 'the chances of distinction are so great and the hazard so slight that the heart of even a wren would be gladdened by the prospect'. In short he was out for honours. He reached Khiva in June 1840 two months after Abbott had left. Unlike his predecessor who hid his intentions by saying nothing of value in his main despatch, although he was most expansive in his subsequent book, Shakespear's three despatches were tersely professional and described his route with a strictly military eye. He journeyed for 185 miles along the Amu Dar'ya and noted its navigability and the fertility of its countryside. He was not surprised that Russia coveted the region: Russian merchants had all the advantages and he did not think India could hope to compete with them there.

Abbott having done so much to prepare the way, Shakespear was comfortably housed and had little difficulty in obtaining audiences of the Khan, although besides Todd's letter, he only carried that from MacNaghten. His instructions were the same as Abbott's with the addition that he was to obtain the actual release of the Russian slaves. It was only at Khiva that he learned that the Russian campaign had failed.

Shakespear spent two months there and had several frank and friendly talks with the Khan. His conclusions were that Khiva was bound to fall to the next Russian attack, but that Bukhara would welcome a Russian force. His suggestion for releasing Stoddart was that Britain should support Khiva and that a combination of Kabul, Herat, Kokand and Khiva would be 'far from impossible if force became necessary to liberate him'. Meanwhile, however, he thought, as had Abbott, that it might still be possible to negotiate his release through good relations with Khiva.

Shakespear found that there were several thousand slaves in Khiva of whom 350 were Russian; like Abbott he drove home the argument that their release would stave off a further Russian attack. The Khan claimed that Russia held 600 Khivans. He was disappointed when Shakespear said India could not supply him with the artillery he had asked for, but nevertheless he reiterated his undertaking to release the slaves and he also accepted Shakespear's offer to act as mediator. At this time neither of them knew what Abbott had achieved at Orenburg and St. Petersburg, so Shakespear addressed a letter to the 'Officer commanding the Russian Forces' conveying the Khan's terms and repeating Mac-Naghten's permission to negotiate an amicable settlement.

Having with difficulty and considerable perseverance collected all the Russian prisoners held at Khiva and assembled enough camels to mount them, Shakespear set out on the 5th of August. Before leaving, either some of his papers were stolen or he forgot to destroy them. They were found by the Russian Khivan expedition in 1873 and the Soviet historian, N. A. Khalfin, has since made great play with them. The distance across the steppe to Novo Aleksandrovsk (now Fort Shevchenko) is nearly 600 miles and on the last part of the journey wells were respectively 30, 40, 60 and 70 miles apart. In bringing all his charges safely to Novo Alexandrovsk in 25 days of high summer temperature Shakespear accomplished a truly remarkable feat. Extracts from his letters add interesting details, and demonstrate his own elation at his success.

Much of his correspondence dating from 1832 is in the archives of the Royal Society for Asian Affairs. Some of his letters written during the journey were printed in 1910 in the Journal of the Calcutta Historical Society, *Bengal Past and Present*. One document therein is worth quoting in full, it reads as follows:

'Commandant at Novo Alexandroffsk Fortress. 5 Sept 1840 No 4097. To the Envoy to the Khan Akhun and of the Englishman Shakespear.

On the 30th Aug. last you delivered here from Khiva, Russian prisoners in number according to a detailed list, males, females and children under age, four hundred and sixteen. When you collected them from amongst the Khivans, Turkomans and others you gave to each one ducat and fifty pounds weight of flour.

On their arrival at this fortress, in answer to my enquiry, they expressed themselves unanimously grateful to you, as Father and Benefactor, from the time of their being taken out of bondage, during the journey from Khiva to this fortress, of which I shall make a report to the Governor-General of Orenbourg, Adjutant General Peroffsky.

Signed Commandant of Nova Alexandroffsk Fortress, Colonel of Artillery Sikhoshiostoff.'

Apart from his official despatches Shakespear also kept a log of his journey, from which however he omitted all references to his delicate negotiations lest it should be stolen by the Khan: for instance the Khan was very suspicious of survey work. On the other hand his letters to friends and relations were remarkably descriptive. From Khiva he wrote to his sister Emily on the 14th June 1840 saying he had arrived there safely and that the Russian force (i.e. the Perovskiy expedition of 1839) had been driven back by sickness. On the 14th September he wrote to her from Dust Kulla[1] on the Caspian telling how he had released the Russian captives and had accomplished his journey 'not a horse or a camel even has been lost! The Russians [prisoners] are at a loss to express their gratitude'. He expected to secure the release of 600 Khivans on his arrival at Orenburg. From Orenburg on the 8th October he wrote to Major Irvine at Calcutta saying he did not expect much pleasure from his trip to the Russian capital and would have preferred to return to Khiva. 'So far the object of my mission has been gained but the Russians will not acknowledge me as anything but a private traveller'. He said he had released 416 Russians and 600 Khivans from slavery and he believed that his agreement with Khiva prohibiting the seizure of Russians and 'Herautees' would save at least 3000 more in future. Somewhat reluctantly but in order to keep faith he had had to accompany the released Russians all the way by sea and land to Orenburg, the total distance from Khiva being about 1000 miles.

Carrying more money than Abbott, who was forced to travel by the 'post', he bought two carriages for part of his journey to St. Petersburg. On arrival there he noted how anxious Russians were to be thought well of in Britain and like Abbott he was lavishly entertained. At a ball he was presented to the Tsar and kissed the hands of members of his family. Elsewhere he said 'The Russian Government refuse to acknowledge me in a public capacity, but they have done all we wanted in publishing their intentions of forming friendly relations with Khiva and *not* invading that territory'. To set the seal on his success he too received the public thanks of the Tsar. The latter also ratified the treaty with Khiva, based on the letter Abbott had brought from the Khan. Besides endorsing the exchange of prisoners it also undertook that the Governor of Orenburg should withdraw his army within the limits of the Russian empire.

Many years later in 1920 Shakespear's son John explained in a letter to Colonel A. C. Yate that 'the Russian Government was

---

[1] Properly Dasht Kila, i.e. desert fort.

horridly embarrassed by my father's success, as it preferred the good excuse for absorbing Khiva which the continued presence of the prisoners afforded'. That was one aspect, but Abbott saw another equally valid one. He wrote 'The promise of the Khan to release all the Russian slaves on assurance from the Emperor that he would set free the Khivan captives had been communicated by me to the Court of St. Petersburg. To have released the Russian slaves while a Russian army was in full march upon Khiva would not have stayed the advance of that army. When however the severity of the season had discomfited the Russian army....the fitting time for their release had come'. He generously acknowledged Shakespear's feat, but ascribed most of the credit for the success of the two missions to Major Todd, 'For he it was who by effecting the release of captives on either side enabled the Emperor of Russia to free himself with honour from a painful dilemma'. This strangely modest man claimed no credit for his work.

Competent soldier as he was Perovskiy knew only too well the difficulties of another campaign and neither the Tsar nor Nesselrode wanted to risk another débacle so soon after the recent damaging blow to Russia's prestige in Central Asia. Shakespear saw no preparations for a renewed campaign whilst he was in Orenburg although Abbott had earlier seen obvious signs. The probability is that the Tsar had already rescinded his order as a result of Abbott's negotiations.

Once in England the ambitious Shakespear boldly applied for a knighthood and Palmerston saw that he received it. He was also promoted to Lieutenant Colonel. Abbott got no recognition at all although he had borne all the heat and burden, and by his delicate and patient negotiations had made possible the actual release of the prisoners by Shakespear. Ultimately however he rose to the rank of general, received a KCB and he named the town of Abbottabad after himself. Todd got no recognition either: in fact he was dismissed by Auckland shortly afterwards and was killed in a subsequent campaign whilst serving with his regiment; hence perhaps Abbott's posthumous tribute.

A contemporary letter in the *Calcutta Review* commented that Abbott was just as deserving of recognition as Shakespear. That drew a sharp riposte from the latter, claiming that it cast an aspersion on his integrity. Nevertheless posterity may think the honours should at least have been shared. Shakespear's only published account of his mission appeared in *Blackwood's Magazine* of June 1842. He said precisely nothing about Abbott's successful negotiations and referred only to the Kazakh attack on him. The contrast between the characters of the two men is vividly shown in Abbott's book, *Journey from Heraut to Khiva, Moscow and St. Petersburg*. First published in 1843 it was so successful that a third edition appeared in 1884. He told his story in much purple prose and expounded his views not only on Russian strategy and designs on India, but on Russian government, social life, art, character and much else that he saw during his short stay. For obvious reasons the missions of Abbott and Shakespear were ignored by pre-Revolutionary Russian historians. Their success had no effect on the defence of India; it was the Russian government that reaped the benefit of their unsolicited intervention. In recent years the Soviet historian, N. A. Khalfin, has re-told the story but has falsified the facts for a Soviet propaganda motive which will be discussed hereafter; one example from his version will suffice here. He wrote '(Abbott) with a large detachment of Khivan soldiers was held off by Russian forces near the Novo Alexandrovsk fortress and was then arrested'!

Because of his achievements Abbott cannot be excluded; otherwise with the exception of Shakespear, the men chosen to carry out India's ephemeral policy in Bukhara, Kokand and Khiva compare most unfavourably with Burnes and the men selected by him. Being temperamentally unsuited to their tasks they too often exacerbated the khans and the tribes instead of, as intended, improving relations with them and raising British prestige. Naturally their activities fed Russian suspicions as to British intentions in Central Asia. It was neither their duty nor had they the experience to discuss British strategy as they all did.

India's fallacious idea that Russia would forego any further interest in the region once her captives were released was a part of the complete incomprehension of what Russia's real interests were. As for the talk of evangelization, Russia was no less a Christian nation than Britain, and in general the visionaries amongst the early explorers proved themselves to be the poorest diplomatists. The casualties suffered by the Political Officers were severe. Wyburd, Burnes, Lord, Stoddart and Conolly were only the best known of the losses; Burnes's brother and both of Conolly's were amongst others less publicized. Perhaps their most admirable common characteristics were immense courage, fortitude and a deep sense of responsibility.

After the Afghan War the Political Service set about improving its status. Up to that time its members, as Kaye said, had bad reputations as being 'wild, addicted to keeping fierce dogs and native harems, and in general as being as uncivilized as the tribes they worked with'. But Kaye also added that their temptations were great. Twenty years later their ability and status had been changed vastly for the better. After the Mutiny only the best men were chosen for the Political Service.

If Russia was somewhat slow to send out trained men – at any rate so far as we know – it was because she saw no need. Central Asia was not nearly so important to her as the Near East. The Kazakhs and the khanates presented no serious threat or defence problem; they were merely an inconvenience and could be dealt with at leisure. Far more important to her was to increase her trade in these parts, preferably with organized states, but the trade needed protection if it was to prosper. In the eighteenth century a few Russian missions had reached Bukhara. They must have been commercial missions and entrepreneurial in the strictest sense of the term for they do not seem to have given the Russian government any useful political picture.

A large quantity of detailed and valuable material was provided by the Russian mission of Negri which visited Bukhara in 1820. Three of his companions published their observations; particularly important was the monograph written by Meyendorf; important, too, were reports by P. Yakovlev, who produced plans of Bukhara and Khiva, and by Budrin, a priest attached to the mission.

After Burnes there appeared in Bukhara a Tatar mulla named Ja'far. He was followed by Demezan, who was in reality a Frenchman named DeMaison in the Russian service. An article based on information supplied by DeMaison was published by P. Savel'yev in 1837.

In 1841 the mission of N. Khanykov and A. Leman visited Bukhara. Khanykov's work *An Account of the Khanate of Bukhara* is considered by the Russians to be the most important book on Bukhara produced before the Revolution.[1]

The latest mission to Bukhara under Colonel Butenov may have been the first with any real political or military motive. It was one of Russia's first reactions to British activities and it appears to have achieved reasonable relations with the Amir. Butenov himself was a mining engineer and the Amir hoped he might find gold in Bukhara. His endeavour to negotiate the release of Stoddart was the result of an urgent appeal to the Russian Government by Palmerston. In the circumstances it was the most likely way of achieving his release and it might well have been successful if it had been backed by Auckland with an order to Stoddart to withdraw. As it was, Butenov withdrew his mission after Stoddart had refused his help.

Turning to individual travellers on the Russian side, our knowledge of one, the Italian Giovanni, suggests that he was simply one of those freelance adventurers who were drawn to Central Asia. Arthur Conolly was the first to mention him: they had struck up a friendship in 1829 in Istanbul. He reappears in a despatch from Shakespear who met him in Khiva. He was an itinerant maker of plaster statuettes and a watchmaker; having failed to sell statuettes in Khiva because images offended Muslim law he was trying to sell clocks instead. Todd's comment was 'From numerous specimens of this class of adventurer whom I have met with in Persia and elsewhere I think it by no means improbable that the individual in question is a secret agent of Russia'. However it is highly unlikely that the Russians would have employed such a man. It is said that he built a clock for the Amir of Bukhara but was afterwards murdered for refusing to turn Muslim.

There are no doubts concerning Lieutenant Yan Vitkevich, although there is a final unsolved mystery about his end. He was a Lithuanian who as a mere schoolboy had been deported from Vilna to Omsk for his Polish sympathies. Harshly cut off from his parents he studied languages and became fluent in French, Persian, Turkish and other Turkic languages. He was subsequently reprieved and commissioned in the 1st Orenburg Cossack Regiment. In about 1833 he came to the notice of the Military Governor

---

[1] See *Bukhara 1800 to the beginning of the XXth Century* by Olga Sukhareva. Moscow 1966.

at Orenburg, Perovskiy, who employed him on missions into the steppes. His first visit to Bukhara was in 1835 – thus following Burnes's mission and probably as a consequence of it, but he may have gone more than once.

In 1837 when Dost Muhammad, with his eye partly on Peshawar, opened negotiations simultaneously with Calcutta, St. Petersburg and Tehran, Burnes reached Kabul first. Vitkevich followed shortly afterwards. Both Burnes and Rawlinson met him: they described him as a gentlemanly, agreeable young man of about 30, wearing Cossack uniform which was a novelty in those parts. Burnes would have liked to make his better acquaintance but deemed it wiser to forbear. Vitkevich had been sent by Simonich, the Russian envoy at Tehran, with instructions to reconcile the Afghan rulers. He carried a letter from the Tsar which the Amir showed Burnes; although unsigned it appeared to him to be genuine. It advised the Amir to take advantage of Iran's protection 'inasmuch as Russia however benevolent is at one remove away'. Vitkevich was empowered to offer better terms than Burnes; he was instructed to offer a large loan as well as a considerable quantity of goods. Whilst Burnes's talks were going well, Vitkevich made little progress but when Auckland repudiated Burnes Dost Muhammad turned to Vitkevich and agreed to make common cause with Iran and Kandahar and to increase his trade with Russia. With that highly successful achievement Vitkevich reported back to Simonich, visiting Herat on the way. It was at that point that Palmerston threatened force against Iran and made a formal protest to Russia against the activities of both Simonich and Vitkevich, as a result of which they were recalled. The Vitkevich affair aroused great public animosity against Russia in Britain. Count Nesselrode, as Foreign Minister, disclaimed all responsibility for Vitkevich when he reached St. Petersburg, whereupon the unfortunate young man committed suicide after destroying all his papers. The note which he left gave no reason for his decision to shoot himself.

Hitherto that has been the accepted version of his end. But recently N. A. Khalfin has re-opened the subject after studying State papers. He says Vitkevich carried out his orders to the letter and was well received in the highest circles on his return to St. Petersburg. Khalfin recalls that both pre-Revolutionary and Soviet historians have suggested that Vitkevich's papers would have been so valuable to the British that it would have been worth their while to assassinate him. None of them however had any substantive evidence to offer and the story is in the highest degree unlikely. It seems at least possible (if also just as unlikely) that given his dissident past Vitkevich and his papers were disposed of by Russian agents lest, having been disowned, he should offer his services to the British. That however is not put forward as a serious conjecture. Lady Clanricarde, the wife of the British ambassador, told Sir John Hobhouse that Vitkevich left a note addressed to one of the Tsar's principal advisers which said 'Come and contemplate your handiwork.' As Khalfin says the mystery of his suicide remains unsolved.[1] At any rate there is no doubt whatever that Russia lost a very skilled man who might well have gone on to far higher achievements.

Thereafter Russia was to send out a series of explorers and missions of resource and determination who contributed not only to the expansionist policies of General Perovskiy's great successors, but to the geographical and scientific knowledge of Central Asia as well. Their often independent activities fed the suspicions of successive British governments and sometimes embarrassed their own; although the embarrassment was generally more assumed than real.

---

[1] A translated and abridged version of his article entitled 'Drama in a Hotel Bedroom' (*Voprosy Istorii*, No. 10, 1966) appeared in *Central Asian Review* No. 4, 1967.

CHAPTER SIX

Interlude

Lord Ellenborough's campaign against Kabul to restore Britain's sadly damaged prestige, his subsequent withdrawal and the failure to prevent the execution of Stoddart and Conolly in Bukhara marked the end of Britain's first round in the Game. It had fallen far short of its objectives in securing India's defence and the development of trade in Central Asia; indeed it was a collapse. On the Russian side the disaster of the campaign against Khiva, followed by the largely unwanted success of the missions of Abbott and Shakespear in negotiating the release of Russian prisoners and other slaves marked the end of Russia's first round, and left her temporarily without an explicit initiative. There was an intermission in Central Asia during which neither of the rivals made any threatening moves against each other. Instead their interests clashed in the Near East. That is not to say that there were no developments of importance in the region but they were not dictated or directly influenced by the two great powers.

From the events of the past ten years there had emerged certain underlying factors which were to influence the Game henceforward. The first of them was common to both sides and was psychological rather than political – it was suspicion. Oddly enough for a nation not prone to suspicion, Britain succumbed to it first – from the days of Napoleon's threat to India – although there were always wise men in high places who remained unaffected. But Russia quickly followed suit because in any case it already was, as it still is, a feature of the Russian character. It is no recent phenomenon brought about by Soviet rule although that may have intensified it. Some believe it was an inheritance from the 400 years of Mongol domination; at any rate it was apparent when, for example, the Marquis de Custine, visiting Russia in 1839, noted that a spy was always attached to any traveller of importance. He remarked that it did not do to become too friendly with one's spy; because in that case the spy, who understood nothing else but spying, was liable to believe the tables were being turned against him![1] It is strange that when an individual complains that he is being persecuted and spied on he is described as mentally ill – a paranoiac – but that the description is never used when a whole nation suffers from this incurable disease: fear and insecurity may well be its source. Both countries could claim a measure of rational cause but suspicion of each other's ultimate motives always bedevilled rational solutions. Agreement was indeed ultimately achieved but not until 1907 at the Anglo-Russian Convention, and even then rather grudgingly. By that time the conflict had lasted for nearly a hundred years with mutual suspicion rife throughout, and with every move followed by a counter-move.

Another common factor also emerged from these early days. It was that neither country wanted a direct confrontation in Central Asia. Junior officers, Russian as well as British, could boast of what would happen when the Sepoy and the Cossack met head on, but even at this time it was becoming plain that the statesmen in London and St. Petersburg had no intention of letting it happen. What Palmerston had stated in his outspoken way was implicitly in the mind of the cautious Nesselrode, and their successors were to follow the same line, although none ever openly expressed it. A third and highly important factor, equally applicable to Russia and Britain, was the need to maintain prestige in Central Asia. In the eyes of native tribes any blow to the prestige of the two great powers indicated a weakness which they were only too ready to exploit. China had always known the importance of prestige and had used it along her outer borders for many centuries – often without any more backing of visible force than an important-looking yamen and a few ill-armed soldiers. Apart from these three common factors, each country found itself forced by circumstances to recognise certain other principles which had emerged during the first ten years and were to govern their political strategy for the next five decades.

First of all it was obviously useless for Britain to continue trying

---

1 See *The Marquis de Custine and his Journey to Russia in 1839*. George F. Kennan. London 1971.

to establish Iran as an outer zone of British influence. The country and its government were far too unstable for her to form any reliable alliance. Their treaty lay in ruins and there was also much antagonism between Iran and Afghanistan. In 1856 Britain was to conduct a campaign at Bushire in the Persian Gulf – in a very unsatisfactory manner – to deter her from continuing hostilities against Herat, but there could be no thought of fighting in the north for that would inevitably bring her into open conflict with Russia. It was a risk which Palmerston, despite his threats, was at pains to avoid. Britain could only strive to hold and develop by commercial means, her influence in the south.

The second British plan, to establish Afghanistan as an inner zone – a buffer state with a puppet ruler under the strict control of India – was also, for the time being, in ruins. Now Britain could only stand by and await events there, hoping meanwhile that at least they would have no serious effect on the peaceful administration and development of India. The fact remained however that Afghanistan was still seen by most men in India as the ultimate answer in one form or another to her western and north-western defences; just as southern Iran with her vital ports on the sea route to India, together with Sistan and Baluchistan, were necessary for her defence on the west. It was the 'forward policy', but in modified form, and it was for the time being in abeyance.

Secondly Britain had done nothing towards establishing any influence in the Central Asian khanates. Whilst Khiva temporarily leaned rather more towards India as a result of the successful mediation of Abbott and Shakespear, Bukhara was leaning away and towards Russia. The Amir was probably influenced by fear of his hereditary enemy Afghanistan and calculated that he might get Russian support against her. The trade through which Britain hoped to exert influence prospered not at all. As the fate of Stoddart and Conolly showed, prestige counted for nothing if it could not be backed by armed force. On the other hand experience in Central Asia had disclosed for the first time that in the fluid conditions which existed there, India would henceforth have to look to her northern defences.

Russia's first round, which had been much more tentatively conducted than Britain's, was also marked by failure. There had been the Vitkevich attempt to arrange a treaty with Dost Muhammad, which was abandoned in the face of British pressure. It had been followed by the inability of General Perovskiy's army to cope with desert conditions in his winter campaign. Neither of these affairs can be seen in retrospect as preliminaries to a planned advance against India, such as the extremists in India foretold. They were really part of Russia's opportunist southward probing policy, always seeking for trade and for settled frontiers, and stimulated by the necessity to forestall Britain. The last principle – not yet formulated in words, but already established by her process of expansion – was the quest for stable demarcated frontiers. She was to achieve it by pushing forward where resistance was weak but stopping short in the face of strong organized opposition.

For the next six or seven years neither of the two powers had the will or the means to launch into new policies in Central Asia. In India the consequence was that those who refused to see Russia as a threat and held that India's north-western defence should be based on her existing borders but ready to move as actual events might dictate, found their policy tacitly accepted, if not officially adopted. That was what became known as the 'policy of masterly inactivity' – the expression borrowed from Sir James Macintosh by J. Wyllie, an official in the Government of India's Foreign Department.

As for Russia she still had her hands full enough in pacifying the Caucasus and establishing her rule there, but events in the Near East were again beginning to occupy her urgent attention. Although Britain may not have recognized it Russia was not nearly strong enough, nor could she afford, to be active on the Central Asian front at the same time. So beyond extending her fortified lines here and there and absorbing a few minor Kazakh tribes, Russia made no important moves.

Meanwhile she initiated one important overture on the diplomatic front. In 1844, Nesselrode accompanied Tsar Nicholas on a state visit to Queen Victoria, who swallowed her dislike of Russians in general and Nicholas in particular, at any rate for the time being. As a result of conversations between the British Prime Minister, the Tory Sir Robert Peel, and Nesselrode, British relations over Central Asia were relieved by a mutual, if rather vague, understanding that Afghanistan and the khanates north of the Oxus should form a neutral belt. That it was never put into precise terms was partly because of the usual suspicion, and probably too because it would have proved quite unworkable in practice. For a single example, friction would have arisen quickly enough through commercial competition. However the détente which had really begun with the Straits Convention of 1841 by defining spheres of influence in the Near East, lasted until the Crimean War. But if the diplomatists in London and St. Petersburg were content to lessen the tension, there was much food for thought in Calcutta and a good deal of significant movement elsewhere in Central Asia. Horizons were beginning to widen and we must take a tour, viewing not only what happened but introducing some new aspects which were to complicate Anglo-Russian relations still more.

To begin with Afghanistan, Dost Muhammad had returned to Kabul in 1842. After Britain had deprived him of his throne in 1838 he had lived in India as a guest of the government. But following the assassination of Shah Shuja he was allowed to go back – a wise decision as it proved. He was still intent on re-unifying his country after the depredations of the Sikhs, Uzbeks and his rival the Saddozais. Rather unexpectedly, yet justifying Burnes's claims for him, he showed no ill-will towards the British. Indeed, whilst recognising that Russia had more men and territory, he realized that India had the better engineers and more advanced technology. Nevertheless, since after all the British had been defeated in Afghanistan, he held aloof from relations with India whilst steadily pursuing his re-unifying policies.

His first major achievement was the re-conquest in 1850 of the Balkh region. This was of great future importance for India because it lay beyond the Hindu Kush, on the possible northern invasion route. Burnes, Lord, Wood and Todd too, had all recommended its annexation by India if Russia annexed Khiva: but that was where the imagination of the early 'politicals' exceeded their knowledge of practicalities. It would have been strategically impossible to launch a campaign beyond the Hindu Kush to rescue Stoddart and Conolly, as MacNaghten threatened, still less so to assert subsequent political control – if that was what he really meant when he favoured the extension of influence up to the Amu Dar'ya. At best India could only have hoped to establish a degree of commercial influence – at the expense of further exacerbating Russia. However Dost Muhammad's political skill saved the Company's government from any future serious consideration of such risky ventures, and his recovery of Kunduz and Badakhshan in 1855 brought further lasting benefits to India. Finally by 1863 he had drawn Herat under his rule and that was a major step towards ending Iranian pretensions, as well as making the main western invasion route more difficult for Russia. In all this work he got no help from India. So in this respect Russia, who would in those days have claimed a pro-British or British dominated Afghanistan as a threat to her interests in Central Asia, had no cause for complaint. Indirectly Dost Muhammad's contribution to the future defence of India was immense.

Dost Muhammad was a strong ruler and he demonstrated a lesson which in spite of their long experience the British seem to have forgotten when they installed Shah Shuja. Much of the expansion of India had taken place through what was called the 'doctrine of lapse' which has already been mentioned. Simply stated the Company moved in to take over any Indian state which was badly governed under a weak or corrupt ruler. The lesson which had been forgotten was that a weak ruler simply encouraged rivals to take over his throne and internal wars were the inevitable result. Russia had already learned the lesson in settling the Kazakh steppes. She had begun by installing khans whose main qualification was subservience to Russian government. By painful experience however she found that a strong khan with a measure of independence, but who governed his subjects firmly in the way that they had been accustomed, was the recipe for peace. It worked all the better because the Russian system of government was a military one, which in itself commanded natural respect.

When Ranjit Singh, the ruler of the Punjab, died the Indian government showed that the lesson had not been altogether forgotten. After much civil strife for the succession, in which French and Italian mercenary officers took an often leading part, Dalhousie and Hardinge, successive Governors General, finally annexed the Punjab in 1847 following the First and Second Sikh Wars. The breaking of the treaty with Sind to enable the army of the Indus to pass through, and its subsequent annexation at the beginning of the Afghan war had been a piece of blatant political expediency. The annexation of the Punjab was the last major step in British expansion in north-west India; in all logic she could go no further. What was needed now was to secure India's frontiers. The Punjab was a reservoir of fine fighting men and, together with

Peshawar as the key military base, it afforded the opportunity to control the dissident tribes in the trans-frontier region between India and the territory recognised as Afghan. The annexation was a step that heartened the protagonists of the policy of 'masterly inactivity', which included all those men of rising influence who had never taken a Russian threat seriously, nor regarded Herat as of prime importance. No steps were ever actually taken to make the Indus itself a defence line, if only for the very good military reason that rivers are unsuitable as defensive positions, especially when they are used by local peoples for everyday trade and travel.

The possibility of the annexation of the Punjab had been pessimistically foreseen by Nesselrode during his discussions in London in 1844 and if Russia saw it differently from India, she can hardly be blamed. The excuse of ending civil strife on her existing borders was how Britain had historically taken over more and more of the subcontinent. Where, asked Russia, would it end? After the Punjab would come Afghanistan, and after Afghanistan perhaps even Central Asia, and all in the guise of trade protection. Why then should Russia be blamed for forestalling Britain in Central Asia by doing the same thing? After all Central Asia was nearer to Russia than to India and she felt, with justification, that she had the prior claim. She had just as much need of stable frontiers as India – in fact as a still emergent major power she saw them more importantly – and even more need of any trade that might be developed there; India could certainly not expect a monopoly. However, from now onwards trade was to become more of a catch-word. Political strategy on a much wider scale was the real factor in the rivalry and the development of trade in Central Asia was to become almost a side issue.

So far neither Britain nor Russia had defined any ultimate political objectives in Central Asia; the only intentions which were beyond doubt were Britain's determination to secure the defence of India, whilst Russia was equally determined to keep Britain out of Central Asia, that is to say primarily the three Khanates of Bukhara, Kokand and Khiva. Concerning Afghanistan, Russia had no clearly expressed policy. Her main fear was that we would use the country as a stepping stone. It seems that broadly at the time she would have regarded the Hindu Kush running from Chitral through northern Afghanistan as the natural geographical boundary of India. With the proviso that Russia would advance no further, Auckland himself had seen the Afghan Hindu Kush as India's natural frontier and said so to Palmerston. But whilst that view was strategically sound for the Chitral end of the range its prolongation into Afghanistan, except in the case of actual war with Russia, would have resulted in permanently dividing that country down the middle. That would have ended any hope of making the country a buffer and would have been an invitation to Russia to occupy the northern half just as it was feared she might occupy north Iran. Yet the concept persisted, for the official Indian publication *Frontier and Overseas Expeditions from India* (Simla 1907–11) had this to say, 'the existing frontier of India has never presented a serious obstacle to invading hordes and the natural frontier of India would appear to be on the Hindu Kush'. Fairly certainly Russia saw herself as entitled to all the fertile land lying between the Syr Dar'ya and the Amu Dar'ya and westwards to the Caspian Sea.

Meanwhile Russia had learned one valuable lesson from recent experience which was to be of great importance. It was that India was the Achilles heel of Britain. Henceforth as she continued to be opposed by Britain and her sometime allies in the Near East she was going to make increasing use of diversionary gestures aimed at giving the impression of threatening India. From Iran to the Pamir and the Himalaya she had an extremely wide field to exploit. To them was shortly to be added Chinese Turkestan (Sinkiang).

Behind the guarded recognition of an undefined neutral zone it is very difficult to say just what amount of activity each country saw as justifiable. What Russia's intentions were as regards the khanates were never expressed, but it was obvious that Perovskiy who was a thrusting forceful governor of independent ideas, or failing him his successor, would wage another campaign against Khiva as soon as he saw the opportunity. As for India there was nothing she could do now about Afghanistan; with the Punjab under the administration of the brothers John and Henry Lawrence, both adhering to the principle of 'masterly inactivity', the defence of India against Russia was for the time being not a matter of urgency. Only in Iran did rivalry between Britain and Russia continue in active form.

But looking at India's defence through the eyes of the brothers Lawrence, Russia was not the only or even the most important danger. All the independent states outside India's control, from

Kashmir in the north, through Afghanistan to Baluchistan in the west, constituted some sort of potential danger to the peaceful internal development of India. What, for instance, if Afghanistan and Iran settled their differences and with or without Russian support launched a joint invasion of India? Prudent soldiers and administrators prepare plans to meet every possible contingency and that one certainly could not be ruled out. There was too the always present fear that some rash Muslim leader would declare a Jehad or Holy war against the British Raj – and India had a large Muslim population which was easily roused. As we shall see, what the Lawrences set out to do in the Punjab after its annexation was to establish a moral rather than a linear frontier. Their policy, in contrast with the Russian notion of strictly demarcated frontiers, was to rely on intimate relationships with the potentially dangerous border tribes. It came to be known later on as the 'close border' policy and was really something of a compromise; but it worked, although it was expensive in terms of punitive expeditions and British and Indian lives.

But whilst Dost Muhammad was pursuing his independent way and the Lawrence policies for India were still in embryo, the Eastern Question once again became the burning issue of the day. Russia made a new attempt to dominate Turkey and so gain access to the eastern Mediterranean. It culminated in the Crimean War. Just as in her campaign against Khiva Russia used the prisoners and slaves as a pretext, so now she backed the claim of the Greek Orthodox Church to control the Holy Land against the Latin Church supported by France. In support of her claim she entered the Balkan States, then like the Holy Land under Turkish Muslim rule. At the same time she virtually destroyed the Turkish Black Sea fleet off Sinop. Seeing that Russia was not going to stop at that, France and Britain for once made common cause in order to block her from the Mediterranean. Louis Napoleon was mainly concerned with the Mediterranean and perhaps with his own prestige. For Britain the issues were far more important. If Turkey were to be overthrown, Russia would quickly gain control of Egypt and the Middle East and her sea communications with India would be at serious risk.

Some in England believed the quarrel with Russia could be patched up, but few believed her protestations that she only wanted to protect the Sultan's Christian subjects. This, from a country ruled by an autocracy and based on serfdom, was too much for the British man in the street to stomach. After his experiences in Tehran, McNeill, Russophobe as he was, had written a book, *The Progress and Present Position of Russia in the East*. He described the Russian procedure of fomenting discontent in subordinate foreign states, then offering mediation and finally absorbing them into her Empire. That for example was how she had annexed the Crimea from Turkey in 1783. Henry Layard, from his intimate knowledge of the Ottoman Empire, described Turkey as being in reality a dominant tribe holding together a variety of Muslim races and tribes in Asia solely by her moral and political prestige.[1] If Turkey fell these tribes would lose all cohesion, and the alternative to Turkey would be Russian domination. That would irreparably damage British prestige and power in the East. The views of these men of experience must have carried some weight in a Parliament put in power by a mainly Russophobe electorate.

For Britain the crisis arose at a time of political weakness when there was a Coalition Government under a somewhat indecisive Lord Aberdeen. Lord Clarendon was still at the Foreign Office, but Palmerston was then helpless at the Home Office. For a time the Government was undecided whether to treat Russia as friend or enemy. This indecision was no doubt faithfully reported to St. Petersburg by the greatly experienced Ambassador von Brunnow, and it encouraged Russia to press on. Turkey declared war in 1853 and it was generally believed that Constantinople would soon fall. At last in 1854, Britain and France declared war, finally preferring the risk of supporting a tottering Turkey to the alternative of Russian expansion westwards. If Palmerston had been at the Foreign Office he might well have averted the war. As it was it was a sorry tale of bad planning and faulty execution. Before it ended Palmerston, then over 70, had become Prime Minister and he instilled some vigour into its prosecution. It was fortunate for the allies that Russia had to maintain large forces in Poland and the Baltic States, and an army of 200,000 men in the Caucasus against a possible Turkish invasion. Lobanov-Rostovsky, the émigré historian of the Tsarist period, whose father had been Foreign Minister under the Tsarist régime, describes Russian strategy as based on the fact that her coast line was open to naval attack, whilst Britain,

[1] Op. Cit: *Layard of Nineveh*

being a maritime power, was invulnerable except in India through Central Asia. He says that at this point Russia revived invasion plans. First Herat was to be captured, then Afghanistan was to be won over and a Russian army was to march on Lahore via Kandahar. The plans were probably more diversionary than serious and he tells us they were dropped after the Crimean War. They do prove however that Russia had already realised the value of threatening Britain in that direction.

The war itself ended with the Russian withdrawal from Sebastopol, and it marked the end for the time being of Russia's Mediterranean aspirations; it had thus secured the British and French political objective. It was scarcely over before British attention was directed back to the East. In 1857 the Indian Mutiny broke out. As every schoolboy used to know, the spark that ignited the charge was the rumour that pig's fat was being used to grease the cartridges of the Company's Muslim troops; but that was only the immediate cause. The morale of the Indian army had already been lowered to some extent by the defeat in Afghanistan, itself a Muslim country. Another factor was that the camaraderie which had formerly existed between the army's British officers and its native non-commissioned officers and sepoys had weakened. British officers had become either unaware of the faiths and susceptibilities of their men or they ignored them. It has been suggested that part of the blame for this state of affairs may have traced to the arrival of British wives in India who disapproved of the old easy relations: at any rate up till then officers had shown much more interest and understanding.

The great fear was that restlessness might spread throughout Islamic Asia: it was nevertheless probably only a coincidence that at about the same time China's Muslim population rose against her Manchu rulers. However Dost Muhammad in Afghanistan notably held aloof and restlessness did not spread. It was indeed timely that Lord Dalhousie had just signed a treaty with him whereby his friends would be Britain's friends and that she should respect his possessions and never interfere therein. More debatably it undertook to recognize his heirs. The actual terms of the treaty had been negotiated by John Lawrence. Russia looked on with close attention. She too had a growing Muslim population and she also had much first-hand experience of riots, insurrections and dissidence in the home lands. In fact like most other onlookers she tended to exaggerate the strength of the Mutiny and of the unrest in India. Only a third of the Company's soldiers revolted and when, after much savagery on both sides, the revolt was quelled, there was relatively little aftermath. The wounds healed and British prestige did not suffer. Only Russia continued to believe optimistically that there was chronic unrest in India which might one day be exploited.

The Mutiny spelled the end of the rule of the East India Company. The India Act of 1833 had already closed down its monopoly of commercial business. After the Afghan War, the British Parliament had realised that the Company could no longer be allowed to follow a more or less independent foreign policy. The inconsistencies of its policies and the difficulties in which it had placed the home Government in its relations with Russia had forced Parliament to put some constraint on its dealings with foreign countries. Now after the Mutiny the Company was wound up and India was to be governed by Parliament through the India Office, with its own Secretary of State advised by an India Council. Henceforth the Foreign Office became the major foreign policy maker for India. It was entirely logical, although one important consequence was the constant complaint of the Government of India that the Foreign Office neither understood India's problems nor consulted her government. It was a complaint which was to continue in one form or another until India acquired independence in 1947.

CHAPTER SEVEN

Russian Missions to Kashgar, Bukhara and Peking

The end of 1840 left Russia at the beginning of a somewhat tentative period of détente with Khiva. Khiva's agreement with Russia to abolish the slave trade did not last long. In the 1860's, in a paper *Russia in Asia,* the historian Professor V. Grigor'yev wrote concerning Perovskiy's campaign, 'It is true that terrified by this movement and still more by the detention of the Khivan traders in Russia....the Khivan Khan gave up a part of the Russians who were kept there as slaves; but immediately after affairs went on as before. The Khivans again robbed our caravans; again bought up the Russians who were captured by the Turkomans and the Kirghiz'. Like other Russian historians he avoids mentioning the parts played by Abbott and Shakespear. The release of the Russian slaves and prisoners had of course never been the true principal object of the campaign.

Perovskiy being a competent soldier, the lesson was not lost on him that the Kyzyl Kum desert was a much greater military obstacle than was supposed. He recognised that another desert campaign must be avoided at all costs; hence future operations against Khiva would have to await the introduction of shipping on the Syr and Amu Dar'ya and on the Aral Sea as well as bases nearer than Orenburg. It was essential therefore to gain control of Fergana and Kokand, both of which fertile oases would support an army. However, the British policy in Afghanistan, which had hastened the Tsar and hence Perovskiy into precipitate action against Khiva, having failed, there was now less urgency. For the time being Perovskiy took another post, and his far-sighted plans were in abeyance.

Study of the works of Russian historians, whether pre-

Revolutionary or Soviet, leaves us in no doubt of Russia's genuine fear that the British conquest of Afghanistan would be only a preliminary step towards the control of Western Turkestan. As it was then seen, and as Soviet historians still affect to see it, Britain's next step after capturing Herat would be to move on Khiva via the Merv oasis. Russian extremists of the day such as Prince Barya-tinskiy, Viceroy of the Caucasus, believed that Britain would also advance through the Iranian province of Khorasan and ultimately try to gain control of the Caspian and even Trans-Caucasia.

In the light of this supposed grand design on Britain's part it is easy to explain the alarm which followed MacNaghten's threat to send a brigade to release Stoddart and Conolly in Bukhara and to occupy Balkh, rumours of which had probably reached Orenburg. The stated object of simply releasing two prisoners was seen as the same kind of cover as Perovskiy's proclaimed objective for his own campaign. The only difference was that whereas Britain naively believed Perovskiy, the Russians did not believe Britain.

Little occurred on Russia's 'open frontier' during Perovskiy's short absence except further small encroachments into the Kazakh steppe. But when he returned for his second tour of duty he began to initiate his plans which were distinctly realistic. Between 1847 and 1850 a line of fortifications was established along the Syr Dar'ya. Because it constituted no direct threat to Khiva or Bukhara these two Khanates remained on reasonably amicable terms with Russia. Kokand however felt the danger, and stationed troops in Tashkent with the hope of stemming the Russian advance. But in 1853 the Russians occupied Ak-Mechet' (now Kzyl-Orda) and extended the Syr-Dar'ya line. They also advanced from Western Siberia and a line of forts linked Semipalatinsk with Vernoye. Tashkent was now within striking distance, but the Crimean war delayed further operations.

These forward moves were valuable not only strategically, but economically too. So far and for a long time to come the advances into Central Asia had shown a financial loss. In terms of future trade and industry Kokand was potentially the most important of the three major khanates. The development of trade in Central Asia was essential, because Russia's major economic disadvantage was that she could not compete with the industrial expansion of Western Europe, especially Britain's Industrial Revolution. Fer-gana offered encouraging prospects of developing the cotton industry, besides its potentially valuable minerals. Hitherto China had offered the most scope for trade but here too Russia was beginning to face competition with Europe.

The Crimean war left Russia temporarily weakened, but more importantly it narrowed her field of expansion solely to Central Asia. Movement there had been slow hitherto and was to be further complicated by China's loss of control in Sinkiang. The end of the Crimean war also saw a complete change of men and policies at St. Petersburg; only at Orenburg was there any continuity of ideas.

Tsar Nicholas I had died during the war. He had been a soldier rather than a statesman; but though he put down mutinies with severity he had also made some attempt to emancipate the serfs. His foreign policies had brought him trouble and with the exception of Nesselrode he was ill-served by his ministers. Nesselrode was a peaceable man, somewhat in fear of his Tsar. He did not always agree with his master, especially concerning his designs on Turkey.

Alexander II who succeeded Nicholas was a man of very different stamp. He was not a militarist, but though he began as a liberal humanist his outlook in due course narrowed considerably. Yet although there seems to have been as much corruption during his reign as in his predecessor's he was served by some outstanding ministers and military governors. Foremost amongst them was Prince Gorchakov who succeeded Nesselrode as Foreign Minister, having previously been Governor General of Western Siberia. Of noble birth he was intelligent and shrewd and possessed an intimate knowledge of the recent diplomatic history of Europe. He was to take a much more independent line with his Tsar than had Nesselrode, but he too was cautious in his approach to Europe. He was to urge the Tsar to steer clear of intervention in European affairs and to remain free to choose his future friends. In his view the first need was to end the nuisance of the nomads on Russia's open frontiers, without which there could be no real development of trade and industry.

At the same time Gagemeister, the Finance Minister, urged the need for more export markets in Central Asia and for stability to enable them to be developed. He pressed for the development of the Amu and Syr Dar'ya basins, and for the appointment of Russian consuls in the Central Asian states. In line with Gorchakov he made it clear that Russia could not afford extensive strategic commitments such as would involve her with Britain and India. In accord with the new policy, Kovalevskiy was appointed head of the Asian Department in 1856. This was a significant appointment because he had served in the Khivan campaign and subsequently in 1851 had negotiated the Kuldja Treaty with China. That gave Russia important trading concessions in Dzungaria, and the right to appoint consuls at Kuldja the capital, and elsewhere. He was thus very well-versed in Central Asian affairs. Perovskiy died at Orenburg in 1857 but his designs for Central Asia were not forgotten. He also left a legacy of incipient independence of St. Petersburg which future Governors General were to exploit, sometimes to the embarrassment of the Foreign Ministry and sometimes to its advantage.

To sum up, the new Tsar accepted the more cautious policies of Gorchakov and Gagemeister rather than those of the more militaristic Viceroy of the Caucasus, which were also opposed by Perovskiy before his death.

The immediate fruits of the new direction were the despatch of three missions. The first was ostensibly sponsored by the Imperial Russian Geographical Society which from now on was to play an important part collaborating with the government in the collection of scientific and political information. It was despatched in 1858 to the Iranian province of Khorasan with a view to investigating trade possibilities and resources, and promoting Russian influence in this borderland with Russia. The matter of extending Russian influence was now recognised to be of urgent importance not only for the sake of prestige, but in order to counter Britain's precisely similar aim. Iran presented to Russia the possibility of a stable frontier. If as she feared Britain moved in, that possibility would be denied to her. It was therefore in Russia's interest to play off Iran against Britain and at the same time extend her commercial influence, especially in the north. It was also useful to Russia to maintain the Shah in power so that she could bully or cajole him as the occasion required. The leader of the mission was N. V. Khanykov and the instructions he received from Kovalevskiy went well beyond the scientific exploration of Khorasan: he was to develop influential relations not only with the Shah of Iran but also with Afghanistan. Khanykov was away for a year and a half during which time his mission visited Tehran at the Shah's invitation, and also Herat. But

Dost Muhammad, having previously concluded a treaty with Britain, refused to receive him. Whatever the scientific results, the political ones were not particularly successful.

The second mission brings the last of Russia's still 'open frontiers' into our direct view for the first time – that of her province of Western Siberia marching with Eastern Turkestan. It was a confused frontier because it was straddled by many tribes, most of them Muslim, who came and went as they pleased, whether herding flocks or in trading caravans, or merely marauding. The southern province, Kashgaria, concerned Russia most at the time.

The whole of Eastern Turkestan was under the nominal rule of China whose Ambans, the equivalent of British Residents in the Indian states, represented the Emperor and kept order within certain limits of recognized protocol. They were assisted by a Chinese garrison of troops who were inferior even by oriental standards of the day. Chinese authority was really little more than an elaborate pretence normally accepted by the indigenous population, who were ready enough to pay their taxes provided the Amban did not exact too much and allowed them to pursue their customary avocations in peace.

The majority of the population in Kashgar, Yarkand and other oasis towns was Turkic. They were a peaceable settled Muslim people who were either traders or small farmers. In the mountainous regions, particularly along the Russo-Turkestan frontier region, the bulk of the sparse population was Kazakh, a nomadic Muslim race, although there were many lesser tribes as well. By this time Russian expansion had brought many Kazakhs under Tsarist rule, though they still came and went as they pleased between the two countries.

In 1857 the Chinese hold over Kashgaria had become so lax and corrupt that there was an insurrection by the Muslim tribes. A hereditary sect of priest-kings called Khojas hailing from Kokand had tried to assume control. The consequence was much lawlessness on the frontier which spread to the Russian Kazakhs. Gasford, the energetic Governor-General of Western Siberia, saw this as an opportunity to invade Kashgaria and help it to become independent, but the government decided it was too risky a venture at that stage, and preferred a more cautious policy. So Gasford was instructed to send someone to Kashgar to find out what was going on.

His choice for this hazardous job was his adjutant, Valikhanov, who was uniquely qualified. He was a Kazakh from a ruling line tracing its descent to the Golden Horde and his true name was Sultan Vali Khan. For some years Russia had been trying to educate the more intelligent of their Russianised Kazakhs. Most found the transition too difficult but Valikhanov was an exception. He had been sent to the Omsk Cadet Corps where he learned European languages and entered Russian service. No Russian could have hoped to reach Kashgar at this time, but Valikhanov, brought up in the steppes and accustomed to tribal ways, dress and language, was an obvious choice.

He set off for Kashgar with a merchant caravan in which he posed as a relative of the caravan-bashi (leader). It was an arduous and most dangerous journey crossing high mountain passes and encountering many tribes en route, all of them suspicious and liable to exact unjust dues. The caravan had started with 37 personnel and 101 camels, but by the time they reached Kashgar only 36 of the latter had survived. At Kashgar they represented themselves as Andizhanis and Tatars from Kokand; although constantly suspected by the authorities they nevertheless managed to sell their merchandise at a profit. Valikhanov made many friends and acquired much valuable information. The initial difficulty he had had to overcome was that some of the caravan's members did not take kindly to the local custom which obliged all travellers to acquire Kashgari wives whilst in the city. In all Valikhanov was away for 11 months. He wrote a description of his journey, of which an abbreviated account appeared in the Imperial Geographical Society's journal. Some years later this was translated by Robert Michell, the official translator at the India Office and the only Russian expert there except for his brother John. Michell's comment was that 'it was a delicate and prying political mission and Valikhanov was essentially a political agent, venturesome, brave, observant' – a judgment with which anyone who has read Valikhanov's report would agree.

At the time of his mission Britain was not interested in Kashgar, but she was soon to be closely involved, and the English translation appeared just as Douglas Forsyth was about to start from India in 1870 on the first of his two missions to Kashgar. By then it had become an extension of the zone of rivalry to the annoyance of the Russian government who regarded it as a Russian preserve.

It is sad to have to add that, after taking part in operations against the town of Turkestan, Valikhanov subsequently became deeply embittered at the harsh Russian handling of his Kokandian kin and decided to forsake all 'civilised' society. He left the army and devoted himself to scholarship. Further examination of events in Chinese Turkestan must be deferred whilst we return to the main field.

The third mission (and possibly the first two as well) was inspired by a man of considerable genius who was also chosen to lead it. He was Count Ignat'yev who had joined the Asian Department in 1857. Previously he had been Military Attaché in London under Count von Brunnow. It is a pity von Brunnow is such a shadowy figure in this story. He must have been one of Russia's key men, for he was appointed Ambassador in 1840 and, with a break when he was recalled during the Crimean War, he continued in the post until 1874. During all that long period, in contrast with Prince Lieven and his celebrated wife, he seems not to have moved much in London social circles of the day; but we may be very sure he had an accurate understanding of the British political scene and that St. Petersburg relied on his views on likely British reactions when any major move in Central Asia was contemplated. Ignat'yev could have had no better mentor.

Unlike his superior, Ignat'yev made himself popular in London society, and successfully disguised any anti-British feelings he may have then had. They seem to have emerged in his dispatches on the Indian Mutiny, which Khalfin tells us were read attentively and with no little satisfaction in St. Petersburg, where reports of mutinies and insurrections in Russia were by no means unusual. But the Foreign Office marked his dossier as a man to be watched when a London map dealer reported that he had been buying up all the available maps of English ports and railways!

Ignat'yev's instructions were to study existing conditions in Central Asia, to strengthen Russian influence in Khiva and Bukhara and to improve trade there. He was to eliminate British interference and secure permission for Russian ships to move freely on the Amu Dar'ya. At Khiva he was to obtain an undertaking that the Khan's Turkmen and Kazakh vassals would not be incited against Russia. At Bukhara he was to demand the release of all Russian prisoners, put trade on a firm footing and find ways of securing priority over British trade there.

He took a large mission of 83 strong and reached Khiva in July 1858. But after prolonged discussions he was unable to make any headway. The Khan, a successor to the man Abbott and Shakespear had dealt with, saw any concessions to the Russians as a threat to his dignity. So after his failure there Ignat'yev moved on to Bukhara. The Amir was more concerned with his wars against Kokand and Khiva than with the Russians and Ignat'yev was only able to extract an agreement, for what that was worth, about shipping on the Amu Dar'ya, otherwise he could do little but bolster the Amir's anti-British feelings.

He reported that shortly before his arrival two Englishmen disguised as Afghans had visited Bukhara and that three more posing as Indians were then in the city. Valikhanov was always careful to cross-check his information but Ignat'yev does not seem to have done so. A careful search of the India Office Records reveals no evidence that India had sent any Englishmen or Indians to Bukhara. If Indians were there they were probably traders such as were to be found in any Central Asian centre of trade. As quoted in *Canadian Slavonic Papers* Vol XVII, 2 and 3, 1975, *'The Ignat'yev mission to Khiva and Bukhara in 1858'* by John W. Strong, Ignat'yev wrote:

> The most important and essential result of our mission to Central Asia in 1858 consisted in dispersing the fog shading the Khanates from the eyes of the Russian Government and in finally recovering the sight and understanding of the real price of 'diplomatic relations' with the Khivan Khan and with Bukhara. Information obtained by our mission and the conscientious destruction of the former mirage, provoked a sudden shift in the character of our relations with these crafty and treacherous neighbours, and contributed to the establishment of a more correct view of the meaning and basis of their power, of their real strength, and in particular, of that position which we must, and may, occupy in Central Asia ... and equally of that goal which we must pursue for a more unfailing and powerful defence of our essential interests.

In the course of his subsequent career, although he never served in Central Asia again, Ignat'yev continued to be concerned with Anglo-Russian relations in Central Asia to an important extent. In 1859, a year after his Central Asian mission and now a general although still only 27, he was sent as envoy to Peking. His presence there requires some explanation. During the Crimean War the British and French had made a diversionary attack in the Far East by sea against Kamchatka. It was an abortive affair but it gave Russia the excuse to extend her hold along the Amur river. Hitherto she had long been the leading foreign power in China; she now saw the chance to strengthen her position by offering support to China against Britain and France – naturally, at a price. Palmerston had very little idea at this time about Russian objectives in China and took steps to find out through the British Ambassador in St. Petersburg.

At that time earlier tripartite treaties with China had broken down and the allies decided to send an expedition to force China into re-establishing the commercial position of both countries. The U.S.A and Russia were invited to participate with representatives. Russia's envoy was Putyatin who had been Naval Attaché in London; he shared Ignat'yev's anti-British views, and some of his guile. The allies bombarded the Taku Forts and forced China to negotiate. Putyatin supported the demands of the British and French representatives, Lord Elgin and Baron Gros, but also tried to mediate with them on behalf of China whilst offering to train an army for her. At the same time he was secretly negotiating a separate treaty with China concerning the Amur. China signed the Treaties of Tientsin although Putyatin had over-played his hand to the disgust of Peking and one of the unfortunate Chinese delegates was ordered by the Emperor to commit suicide. (Later delegates, recollecting his fate, showed considerable reluctance to negotiate with the allies.)

But when it came to ratifying the Treaties China refused ratification to the British and French: she did however ratify that with Russia, a fact of which Gorchakov did not trouble to inform the British and French. Nevertheless China did repudiate her separate Russian Treaty of Aigun which concerned the Amur frontier.

The consequence of China's refusal was a new allied expedition under the same commanders but with Count Ignat'yev as the Russian envoy. Gorchakov tried to dissuade France from joining the second expedition. He also offered the services of Ignat'yev as mediator, but the Foreign Office had not forgotten the latter's escapade in London and refused the offer; Lord Elgin was warned that he was a 'clever wily fellow'. Having by then learned more about Putyatin's activities the allies were on their guard and Ignat'yev faced a harder job; but he adopted the same tactics as Putyatin. To Elgin he was sweetly reasonable, pointing out that Russia was not out for aggrandisement and encouraging the allies to push on with the expedition. Such was his charm and plausibility that Lord Elgin took a liking to him, and only became suspicious when it was found that he was trying to put Elgin and Gros against each other whilst listening sympathetically to their mutual complaints when they temporarily fell out.

To the Chinese Ignat'yev offered his services[1] in the role of honest broker, although like Putyatin he too finally made himself unpopular. His separate objectives were to get as much control as possible over Mongolia, Manchuria and Eastern Turkestan (Sin-kiang), to enlarge on the Treaty of Tientsin, and to embody in it clauses giving Russia more territory on the Amur-Ussuri frontier, with more trade and consular facilities. He particularly hoped to prevent the allies from achieving permanent ministries in Peking.

The second expedition had a much harder task than the first: the Taku forts had been re-fortified and had to be destroyed again. Elgin then destroyed the Summer Palace and even threatened to sack Peking, which seriously alarmed Baron Gros. Thereupon Ignat'yev played his trump card: he agreed with the Chinese government to mediate on behalf of China – provided all Russia's demands were met. In the upshot China was forced to meet all the allied demands and most of Ignat'yev's, though he kept them secret from the allies. The new Treaties were re-named the Treaty of Peking and it was signed and ratified in 1860. From then on, in spite of Ignat'yev's efforts, it was the British and not the Russians who were to become the dominant foreign power in Peking. Much of the credit for this improvement in British status in Chinese eyes was due to her first Minister there, Thomas Francis Wade, whom the Chinese came to trust and respect. After the performances of Putyatin and Ignat'yev, China remained suspicious of Russia. Meanwhile however part of the spoils for Russia, in addition to great gains in the Amur region, was permision to establish consulates at Urga and Kashgar in addition to Kuldja. The

---

[1] See R. K. I. Quested. *The Expansion of Russia in East Asia 1857–1860*. Singapore 1968.

Kashgar consulate was later to become a focal point of Russian intrigue in Sinkiang, an embarrassment to China and a source of continual friction for India.

After his Peking success Ignat'yev was appointed head of the Asian Department where he was able to form a strong combination with the aggressive Milyutin at the War Ministry. Between them they were able to exert pressure on Gorchakov whom they regarded as much too pusillanimous a Foreign Minister in his Central Asian policy.

Even whilst Ignat'yev was only a member of the Asiatic Department, but particularly in the three years 1861–64 during which he was head of it he continually advocated a strong policy in Central Asia. All the same it does not appear that he ever contemplated an invasion of India. In 1857 he had written 'In the event of a breach with Britain it is only in Asia that we can fight her with some chance of success and can harm Turkey into the bargain. So long as peace endures, the difficulties created by Britain in Asia and the growth of our prestige in the areas separating Russia from British territories will be the best guarantee of our avoiding war with Britain'. 'Asia', he wrote 'is the only field left to our commercial activity and for the development of our industry, which are too weak to enter into competition with Britain, France, Belgium, America and the other states.... Research into Central Asia, the strengthening of our relations with that region and the weakening of British influence there are matters of such obvious advantage to Russia that it should not be difficult to meet the expense of an expedition....' He saw the necessity for the ultimate annexation of the three Khanates, and the opening up of the Amu Dar'ya for Russian shipping as a step towards that end.

In 1864 just before the campaign against Kokand was about to be launched he was appointed Ambassador at Constantinople. In view of Russia's aspirations in the Near East this was a key appointment. His most important task was in 1877 when he toured the European capitals trying to ensure the neutrality of the powers during the Russo-Turkish war of 1877–78. He was mainly instrumental in drawing up the Treaty of San Stefano, drafted when the Russian army was almost within sight of the Turkish capital. Turkey asked for mediation and at the Congress of Berlin the powers, headed by Britain, objected to it considering that it put Turkey too much under Russian power, as indeed Russia intended.

Before the war, Lord Salisbury had been sent to Constantinople on his first mission abroad to try and reach a peaceful settlement. Here he fell for the charms of Ignat'yev: they were constantly together, even indulging in long walks to the exclusion of the frustrated British Ambassador. But once again Ignat'yev's tendency to over-play his hand showed itself. After Salisbury and he had agreed a boundary on a map, Ignat'yev tried surreptitiously next day to substitute a map with a different boundary on it more favourable to Russia. It was only by mere chance that Salisbury noticed it, whereupon Ignat'yev, with a disarming smile took it back and replaced it with the agreed copy. Salisbury had very nearly been fooled by the man whom his biographer A. L. Kennedy says was considered to be 'the most talented liar on the Bosphorus'. Although he had been unable to prevent the war he had learned a lesson about Russian diplomatic methods which he never forgot.

Henry Layard, who became Ambassador at Constantinople just after this episode, wrote subsequently that his experience of Russian diplomatists 'has led me to believe that they are so trained to the habits of deception and dissimulation that their word can rarely if ever be relied upon'. At the same time the British negotiations at the Congress were not above criticism. Disraeli announced the result as 'Peace with honour'. His critics called it, 'The peace which passeth all understanding and the honour that is common amongst thieves'. Bismarck, the German Chancellor, wrote in his autobiography, 'England is one of those dexterous powers with whom it is impossible to form any lasting alliance ....and who cannot be relied on with certainty.... because the basis of all political relations.... is the product of elections and the resulting majorities'.

The Berlin treaty marked the end of Ignat'yev's diplomatic career. In 1881 the Tsar appointed him Minister of Internal Affairs. In that post as a conservative and a strong Pan-Slav he condoned, if he did not actually instigate, the first Jewish pogroms in Kiev, Odessa and Warsaw, besides combating revolutionary movements. These pogroms aroused much anti-Russian feeling in Britain. When interviewed by the journalist, Charles Marvin, he expressed no regrets. Looked at in any light Ignat'yev's career was an outstanding one and the part he played in Anglo-Russian rivalry was unique. It seems rather unfair that his nephew, A. A. Ignat'yev, who rose to be a lieutenant general in the Red Army, should subsequently, in his autobiography, have written of his distinguished uncle, albeit with affection, as if he had been simply a swashbuckling adventurer.[1]

Because so much was written and believed in Britain and India about Russia's ultimate intention to invade the subcontinent, Ignat'yev's expressed views are of importance. His writings have never been translated into English; the quotations above, and those which follow, have been taken from the works of N. A. Khalfin who has made a study of them, together with archives of the day. This historian tells us that as the result of a letter written to the War Minister in 1857 from the Viceroy of the Caucasus the War Ministry drafted a memorandum, *The Possibility of a Clash between Russia and Britain in Central Asia*. He tells us that the memorandum considered that Britain could not undertake large military expeditions into continental hinterlands, but that her 'powerful fleet only enabled her to establish herself along sea coasts'. At the same time Britain would try to damage Russian political interests by intrigues in Russia's Muslim provinces and the Caucasus. The memorandum examined projects for an Indian campaign and condemned the idea. He also quotes Gorchakov who had just become Foreign Minister as writing to the War Minister that the very talk of the invasion of India might provoke a clash with Britain, a possibility which 'seems to me so incompatible with the condition of our finances, our exhaustion after the war and the political situation in Europe that I find it impossible even to think about it'. Gorchakov seems here to be following the advice of the always pacific von Brunnow who had written 'Any undertaking in the East which might in some ways affect British interests or even give a pretext to the British Cabinet to object would be dangerous'. Khalfin's interpretation of history is frankly propagandist, but there seems no need to doubt the accuracy of the above quotations which, in the context, he is using to refute British extremists such as Henry Rawlinson. His testimony is therefore important.

Perovskiy had learned by his experience; but in general what must strike any military student of the period is the complete failure of strategists both British and Russian to carry out any form of logistical appreciation, either of their own capability or that of

[1] A. A. Ignat'yev. *A Subaltern in Old Russia*. Trs Ivor Montagu. London 1946.

their opponents, to mount and sustain operations in Afghanistan, Central Asia, or for that matter in Iran. True British and Indian surveyors reconnoitred roads and passes but nobody tried to assess the geographical and climatic factors, the problem of supplies along lengthening lines of communication, or the effect of a foreign army on the susceptibilities and economy of the indigenous peoples; still less the strength of the forces likely to oppose them. If any such systematic appreciations had been made, less would have been heard from the extremists on both sides; they simply took it for granted that Russia intended ultimately to invade India or conversely that Britain would in due course invade Central Asia.

It might have been expected that even by this time the British and Indian governments would have undertaken a detailed analysis of the feasibility of a Russian invasion: but it seems never to have been done, mainly because not for many years was any department of Military Intelligence set up whose job it would be to study such matters. This failure will be examined in more detail hereafter.

CHAPTER EIGHT

Lawrence's Non-interventionist versus Rawlinson's Forward Policy

It was just as well that there was no powerful political school in India to press the claim that the Hindu Kush should become the frontier of India. The men who thought on these lines were chiefly to be found in the senior ranks of the Indian Army and their thinking was based naturally enough on considerations of strategy not politics. Even Henry Rawlinson recognised that such a frontier would lead to endless Anglo-Russian recriminations, although his own solution would simply have substituted the Amu Dar'ya for the Hindu Kush. From the earliest stages the general tendency was towards keeping Britain and Russia as far apart as possible in Central Asia, and that tendency crystallised ultimately at the point where agreed borders actually achieved this result, but that is looking a long way ahead; only if Britain and Russia had come to blows in Central Asia would the Hindu Kush have become a dominating influence in British military strategy.

As it was, quite enough voices were raised and ink spilt by the rival supporters of the two chief schools of thought. In the stage before party lines emerged, British foreign policy was still really governed by the views and actions of the Prime Minister of the day and his Minister for Foreign Affairs. As for India the Chairman of the Company's Board of Control was, until the Company was abolished, always a member of the British Cabinet whoever the Prime Minister was. On the other hand Governors General and Viceroys of India were selected by the Prime Minister. When a Prime Minister fell the Governor General in office sometimes found the policy he had been instructed to pursue was no longer favoured, because the new Prime Minister himself had different ideas: but that had nothing to do with his party.

What really affected the policy of successive Prime Ministers towards Central Asia, and hence to a great extent the ebb and flow of the two rival policy schools, was their view on how best to contain Russian expansion in the Near East; Central Asia was for most of the time a secondary matter. As Iran was geographically between the Near East and Central Asia, responsibility for British policy there tended to be a shuttlecock between the Government of India and the Foreign Office in London. When the India Office was set up under a Secretary of State after the Mutiny that introduced another interested party. It is small wonder that there were such marked vacillations in British policy over the years – that often enough there was none at all other than a purely pragmatic one. Palmerston was perceptive enough to see that the one absolute essential was to keep open sea communications with India via the Persian Gulf. Otherwise he had lost interest in Iran itself because he could see no promise in becoming immersed in such a fathomless morass. Britain had neither the military resources nor the desire to support her against a Russian invasion from the north. (It was fortunate for her as well as Iran that Russia took the same view and did not want to get herself totally involved either.) That was why Palmerston left the Calcutta government to deal with Tehran. His attitude, and that of succeeding Prime Ministers, must have been the despair of the Shahs who were continually pressing Britain for a guarantee of support for Iran's independence against Russia. The comment of a contemporary English writer was that, 'Persia is attracted to Britain by her hopes, driven towards Russia by her fears'. The fact was that Iran was in a permanent state of near collapse, yet in the long run, despite Russian machinations in the north and with the help of British financial and commercial support – always with the best intentions but sometimes rather shady in its methods – Iranian national resilience ensured the country's ultimate survival. One is reminded of Metternich's comment about Austria, 'I think that the situation is hopeless but not serious'.

In general it is apparent that the policy of successive Foreign Ministers, from Palmerston onwards, was not to get too embroiled in Iranian affairs. That, however, did not suit Calcutta because India after all would have to bear the brunt of serious trouble and it was her defence that was at stake, and the same remark applied to Afghanistan. Nevertheless it is an astonishing commentary both on British policy and the British Parliament of those days that

when the Anglo-Persian war of 1856–57 was launched to forestall
the threat by the Shah to seize Herat, Parliament was not informed
till six months later. True it was mainly an Indian government
affair but British as well as Indian troops were involved. Palmerston was then both Prime Minister and Foreign Secretary. In the
same year Lord Clarendon was appointed as the first Secretary of
State for India.

From among the supporters of the forward policy in Central Asia
Rawlinson may be taken as the archetype, although supporters and
sometime executors of the policy did not always have the same
views. He had had active experience in the field when he first
formed his views and for the next thirty years was their most active
exponent. He is usually regarded by both Tsarist and Soviet
historians as having influenced successive Prime Ministers and
Foreign Secretaries. We shall see to what extent they were justified.

After his second spell of archaeology in the Middle East
Rawlinson returned to the political field. At that time Dost
Muhammad was pursuing his process of unifying Afghanistan and
Calcutta was watching his progress with interest, at first neither
supporting nor ostracising him. Admittedly Rawlinson did make
some adaptation to events. Thus he saw that the acquisition of the
Punjab and Sind had greatly improved India's defensive position.
It had brought the frontier zone 500 miles or more nearer
Afghanistan and Herat and he correctly saw the need for the
development of road and rail communications in the region to
make the best strategic use of the new base. But he still disliked the
idea, favoured by the opposite school, of making the Indus the
main line of a passive defence system, because he believed it would
have an adverse moral effect on India. On the other hand he was
not concerned about any possible advance from Eastern (Chinese)
Turkestan. He was making a different point when he wrote that
'Russia has always dreaded the effect on her inflammable Asiatic
subjects of the formation of a strong and prosperous Muslim power
in the neighbourhood, hence one reason for her jealousy of
England'. He saw the same danger facing India from an Afghan-
Iranian Muslim alliance fomented by Russia. His primary and
almost obsessive concern was always to forestall a Russian advance
through Iran, for which he saw the development of Russian bases
on the Caspian as a preliminary step which could only be
prevented by active British interference.

In the .early stages of his career Rawlinson had assumed Badakhshan to be independent of Afghanistan. It is to his credit that once he found that Afghanistan had historical claims to the territory he promptly saw the strategic value of the link: especially because he had already begun to take very seriously the possible use by Russians of the northern route to India. In 1869, at Lord Mayo's request, he sent him a memorandum. It was a somewhat muddled document but he made two valuable points in it. He wrote 'on no account should the dependence of Afghan Turkestan and Badakhshan on Kabul be called in question'. Looking ahead in this memorandum Rawlinson visualised that just as Russia would ultimately absorb Bukhara so India would absorb Afghanistan: thus the two Empires would have a common frontier along the Amu Dar'ya. That was why he considered it necessary to establish Afghanistan's northern boundary along the Amu Dar'ya once and for all, and the sooner the better. It was a cardinal mistake on his part that he made no distinction between the weak khanate of Bukhara and the fanatical fighting tribes of Afghanistan. He should have known better from his own experience of the latter: Lord Lawrence did.

Meanwhile Rawlinson was to continue to sound the alarm at every advance by Russia south-eastwards from the Caspian which brought her nearer to Herat. Although he claimed to favour a unified Afghanistan he still thought it so unlikely to happen that he would have preferred to detach Herat and Kandahar and to man these outposts with garrisons from India. But he did not discuss the practicalities; indeed he seems to have learned little from the First Afghan War.

He had noted Ignat'yev's mission to Bukhara and the Khanykov mission to Herat and he realised the constant Russian threat to Bukhara. In his view Russia's 'manifest destiny', which would include Turkestan and the fertile Amu Dar'ya basin, could only rival Indian prosperity. Having begun by preaching Russia's ultimate intention to invade India it took him thirty years during which she had not done so to modify his opinion. But he never changed his view that Russia would use Iran as a stalking horse linked with Afghanistan, or that Herat was the vital gateway which must be denied to her at all costs. In spite of that for a short time he entertained a novel idea, not for denying Herat to Iran, but for actually giving it to her.

Whilst British policy towards Iran was still under the control of the Indian government, Rawlinson was sent in 1859 as Minister at Tehran. Because of his experience and his knowledge of Iran it was thought the appointment would please the Shah, and that was what he set out to do. Originally he had wanted to occupy Herat. Now his plan was first that Dost Muhammad should be bought off from taking it; Britain should then either turn Herat over to Iran or keep it independent. In either case Britain would assure the Shah of support for Herat if his country was threatened from the north; this would give Iran a sense of security for Khorasan, her most vulnerable province and would be tangible evidence of British support. Such a plan would have had little prospect of success, but it got nowhere because after nine months Rawlinson left Tehran. Lord John Russell as Foreign Minister had decided that the Foreign Office must resume control of Iranian policy because Russia was being awkward again. Rawlinson's biographer, his brother G. A. Rawlinson, says he resigned because, having been appointed by the India Office, he could not continue under the change. It was a fact however that Russell feared the adverse effect on both Iran and Russia of any Indian interference with Herat. On the subject of British policy towards Russian aims in the East, he is quoted as having said 'If we do not stop Russia on the Danube, we shall have to stop her on the Indus'.

At heart Rawlinson was still opposed to an Afghanistan united under Kabul. He thought India would suffer from the chaos that would follow Dost Muhammad's death. He believed the country would be an adequate barrier provided India annexed Kandahar, thus effectively masking Herat; at the same time he said he was against interfering with Dost Muhammad's government, which sounds somewhat ingenuous. In fact the chaos which indeed followed Dost Muhammad's death did not at all affect India.

It was only natural that Rawlinson with his aggressive approach disliked the masterly inactivity policy and in 1865, two years after Dost Muhammad's death, he challenged it in a memorandum to Lord Lawrence. He asked 'Should Russia be allowed to work her way to Kabul unopposed and then establish herself as a friendly power prepared to protect the Afghans against the English?' He considered India could have had a strong and friendly power on her north-west frontier if Dost Muhammad had originally been supported, but that there could still be one if Sher Ali, then struggling for the throne, were now supported. Here for the time being we may leave Rawlinson with his extreme, but hitherto unacceptable, views. They must be compared with those of other, less extreme, forward policy supporters, all of whom, unlike Rawlinson, were in positions of responsibility.

In 1846 Palmerston had urged on Hobhouse 'the necessity of preventing Persian, and in other words Russian, authority from establishing itself in Herat'. Hobhouse advised him to leave India out of it. The acquisition of Sind and the successes against the Sikhs had caused him to change his mind again and he did not think India should go beyond the Khyber Pass, still less the Hindu Kush. Subsequently, when the Foreign Office wanted Herat to be independent and a permanent representative to be appointed there, Dalhousie as Governor General was against it.

Lord Canning who followed Dalhousie wanted Afghanistan, including Herat, united under Dost Muhammad. He did not think the Persian War would solve the Herat problem, and now that India held the Punjab and Sind he did not foresee any danger from Afghanistan united under one ruler. It was Canning who negotiated the treaty with Dost Muhammad. However in the Anglo-Persian treaty of 1857, following the war, the future of Herat was left open. All these men held forward policies which were more practical and flexible than Rawlinson's. An important difference between them was that whereas they held posts of responsibility, Rawlinson had none. Even when he joined the Council of India formed by the new India Office he was only a voice.

The renewed interest of the Foreign Office at this time in Iran and in the independence of Herat was the result of the fear that, foiled in the Crimea, Russia would turn to Iran and Central Asia. Either the British Ambassador at St. Petersburg did not advise the Foreign Office that after the Crimean War Russia was in no financial position to indulge in costly adventures elsewhere, or else he was ignored. Another interesting light is thrown on relations between London and Calcutta in 1853 when Iran had engaged with the Foreign Office not to send troops into Herat unless the latter was attacked from Kabul or Kandahar: Calcutta was not informed although it was in conflict with Dalhousie's plans. In 1855, a year after the treaty of friendship with Dost Muhammad, when Dalhousie was still hoping he would bring Herat under his control, Iran once more besieged and captured it.

To this conclusion a further suggestion is offered, namely, that the fertile province of Khorasan was itself the key to Herat. It had been an essential supply base for all the historic invasions that had passed through it, but for Russia to attempt its occupation would have been beyond her resources and the risk of extending the conflict too great. No Russian documentation is available to support this view, but when Russia launched her short campaign against Geok Tepe forty years later, all the supplies had first to be obtained from Khorasan and that alone took five months.

G. J. Alder, the reliable authority on the history of India's northern and north-western defence, has devoted some detailed research to the subject of Herat and has given us the benefit in an article *The Key to India? Britain and the Herat Problem, 1830–1863.*[1] He has deduced that Captain Arthur Conolly was the first man to describe it as the gateway to India. It was of course a fertile land and no doubt Alexander of Macedon and others had reaped the benefit. Conolly believed that in Russian hands Iran would move on India via Herat. He impressed that belief on Palmerston who never departed from it. Auckland and his successors had all followed Conolly, and Rawlinson himself obviously never questioned the theory. Only a few realists did, although by implication, Hobhouse in his later days seems to have recognised its lesser importance. The first real doubter was Canning. Canning wanted Afghanistan to be a firm defensive barrier, but he also appreciated the strategic importance of the Punjab, and he thought it was a poor outlook for India if her defence really depended so completely on Herat.

After him came John Lawrence whose policy will be discussed hereafter. As Alder concludes, the fact of the matter was that Herat never was the gateway to India. That it was the key to Afghanistan was a very different proposition. No Afghan Amir would have rested content till he had annexed it, for whether independent or under Iran it would always be a threat to the goal of Afghan unity.

*   *   *   *   *

Nobody can study the period of 'masterly inactivity' against which extremists of the opposite school tilted in vain for twenty five years, without being impressed by J. L. Morison's Raleigh Lecture to the

---

[1] *Middle Eastern Studies.* May and October 1974. Vols I and II.

British Academy in 1936 – *From Alexander Burnes to Frederick Roberts – A study of Imperial Frontier Policy*. Masterly it was, inactive it certainly was not.

Two events had begun the transformation of India's defence capability on the north-west frontier and taken it out of the original *status quo* category. They were the treaties with Ranjit Singh and with the rulers of Sind which led in turn to the annexation of both countries. The Punjab and Kashmir were destined to play an important part in India's northern defence strategy as well: hence the importance of retaining friendly relations with the latter state which under hostile rulers could have proved a costly liability to India. In the long run it was the Punjab, not the Hindu Kush which was India's natural north-west frontier.

Two men who saw the strategic significance of these events and set about developing them were the brothers Henry and John Lawrence, both of them supporters of the original *status quo*. These two Political Officers (a third brother, George, played a minor part) marked a new and powerful generation of frontier administrators. In spite of the re-organisation of the Political Service and against the views of old soldiers like the Duke of Wellington, who said they deprived army commanders of their proper initiative in the field, Political Officers still had plenary and discretionary powers to make military dispositions. The Lawrences were perhaps lucky in that Dalhousie and Hardinge, the Governors General of those formative years, were largely pre-occupied with other matters and left them very free hands. They made the best use of their great powers.

The two brothers resembled Burnes in one respect: they both achieved a remarkable rapport with native rulers. Otherwise they had the stability which Burnes lacked and where he was ambitious they were selflessly dedicated to the service of the Punjab. Members of an Anglo-Irish family of twelve brothers and sisters they were devout Christians although by no means evangelistic and Henry in particular, gaunt and aged through frequent illness, even in his fifties resembled an Old Testament prophet. Whilst John was the sounder administrator, Henry was the virtual ruler of the Punjab from 1847 onwards, but both men inspired the loyalty of the Sikhs. They assembled under them a team of like-minded dedicated men, amongst them James Abbott who ruled Hazara from Abbottabad, all of whom adopted the same highly personal fatherly style of rule which was sometimes known as the Lawrence

System. Henry left the Punjab in 1852 because he disagreed with John who wanted to introduce into the province fairer and less corrupt methods of administration and justice than the indigenous variety, but not before he had established a policy of frontier political administration which was to leave a permanent mark on all his successors for the next sixty or more years.

Neither man ever wanted a properly demarcated frontier on the north-west which, as they rightly saw, would never be observed by the lawless hill tribes in the territory between the Punjab and Afghanistan. They were also against frequent punitive expeditions such as Napier the Commander-in-Chief in India had always been accustomed to. Henry expressed his very definite ideas on the subject when he wrote 'With a *carte blanche* I could guarantee at a less expense than at present to pacify the frontier....that is to make it as quiet as is consistent with the character of such a people. Now they like us but do not fear us. I should try to reverse the case – to conciliate them when quiet and hit them hard when troublesome'. However in the aftermath of Ellenborough's campaign such severe treatment would not have been supported at home. Consequently after the Lawrence days there were many more expensive expeditions in the Napier tradition which yielded only short-term results. When it came to the final settlement of her transcaspian frontier with Iran, it will be seen later that Russia adopted the opposite policy. She dealt so ruthlessly with the recalcitrant Tekke Turkmen tribes that they never caused trouble again.

Henry was fully aware of the strategic importance of the Punjab vis-à-vis Afghanistan and Central Asia, and in particular of Peshawar commanding the Khyber pass. From this advanced base anything from a punitive raid to a major expedition could be launched and supplied. In his view there was even less need than before to fear Russian expansion in Central Asia and hence less need than ever to aim at active control of Afghanistan. From merchants passing through Peshawar India should always be able to collect news of events in Afghanistan and Central Asia. Finally it was Henry who formed the body of troops called the Corps of Guides into which were recruited those very tribesmen who could otherwise be formidable enemies. It was a tribute to Henry's rule that later, under his brother, the Punjab remained loyal during the Mutiny. They shared the same strategic views but it was John who ultimately became Viceroy. Portraits of him suggest an imposing man with great strength of character and breadth of mind; in some there is too a hint of the visionary. His career did not belie the impression.

In 1857 Dost Muhammad proposed to John Lawrence at Peshawar that he should send an expedition to recover Herat and he asked for British financial help. The expedition was not sent but the Indian government granted him twelve lakhs of rupees per annum to help him to hold Balkh, Kabul and Kandahar against possible attack by Iran. Lawrence's negotiations coincided with the Indian expedition against Iran in the Persian Gulf. By the treaty subsequently negotiated with Iran, the Shah undertook to relinquish his claim on Herat – an undertaking which was however almost immediately broken. Dost Muhammad died in 1863 only a few days after he had finally captured Herat. His death threw Afghanistan into the turmoil which the forward school feared would be exploited by Russia, with rival claimants fighting for the succession. It was to be five years before the succession was settled.

In the same year John Lawrence was appointed Viceroy, succeeding Lord Elgin who had died after only a year in office. If we exclude Metcalfe who acted as Governor General for a year Lawrence was the only Viceroy to serve almost his whole career in India, and the only man to rise from the rank of Political Officer to the status of statesman. Like his brother Henry, he had an unusually intuitive understanding of the north-west border tribes, and how to deal with their leaders in a way they understood: it was a faculty of immense value throughout his Viceroyalty. In the four years prior to his appointment, he had served, probably unhappily, on the Council of India in London, together with Rawlinson. The clashes between these two men of diametrically opposed views must on occasion have enlivened the Council's proceedings. At home Palmerston was still Prime Minister but the new Viceroy was to make no concessions to Palmerston's more forward policy. Indeed his own views coincided with the liberal school of thought which was beginning to make itself felt in England with its concentration on domestic policies rather than foreign interventions.

In October 1867 when Lawrence had been four years in office he wrote a minute[1] which was virtually his credo and there are signs

---

[1] See Appendix 2.

that he also intended it to be an answer to his critics of the
Rawlinson school. Bearing the marks of deep and prolonged
thought, the minute fell into three parts. In the first he drew his
conclusions from the policy leading up to the First Afghan War
and its aftermath, which have already been discussed in Chapter 4.
In the second part he asked whether India should repeat the series
of errors by re-occupying Afghanistan. He believed she could not
'advance a force permanently beyond our present frontiers
....without the Afghans believing that it is intended to be the
forerunner of an occupation of their country. Indeed this is the very
object which those who encourage such a movement openly
avow.....In a political or military point of view I do not think we
could occupy Herat or Kabul with any real degree of security
without constructing fortifications for the preservation of our own
people and to overawe the population'. He believed it would
require 30,000 men of whom half at least would have to be British.
He then considered the cost including followers, carriage, supplies
and ammunition, none of which could be spared from the present
establishment of the army in India. On financial grounds alone
there was no justification for raising and maintaining such a force.

Politically he said 'The Afghan will bear poverty, insecurity of
life; but he will not tolerate foreign rule.... Whether we advance as
friends or foes would make little difference.... (they) do not want
us; they dread our appearance'.

As to sending British officers as commercial agents, which the
Indian Press proposed, he had been against that ever since his talks
with Dost Muhammad in 1856. Dost Muhammad had then said, 'If
we are to be friends do not force British officers on me'. The fact
was, said Lawrence, that their motives would always be mistrusted
and their lives would never be safe. Pointing to the fate of Stoddart
and Conolly he said that in such circumstances, by the inability to
rescue them except at extravagant cost and even then the risk of
failure, 'our prestige is over-shadowed and England's power is
called in question'. It is consistent with Dost Muhammad's request
that he had just previously refused to accept the Russian Khanykov
mission after its visit to Herat. Lawrence also recalled a mission
which had been sent to him from Kokand in 1853 asking for arms,
guns and ammunition and British officers to help train the Kokand
army. The army he said was non-existent and Kokand was only
able to retain its independence because of its distance from the

Russian base at Orenburg. The Viceroy had accepted his argument that to send help would be bound to end in the loss of British lives.

Lastly he looked at Central Asia from the Russian view point which the opposing school always overlooked. 'I do not pretend to know what is the policy of Russia in Central Asia: what may be her views hereafter in India. But....common sense suggests that her primary interest is to consolidate her hold on those vast regions now in her possession....Russia has indeed a task before her in which she may fail and which must occupy her for generations. To attempt to advance until her power is fully established is to imperil all she has hitherto accomplished. If we proceed to meet Russia to prevent her approach to India we give her so much vantage ground. Instead then of advancing as the allies and supporters of the Afghans....we should be the party against whom they would seek deliverance....May not also the advance of England into or even towards Afghanistan be looked on as a challenge to Russia? May it not bring on the collision we wish to avoid?'

Lawrence continued 'Supposing Russia has the desire and the means to make a formidable attack on India....which appears to me very problematical....In that case let them undergo the long and tiresome marches which lie between the Oxus and the Indus and wend their way through difficult and poor countries where every mile can be converted into a defensible position. Then they will come to the conflict toil-worn with an exhausted infantry, a broken cavalry and a defective artillery'. Then, he said, 'we could meet them on ground of our own choosing'. Finally he asked if it was really in Russia's interest to occupy countries adjacent to India's western border: the further she extended her border the greater area she must occupy. 'The mountain country between our border and Afghanistan....is inhabited by races who are as ill-disposed to subject themselves to one master as to another. They have no desire to be ruled by the chiefs of Kabul. There is not one of these tribes who would not earnestly seek aid if their leading men found themselves over-matched. Which party would then win them to its side; we, or the Russians?' In short, the independent tribes in the zone between Afghanistan and India would, even without any help from India, have formed a kind of inner buffer or zareba – and a very prickly zareba at that.

That masterly minute by a great soldier statesman was a distillation of all Lawrence's experience and wisdom. It is hard to believe that less than ten years later it should have been forgotten – but it was. Elsewhere he suggested that Britain should recognise Russian influence as paramount between the Caspian and the western frontier of China and advocated leaving Russia undisturbed north of an agreed frontier but to oppose any advance beyond it. He had of course less immediate cause to doubt Russian intentions than had Clarendon and his successors at the Foreign Office: all the same his thoughts verged on the prophetic.

In the following year Lawrence did add an important rider to his minute in which he said that Russia could not be allowed to interfere in the affairs of Afghanistan or any other State contiguous to the India frontier. 'If this failed we might give this Power to understand that an advance towards India, beyond a certain point, would entail on her a war, in all parts of the world, with England'. In that at least he was at one with Rawlinson.

Meanwhile he resolutely avoided interference with Afghanistan during the years of internal strife and he refused to establish military posts beyond the new frontier zone. He also resisted pressure to annex any of the tribal territory lying between the Punjab and Afghanistan. On the other hand he had foreseen the need to develop road and rail communications in the Punjab, not only to develop the province but to increase the strategic mobility of the army.

Faced with requests for recognition from family claimants to the Afghan throne, Lawrence maintained complete neutrality. He may have noted with regret that the treaty with Dost Muhammad had pledged the British government to recognise his heirs. When Sher Ali looked like establishing himself, as he ultimately did, Lawrence told a rival relative: 'My friend, the relations of this government are with the actual rulers of Afghanistan. If your Highness is able to consolidate your Highness' powers in Kabul and is sincerely desirous of being a friend and ally of the British government I shall readily accept your Highness as such. But I cannot break the existing engagements with Amir Sher Ali Khan and I must continue to treat him as the ruler of that portion of Afghanistan which he controls'. Later when Sher Ali's hold appeared to be weakening and there were rumours that Britain had given him aid Lawrence told the same claimant 'not to believe such idle tales, neither men nor arms nor money have been granted to him by me. Your Highness and he, both equally unaided by me, have fought out the battle, each upon your own resources. I propose to continue the same policy'. However when the struggle finally ended in Sher Ali's favour at the end of Lawrence's term of office, the Indian government made him a good-will present of £20,000 and promised £100,000 more. To some extent that act appeased Rawlinson who had recommended it in his memorandum to the Viceroy. As a result of his long experience Lawrence had seen the risks of supporting *de jure* rulers; he preferred to deal only with the *de facto*. He had consistently followed what he had said in 1866, namely that 'We should await the development of events. It should be our policy to show clearly that we will not interfere in the struggle'.

Meanwhile we may note the important work which another frontier administrator, Jacob, had initiated some years earlier in Baluchistan. He had a clear picture of its strategic importance when he wrote 'From Quetta we could operate on the flank and rear of any army attempting to proceed towards the Khyber pass; so that with a British force at Quetta, the other road would be shut to an invader, inasmuch as we could reach Herat itself before an invading army could even arrive at Kabul'. Jacob's policy was indeed a forward one but in that hot and arid country he was not faced with the same tribal antagonisms as in the north and his task was easier. It resulted in the securing of India's southern flank, and thus was completed another link in India's defence system.

*   *   *   *   *

Before the end of the Lawrence regime there had been considerable changes in Parliament. Palmerston had been succeeded as Prime Minister in 1865 by Lord John Russell and after a few months he in turn was followed by Lord Derby. Two years later Derby was succeeded for a short spell by yet another Conservative, Disraeli. The experienced Clarendon died in 1870 shortly after opening discussions with Russia for a neutral zone. He was succeeded by Lord Granville, a Liberal of the Gladstone school, who was a good negotiator but said to be somewhat indolent. It was Disraeli who appointed Lord Mayo to succeed Lawrence. Although his was the first truly party political appointment, Mayo was scarcely of the Disraeli mould and he was too great a statesman to be influenced by party politics, even though he was an Irish

Conservative Member of Parliament. Hence the appointment did
not usher in a new era for Indian defence policy. He was a man of
impressive physique with immense stamina matched by considerable powers of application. It was to his advantage that he had
travelled in Russia. Before he left London he paid daily visits to the
India Office to prime himself for the task ahead. From his
background a forward policy might have been expected but when
he had seen the view from India it was Lawrence not Rawlinson
whom he chose to follow.

Mayo adopted much the same broadminded approach to
Russian aspirations in Central Asia as had Lawrence. He even
corresponded on the subject direct with Sir Andrew Buchanan, the
exceptionally able Ambassador at St. Petersburg, which was both
sensible and profitable. Buchanan sometimes passed on Mayo's
views to Gorchakov to their mutual advantage. The opinions of
many other British ambassadors there concerning Central Asia
carried little weight in London; thus, if they tended to play down
the Russian threat there they were liable to be accused of being
pro-Russian. Unfortunately unless briefed by the Viceroy they
tended to know very little about Central Asian affairs; for example,
some seem not to have appreciated the subtle interplay between St.
Petersburg and Russian Governors General in Turkestan.

To Buchanan, Mayo wrote 'I cannot think that if only we
understand each other, Russian interests in Central Asia ought to
be at variance with our own'. He continued 'We cannot view with
any feelings of alarm the advance in Asia of a civilized Christian
power and the establishment of its influence over wild and savage
tribes. If Russia could only be brought to act cordially with us and
say she would not obstruct our trade, that she would not encourage
any hostile aggression or intrigue against Afghanistan...she
would find her mission in Asia would be facilitated'. He concluded
'I am rather inclined to believe Russia is ignorant of our
power....That we are compact and strong whilst she is the reverse
and that it is this feeling of power which justifies us in assuming
that passive policy which, though it may be occasionally carried too
far, is right in principle'. Mayo here took no account of Russia's
jealousy and characteristic suspicion, but lest his views be thought
too idealistic he also thought that a formal treaty binding either
country to non-interference would not be worth the paper it was
written on. He saw too that Russia counted on using her position in

Central Asia as a lever in her European policy, thus turning the flank of the Eastern Question. But Britain could afford, he said, 'to meet force with force and intrigue'.

As a commentary on Mayo's Russian policy it is interesting to conclude with some figures quoted in 1874 by his biographer, W. W. Hunter. In three centuries Russia had acquired eleven million subjects in Asia and the Caucasus. In 100 years Britain had acquired 200 million with 50 million more in the Feudatory States. To secure her Asiatic conquests Russia had an army of something over 163,000. For her 250 million Britain had 180,000 of whom only 60,000 were British troops. Hunter remarked on the similarity of the position as regards native states and races and the difference between the British civilian form of government and the Russian military one.

Mayo's views on Indian defence were based on certain broad principles. 'Surround India', he wrote, 'with friendly independent states who will have more interest in keeping in well with us than any other Power and we are safe'. He was prepared to back these states, amongst which he included Kelat, Nepal and Burma with money, arms and even men. He took the same line over Kashgaria: all of which admittedly was going somewhat beyond Lawrence. He said 'I object to fight for privilege. Every shot fired in anger reverberates throughout Asia... gives to nations who are no friends of Christian or European rule the notion that among our own subjects there are still men in arms against us'. On the north-west frontier he proposed to substitute as far as possible for surprise, aggression and reprisal, a policy of 'constant and neverceasing vigilance and defence of those parts which are liable to be attacked by foreign tribes'. It need scarcely be said that here he was at odds with the soldiers of the day who preferred punitive expeditions to mere policing – an attitude they shared with their Russian opposite numbers.

Towards Afghanistan he departed from the Lawrence policy at only one point. He received Sher Ali in durbar in 1869 shortly after he arrived in India, and before it he had expressed himself as being against any treaty or promise of permanent subsidy and that he preferred to check hostile advances by pushing commerce northwards. Hence he did not give Sher Ali the further £100,000 Lawrence had promised, though he did reassure him that India would extend her frontier no further. Sher Ali had hoped for more support and although he expressed himself as satisfied, later events suggest that he was not. Coming at the time when St. Petersburg and London had begun discussions on a neutral zone, Russia regarded Mayo's durbar with distrust.

Lastly on Iran, Mayo considered it in the interests of all the states concerned that her eastern boundary should be defined, but that it should not be co-terminous with that of India. The result was the demarcation in 1871 of the Kelat boundary with Baluchistan and in 1872 of the Sistan border. Perhaps only in these two achievements and in Mayo's wish that Iranian affairs should be transferred from the Foreign Office back to the India Office did his policies really appease the Rawlinson school. Sad to say Mayo was murdered whilst he was visiting the Andaman Islands, by a tribesman from the north-west frontier who had been convicted of a blood feud murder and had sworn revenge on the British. But by that time he was near the end of his notable term as Viceroy.

The appointment of Lord Northbrook to succeed him in 1872 followed the liberal policy of the British government: Gladstone's first Government had achieved power in 1869 and Northbrook was a truly Liberal choice. The policy of non-intervention abroad fitted well with that of Lawrence's masterly inactivity in India; but Northbrook never acquired any deep understanding of the Central Asian problem. His approach was a somewhat negative one. True he accepted that Afghanistan's interests were identifiable with those of India and that Iran had to be discouraged from taking action against Sher Ali. He also saw that Iran was so unreliable that she could not be supported if Russia attacked her from the north. On the other hand he would, in the last resort, have been prepared to fight to protect British sea communications through the Persian Gulf. Northbrook's passivity naturally met opposition from the soldiers on his Council who wanted a more aggressive policy. It goes almost without saying that the Rawlinson school also disapproved.

One solid strategic gain to India's defence during the Northbrook regime was the acquisition of Quetta at the head of the Bolan pass which had been recommended by Jacob. Mayo had seen how important that would be as a military base on the southern route to Kandahar. On the other hand Northbrook's ban on British officers exploring or game hunting beyond India's borders meant more lost opportunities of gaining any real picture of the extent of Sher Ali's northern and eastern possessions, in particular Badakhshan, Wakhan and Shughnan. The lack of any intelligence organization and reliance on the uncheckable reports of Indian merchants and those of the Pundits of the Survey Department of India were great handicaps to up-to-date reliable knowledge of what was going on in Central Asia. It was a handicap that India was never to overcome fully even by the time of the Bolshevik revolution in 1917. But that is a subject for separate examination and meanwhile we must see what Russia had been doing in Central Asia since Ignat'yev's mission.

CHAPTER NINE

Russia's Subjugation of the Khanates

Following Ignat'yev's mission to Khiva and Bukhara Prince Gorchakov did not lack suggestions for settling Russia's 'Central Asia Problem', but that was only one of three problems which constantly faced him and he must have been a sorely tried man in trying to balance them. As Mary Holdsworth has concisely put it, Central Asia was 'but one sphere of an enormously complicated process of growth and strain at home and penetration into great power politics abroad'. There was 'an outer ring of the powers concerned – Russia, Great Britain (acting directly or through the Government of India), China and, towards the end, Germany'. Within that outer ring was the local ring – Iran, Turkey, Afghanistan and the small khanates, from Kashgar westwards along the northern slopes of the Hindu Kush as far as the Caspian. Not only had Gorchakov to balance all the conflicting problems they presented but he had to deal with clashes of individual opinions and personalities as well – and finally to satisfy his Tsar. It is no wonder that he acted circumspectly, nor that his attitude exasperated the military administration of Central Asia which increasingly tended towards firm independent action.

So far as the problem of Central Asia itself was concerned it seems to have been at least tacitly determined by the Russian government that it consisted primarily in establishing a hegemony over the whole region, with a stable southern frontier behind which trade could be developed in peace. (Except in the Kazakh steppe colonization was so far barely officially envisaged.) A corollary was that Britain and India would be denied any strategic or commercial influence there. There was however no idea as to where the frontier line would ultimately be drawn – that to put it simply was still a matter of trial and error.

Gagemeister, the Finance Minister, put a point of view at St. Petersburg. His argument was the urgent need for industrial development, although he accepted that certain military measures were needed first. His proposals consisted in occupying the upper reaches of the Syr Dar'ya and to put an end to hostilities between Kokand and Bukhara. It was still essential to gain a footing on the Amu Dar'ya to open it up for shipping, to end the Khiva slave trade and to pacify the Turkmen tribes east of the Caspian. The linking of the Syr Dar'ya and West Siberia line of forts was the first necessary step. Grigor'yev, who was then President of the Orenburg Frontier Commission, had made the point that tax discrimination by the khanates against Russian goods must be ended. The fact was that Russia had so far gained no economic advantages from her territorial acquisitions whilst the military administration was expensive to maintain.

Gorchakov may well have recognised the importance of all these recommendations but he continued to oppose open expansion and, so far as any official policy was concerned, he limited it to linking up the two lines of forts. He seems to have been under one belated misapprehension. According to Eugene Schuyler, the thoroughly well-informed American Consul General at St. Petersburg, he still thought the three major khanates were organised states with whom political relations could be established and treaties agreed. If so he cannot have read Ignat'yev's report to the Governor General at Orenburg. Yet Schuyler was not a man to make unsubstantiated statements, particularly as he tells us that the state archives were then liberally open to foreign students – an opportunity of which he obviously made good use, although even he failed to recognize the future economic value of the khanates.

However, the spirit of independence towards the home government was about to show itself in the army of Central Asia. As part of the exercise of linking up the two lines of forts, a thrusting young Colonel still in his thirties, M. A. Chernyayev, was ordered to lead a small flying column from West Siberia. He so far exceeded his instructions as to capture the town of Turkestan. Claiming that he needed to stop Kokandi troops from advancing against him he went on to attack Chimkent, but at that point he was repulsed. Having defeated the Russians the Khan of Kokand set off to attack Bukhara, so Chernyayev decided to try again in his absence. This time he captured Chimkent and set out for Tashkent where his small force of only 1,500 was again defeated.

St. Petersburg let Chernyayev off lightly; indeed the Government was probably very pleased with the results achieved at such small cost. It appears that Gorchakov may have over-estimated the expense of operations against Tashkent and fairly certainly he feared the British diplomatic thunder, which inevitably reverberated. In fact Chernyayev was awarded three medals and promoted. Next year in 1865 in spite of orders to the contrary he again attacked Tashkent, and this time captured the city. After that exploit he was promoted to General. His action had resolved differences of opinion between the Foreign Office and the War Department about attacking Tashkent but it left them undecided as to whether or not it should now be formally annexed. Gorchakov seems to have seen its future as a buffer against Bukhara, but he was in great difficulty in explaining matters to the European powers; partly because he did not know in advance what Chernyayev had intended.

Gorchakov would have found it more difficult still but for the often-quoted circular he had recently sent to his European ambassadors in response to enquiries, chiefly British, about the meaning of Russia's moves. In part he said: – 'The position of Russia in Central Asia is that of all civilised States which are brought into contact with half-savage, nomad populations, possessing no fixed social organization. In such cases it always happens that the more civilised State is forced, in the interests of security of its frontier and its commercial relations, to exercise a certain ascendancy over those whose turbulent unsettled characters make them most undesirable neighbours. First there are raids and acts of pillage to put down. To put a stop to them the tribes on the frontier have to be reduced to a state of more or less perfect submission ...Asiatics respect nothing but visible and palpable force.... The civilized State is thus in the dilemma of abandoning attempts at civilization or lunging deeper and deeper into barbarous countries. The United States in America, France in Algeria...England in India; all have been forced by imperious necessity into this onward march where the greatest difficulty is to know where to stop....' It was a masterly document, for whilst unerringly pointing the finger it most skilfully confined itself to generalities and gave no hint of future limitations to Russian expansion. Its wording must also have given satisfaction to others in the Russian government such as Milyutin; not to mention the army in Central Asia, thirsting as always for campaign medals and promotion. Schuyler does not doubt Gorchakov's sincerity, but many in Britain thought it was just another example of Russia's devious diplomacy. They may have recalled that when the Russian delegate died during the Congress of Vienna in 1815 Metternich was said to have commented 'I wonder what his motive was'.

The fall of Tashkent was of primary importance and the key to future expansion, because it drove a wedge between Bukhara and the rest of Kokand. But the Amir of Bukhara, whose state was in reality very weak, did not read the writing on the wall. During trade negotiations between him and General Kryzhanovskiy, the Governor General at Orenburg, he continued to press his claim to the rest of Kokand, in particular the Fergana valley whose ruler he had installed. Chernyayev, now Military Governor at Tashkent, was not a man to let the grass grow under his feet. Ignoring Kryzhanovskiy he carried out a series of successful operations towards Bukhara which incurred the former's wrath as well as his jealousy. He succeeded in getting Chernyayev recalled in disgrace despite the fact that the Tsar had just awarded him a sword of honour. His successor was General Romanovskiy who also showed his independence by continuing offensive actions against Bukharan troops and presenting his own peace terms to the Amir. These too were refused and Kryzhanovskiy, feeling that his two juniors had stolen enough thunder, reversed his earlier decision not to attack Bukhara. In September 1866 he took direct command and ordered Romanovskiy to 'squeeze the Amir dry and not give in an inch to him'. The Amir was given an ultimatum and on its expiry the city of Bukhara was successfully stormed. Kryzhanovskiy himself negotiated the subsequent peace terms.

Russia still had to decide the future of Tashkent and there were as many opinions about that as the British had about Herat, though the solution, being entirely in their own hands, was reached more quickly. Not only Gorchakov but even Milyutin were at first opposed to annexation; the latter because he did not want the expense of a military administration. But business interests, with their eyes on the rest of Kokand now within reach, argued otherwise. Kokand, and particularly the Fergana valley, was fertile and potentially rich. For instance it grew cotton which, as the

American Civil War had cut off supplies, was badly needed in
Russia. Commercial interests pointed to the expense of maintaining customs barriers and collecting import and export taxes. Finally
there were excellent prospects of colonisation. In face of these
arguments the Foreign and War Ministry's objections were withdrawn and in 1866 the Tsar issued a ukaz announcing the
annexation of Tashkent. To Britain Gorchakov justified the action
simply as a matter of necessity.

The next decision to be taken was how the newly acquired
territories were to be administered. In 1867 on Milyutin's recommendation, although Kryzhanovskiy for obvious reasons opposed
it, a new Governorate General of Turkestan was set up at
Tashkent, taking over from Orenburg the administration of all the
newly acquired territories.

The annexation of Tashkent, the defeat of Bukhara and the
imminent prospect of forcing the rest of Kokand into submission
had marked a new and quickening phase in Russia's southern
expansion. Twenty-five years earlier Perovskiy had correctly assessed the strategic importance of occupying these new territories,
although subsequent Russian historians do not seem to have
given him the credit he deserved. Henceforth Russia had a secure
base in a fertile region with command of much of the Syr Dar'ya.
Orenburg had always been too far away and the intervening desert
too great an obstacle to offer a feasible approach to Khiva. Now
Bukhara could be kept in submission and Khiva and the rest of
Turkestan could be threatened; the latter eastwards from the
Caspian as well. Kokand (whence hailed Yakub Beg, then in
control of Kashgaria), had caused much trouble in southern
Kazakhstan already incorporated in Russia, and Kokandis had
been a constant menace to trade caravans. Russia was now in a
position of influence not only over the rest of Turkestan but also
over Kashgaria and the rich valley of Ili which China had lately
abandoned to Muslim insurgents.

Lastly Russia was in a far stronger position from Kashgar in the
east, to Afghanistan, Iran and even Turkey in the west to counter
British moves and at the least to drive hard diplomatic bargains.
All remaining prospects for Indian trade in Central Asia on equal
terms with Russia had now vanished. The Russian Empire was
drawing level with the British Empire – a prospect to gladden the
hearts of all Russian patriots.

To the disgust of many who had served long in Central Asia, especially Kryzhanovskiy, the man chosen as the first Governor General of Turkestan was Adjutant General K. P. von Kaufmann who had served in the Caucasus but never before in Central Asia. He was yet another Baltic German, although by temperament differing greatly from those others in the Russian service. He was already a favourite of the Tsar, a position which he was to exploit to the full. In his new post he soon became known as Yarym Padshah (lit. Half the Tsar). He was given almost unfettered powers; his task in the broadest terms being to contrive the advance into Central Asia so that trade and industry could be developed. Von Kaufmann was an autocrat and undoubtedly the greatest pro-consul Russia had produced since Murav'yev-Amurskiy in Siberia, though like all autocrats he had his weaknesses. He was a vain man, delighting in etiquette and ceremonial, and although a fine commander he neglected administrative problems. Always seeing the big issues he let the smaller ones take care of themselves. Another failing was his general inability to choose good subordinates at the lower levels and his refusal to dismiss bad ones. Admittedly he had little choice because the standard of personnel serving in Turkestan was deplorable. The consequence was that, as in the Russian bureaucracy elsewhere, there was much corruption. Knowing he had the fullest backing of commercial and industrial interests he quickly staged a trade fair at Tashkent, but otherwise he was slow to develop trade facilities so that for several years to come Central Asia was still a burden on the exchequer.

However, when he arrived at Tashkent there was much pacification yet to be done. Bukhara was still independent but von Kaufmann refused to recognize the peace treaty in force, though he could not negotiate a new one till he had secured his rear by pacifying the rest of Kokand.

In 1868 he captured Samarkand. The significance of this event was in itself more symbolical than strategic. Now it was only an important centre of the Muslim religion, but it had once been the great and flourishing capital of Timur. It was from Samarkand that Timur had invaded Russia and conquered Muscovy in 1405 with his Golden Horde. So at long last Russia had settled the score with their Mongol conquerors. Over the future of Samarkand controversy arose as over Tashkent: Russia assured Britain that the occupation was only temporary; but that too finally ended with annexation. Von Kaufmann concluded a new treaty with Bukhara in 1868 which left Bukhara as a vassal state of Russia but with Fergana still ruled by Bukhara. That situation lasted for an uneasy five years during which the Kokandis with their interminable feuds still proved troublesome and had to be quelled. Finally in 1875 the rest of Kokand was annexed and re-named Fergana. However, Bukhara remained a vassal state with various treaty modifications until 1921. By 1868 it was clear to all that the fate not only of Khiva but all the rest of Turkestan, was sealed.

Soviet historians would have us believe that all the tribes were eager to be taken under the benevolent rule of Russia, of course in strong contrast with the races of India groaning under British rule. But that is simply not true. The contemporary and temperate Russian historian M. A. Terent'yev, with no propaganda axe to grind, states quite clearly that the tribes only begged to be taken under Russian protection if they happened to be on the losing side in their own local wars. The many subsequent insurrections, exacerbated as they were by the uncontrolled influx of Russian settlers and their seizure of tribal lands, support Terent'yev's contention.

It is not to be supposed that Britain accepted this sudden wave of expansion with equanimity. Diplomatic enquiries and protests were of course made and as diplomatically parried. Even Lawrence was moved to action; in 1867 he wrote 'I do not recollect anything of importance which has occurred [in Central Asia] of which we have not heard in very reasonable time'. Nevertheless he had taken a unique step in 1865 in sending a carefully picked party of three Indian spies and one Afghan to visit Badakhshan, Balkh, Bukhara and Khodzhent. The Afghan was actually interviewed by General Chernyayev, whilst another after visiting Bukhara, Samarkand, Kokand and Tashkent, was present for some time during the siege of Khodzhent (now Leninabad). These men were able to bring back useful information about the extent of Russia's latest conquests. Both Bukhara and Kokand had applied for help not only to Lawrence but also to Constantinople and London, but always in vain. When Samarkand fell Lawrence had pressed once more for some arrangement with Russia urging 'that it cannot be permitted to interfere in the affairs of Afghanistan or in any of these States which lies contiguous to our frontier'. Mayo always took matters calmly enough but expressed much the same opinion. He may not have realised the extent to which Britain's strength actually served to stimulate Russian jealousy and distrust, but he still expected a peaceful settlement of the issues involved and optimistically even a share of the trade in Central Asia.

It is interesting to see how von Brunnow viewed the British political scene during these years. According to Terent'yev he had reported in 1867 that the British Press exaggerated Russian strength and that the British government 'although not revealing its alarm by those ill-regulated manifestos such as were given out in Palmerston's day, still in deference to public opinion kept a sharp eye on events'. Next year the Ambassador wrote in a dispatch, 'A rational line of policy however good it may be, in a country like England which is ruled by public opinion cannot be maintained when once it ceases to be popular'. Terent'yev himself noted the opinion of *The Times* that Russia could not successfully attack India through Afghanistan. The newspaper appears to have been fighting a rearguard action for at least some British commercial influence, but although it objected to Russia establishing her authority over the whole of Central Asia it concluded that it was not worthwhile opposing her. One of Baron von Brunnow's greatest assets must have been his ability to explain British democratic processes, expressed through Parliament, to his own autocratic Government. It would be interesting to know whether he ever tried to convey how much this very autocracy exacerbated British opinion. An intelligent Russian once remarked to Count Munster, 'Every country has its own constitution; ours is absolutism, moderated by assassination'.

British suspicions of Russia's advances were bound to die hard whilst her actions in Central Asia so often ran counter to the official pronouncements and assurances which issued from St. Petersburg. For example in 1870 the British Ambassador informed the Liberal Foreign Minister Lord Granville, when the latter had just succeeded Lord Clarendon on his death, 'that the intention of the Emperor was to withdraw his troops from Samarkand as soon as the Amir of Bukhara had fulfilled the engagement which he had contracted towards the Russian government'. Whether or not that was really the Tsar's intention von Kaufmann had decided otherwise and von Kaufmann was skilled at presenting *faits accomplis* to his government – in which it always acquiesced with little or no demur.

Schuyler considered that he did not flout orders though he sometimes embarrassed his government. In any case victories in Central Asia were proving cheap both in money and lives and that was no minor consideration. In the year before he died Clarendon, never prone to give Russia too much rope, summed up British doubts when he told Gorchakov 'we fear not the designs of your government in Central Asia... but the undue zeal and excessive ardour of your generals in search of glory, paying no regard to the views of the Russian government'.

Schuyler considered that Britain's frequent expostulations about Russian movements were undignified; after making her protests she accepted the cause of them without further demur. In his opinion it would have been better for Britain to say in effect 'Thus far and no further'. That indeed was what the government of India always wanted, but the British government never said it. But neither Schuyler nor Lawrence nor anyone else could say where, and expostulations were really the only possibility. All the same the protests may have had some cautioning effect in the long term. The Tsar and his ministers were reluctant to offend British susceptibilities, feeling perhaps that it did not befit a Power wishing to be accepted into the Western comity of nations. Thus Mayo's biographer quotes a letter he wrote in November 1872 to Gorchakov but intended for the Tsar, 'All our neighbours, particularly the Afghans, are filled with the conviction that there exists between Russia and Britain an enmity which will lead us into conflict. I have applied myself to this bugbear. In my relations with Kokand and above all in my letters to Sher Ali, I have always spoken of the similarity of views and the friendship that exists between us. It is this reason which has, up to the present time, determined me not to send officers into those parts with the object of obtaining information respecting the questions put to me by the Imperial Government'. Schuyler, the independent witness, confirms that von Kaufmann was very correct in his dealings with Sher Ali. But it should be added that after the Russo-Turkish War, von Kaufmann so far departed from this estimable attitude as to send a mission to Sher Ali, though he was ordered to recall it on the eve of the Congress of Berlin.

The year 1869 had turned out to be an eventful one for the Game. In March the British Foreign Secretary reported to Sir Andrew Buchanan at St. Petersburg the results of discussions with von Brunnow.[1] Their objective was to decide on a neutral zone in Central Asia. Clarendon had skilfully pointed out that for years Britain had tried to restrain the Indian government from expanding its territory: yet always those on the frontier, far too distant for quick communication and control, had found one reason or another for pressing on. Russia was in danger of making the same mistake and for the same reason. In reply von Brunnow said he was positive of his Government's desire to restrict rather than extend Russia's possessions southwards. He affirmed, with full knowledge of its policy, that no movement disquieting to India need be apprehended. Clarendon said he had earnestly recommended the recognition of a neutral territory between the two countries and that the Russian Ambassador had appeared to think that this would be a desirable arrangement. The Ambassador subsequently gave Clarendon a copy of a letter to him from Prince Gorchakov assuring positively that Afghanistan would be considered as beyond the sphere in which Russia might exercise her influence. Clarendon replied he was not sufficiently informed about Afghanistan to know whether it could be an effective neutral territory. He did not say so in his letter to Buchanan, but he obviously wanted the Indian government's views before committing himself. Mayo in turn consulted Rawlinson who replied with the memorandum discussed in Chapter 8.

Soon after this exchange two important meetings took place. The first was Mayo's with Sher Ali at the durbar staged with immense pomp and ceremony at Ambala. The Russian government had good reasons for viewing with suspicion the British government's support of Sher Ali in recognising him as being in rightful possession of all the territory previously held by Dost Muhammad, and its promise of help against foreign invasion provided he remained faithful to his engagements. The second, a more sober affair, was between the British and Russian Foreign Ministers at Heidelberg and was the result of their earlier exchange of views. There Clarendon developed the proposal that the two countries should agree on some neutral zone in Central Asia. Gorchakov, possibly feeling that Russia was now strong enough to conciliate the British government, made an important gesture in confirming Afghanistan to be 'outside the sphere of our interests and political

---

[1] See Appendix 3 for the text of the Foreign Secretary's letter to the British Ambassador.

influence'. Clarendon reciprocated with the assurance that Britain was ready to abandon all ideas of extending her territory in that direction. In recent years it had become less likely that Russia coveted Afghanistan than that she feared always the influence of a militant Muslim population on the Muslims in her own territory. Thus far thus good, but the talks then ran into trouble because nobody knew for certain what territory actually belonged to Sher Ali, and in particular what the northern boundary of Afghanistan really was.

The Indian government in any case declared itself uncompromisingly against including Afghanistan in a neutral zone. It adhered strongly to Rawlinson's recommendation concerning Badakhshan. On that point Gorchakov demurred and said he must consult von Kaufmann. That delayed the neutral zone discussions as such; meanwhile they were focused on Afghanistan's territorial possessions. It was a long time before von Kaufmann put forward his own views, and when he did they differed predictably from those of the British and Indian governments. It may be that Russia's Military Department had not dropped the idea that the Hindu Kush would ultimately form Russia's southern frontier; in that case Badakhshan would fall under Russian influence – no doubt too for his own ambitious reasons von Kaufmann would have liked to add it to his 'possessions'. But there was in the Russian view a more immediate objection. Afghanistan and Bukhara had long been enemies and Russia feared that, with Badakhshan in Afghan hands, the Amir might one day attack Bukhara, despite Britain's guarantee. There was yet another problem, not fully recognized at the time, namely that Bukhara claimed historical possession of Darwaz, a territory which lay within the northernmost loop of the Amu Dar'ya and thus in Badakhshan. Von Kaufmann, when he finally put forward the Russian view, also claimed that Wakhan, the strip of territory projecting eastwards from Badakhshan between the Pamir and the Hindu Kush to the ill-defined Chinese border, was not Afghan either.

Obviously the British and Indian governments could not accept these contentions. Britain had just recognized all Sher Ali's claims and she could not now back down even if she had wanted to. Nor would it have been strategically wise to give Russia any possible chance of gaining a footing along the Hindu Kush and hence the passes into India. Thus the British were bound to follow Rawlinson's strong recommendation that Badakhshan must be ruled from

Kabul. There was the further point that Bukhara might one day attack Afghanistan through Badakhshan, with or without Russian support. Even Mayo, with his reluctance to interfere in Afghan affairs, realized that Britain might then be forced actively to help Afghanistan to hold her Amu Dar'ya boundary.

In spite of these complications the talks dragged on, with Granville still pressing for a final settlement with an insistence which added further strain to Anglo-Russian relations. They also strained von Brunnow's relations with his Tsar, who thought him too conciliatory. Possibly however Gladstone's known desire to limit Britain's commitments abroad eased matters. At any rate in 1872 Granville, having heard no more about von Kaufmann's objections, put forward the ill-drafted Rawlinson definition of Afghanistan's northern boundary. To appease Britain Gorchakov somewhat reluctantly withdrew von Kaufmann's strictures concerning Badakhshan and Wakhan, on the understanding that the British would use all moral and material means to prevent aggression or further conquest on Sher Ali's part. That conformed appropriately with Britain's previous undertaking to Sher Ali to protect him from invasion. Unfortunately Gladstone promptly repudiated responsibility for armed intervention and said the undertaking implied only friendly advice. As might be expected, Russia regarded Gladstone's retraction as a typical example of British duplicity. The consequence was that Russia refused in turn to guarantee the inviolability of Afghan territory.

The subsequent Agreement of 1873, even though it would have been better spelt without the capital letter, achieved at least some idea of Afghan boundaries but it was obviously not going to last when all the facts were known. These did not all come to light till Abdur Rahman took the Afghan throne. But meanwhile interest had already shifted elsewhere; for the time being the definition of Afghanistan's northern frontier had become almost academic and the relative détente was suffering some severe blows.

Following her successes in north-east Turkestan, Russia began to expand in Transcaspia from the north-west, and Krasnovodsk on the eastern shore of the Caspian was established in 1869 as a fort and base. Operations against Khiva, which was the key to the settlement of the rest of Turkestan, were only delayed because Gorchakov did not want to upset the negotiations he had begun with Clarendon. There is no doubt at all that Russia had thoroughly good reasons for bringing Khiva to heel. Preparations were put in hand and in 1873 the Tsar sent Count Shuvalov to London to explain that the expedition was to be purely punitive and that annexation was not envisaged. The campaign was planned by von Kaufmann and consisted of four converging columns. General Verevkin's column got there first and besieged and stormed the city inflicting considerable indiscriminate slaughter, but it was von Kaufmann himself who entered it and received the Khan's surrender in true pro-consular style. It scarcely needs to be said that Gorchakov was opposed to total annexation, but von Kaufmann had no intention of completely relinquishing his hold and he compromised by retaining the territory on the right bank of the Amu Dar'ya. Khiva itself was reduced to the same state of vassalage as Bukhara. Following this campaign Russia created the new province of Transcaspia, which must have been a disappointment to 'Half the Tsar' who would have hoped for a unified command under himself. This unification was in fact achieved later.

Control of Khiva brought Russia many gains. It ended the Khivan slave trade and it enabled her to control Khivan trade relations with Iran which had existed for hundreds of years. It also brought her a step nearer a stable frontier with the Iran province of Khorasan, with the prospect of developing influence in that fertile province. But before that stage could be reached the rest of south-east Turkestan had to be brought under control. That region was inhabited by the Tekke and other Turkmen tribes, the only really war-like and formidable people in Central Asia, who raided indiscriminately both there and across the Iranian border. A big expedition would be needed to deal with them and Khiva provided a valuable advanced base. Finally Russia was now that much nearer Herat and the rest of Afghanistan and so in a stronger position to stage diplomatic or even military diversions which could be seen to threaten India, thus supporting her future actions in the Near East. It was this last factor which was to precipitate a new phase in the struggle with a return to Rawlinson's long cherished forward policy; this time with Disraeli's Conservative Government in power, following the end of Gladstone's first period as Prime Minister. Whether by intent or luck Russia had certainly made the best use of that period.

*   *   *   *   *

No description of Russia's moves towards the final consolidation of her southern expansion would be complete without mention of a quite different though relevant subject – that of exploration. After the British withdrawal from Afghanistan in the early forties India carried out no more real investigations in Western Turkestan. Free-lance travellers and adventurers there, none of them under the control of the Indian government, included Germans, French, Austrians and one Hungarian, the prolific but politically unreliable writer and traveller Vambéry, but few added much to factual or scientific knowledge. From India the only contributors to geography and ethnology were the Indian surveyors trained and sent by the Survey Department of India. But the valuable information they obtained was often not passed on to the Foreign Deparment or if it was it was ignored. Unlike the Russians the Survey Department's maps were kept very secret. In Chinese (Eastern) Turkestan the situation was rather better. Cayley, R. G. Hayward, who was sponsored by the Royal Geographical Society, and the independent R. G. Shaw (the uncle of Francis Younghusband) had all visited Kashgar. Hayward, who had previously travelled in the Pamir, was later murdered there. Subsequently T. D. Forsyth's two official missions to Kashgar had included trained British as well as Indian surveyors. One of the latter was Faiz Bakhsh (now in the Survey Department) who had been one of Lawrence's spies. But Northbrook further prolonged the period of ignorance by his virtual embargo on British travellers. That was not at all popular with the Royal Geographical Society which considered that all genuine exploration was a contribution to science rather than politics.

Russia, on the other hand, saw very early the need for scientific exploration, and the Imperial Geographical Society sponsored several missions in Central Asia which included not only surveyors, but ethnologists, botanists and mineralogists. Men like W. Radlov, an expert on Ili, Colonel Venyukov, a geographer and a considerable authority on the Turkmen tribes and territory, and P. Lerch, who crossed the Ust-urt and visited Khiva in 1858, were all specialists in their subjects. (Incidentally, writing at the time of the Khivan campaign Lerch shared Schuyler's view. He could see no material advantage deriving to Russia from its fall – only fresh cares and expense.) The reports of all these and others were regularly published by the Imperial Geographical Society and the

Turkestan Gazette. Many were also translated and published in the German *Russische Revue*. In the 1870s they were still the main source of knowledge for the Indian government. Russian maps were particularly good and unlike British maps they were freely available. The situation was of course more difficult for would-be British travellers: in Afghanistan for instance their lives would have been in the greatest danger. But provided they kept out of territory under direct Russian rule or influence they had as much right to go elsewhere in Turkestan as Russians. The lesson taught by the fate of Stoddart and Conolly had been too long remembered; for by the 'sixties the picture had changed. By that time India had prudent and experienced professionals available in the Political Service, yet they were never given the chance to gather essential information until it was almost too late, and both the home and the Indian governments paid the penalty. The subject of exploration leads inevitably to an investigation of British espionage, always a favourite target for Tsarist and Soviet historians.

CHAPTER TEN

Espionage

In the atmosphere of mutual suspicion which continually manifested itself it is easy to see that charges and countercharges of espionage played their part. Indeed at a stage in the present assessment yet to be described, alleged espionage was the direct cause of one of the more serious crises in Anglo-Russian relations. The whole vexed subject merits examination even if only to clear up certain misconceptions which were general at the time and which are being resuscitated today by Soviet historians. They have their reasons, but modern British writers have no excuse for repeating the old fallacies. An initial difficulty arises from the characteristically different attitude to spies which has always existed in Britain and Russia. On the whole the British do not like spies; they regard their profession as a nefarious one and the less they know about their activities, at any rate of those who spy for Britain, the better. In his day Hobhouse illustrated the point very well in choosing, as the subject for his maiden speech in Parliament, to speak against their employment. But if the British do not like spies they certainly enjoy reading about them, in fact as well as fiction. A long line of writers from Kipling in *Kim*, through John Buchan, to the present day, shows the popularity of spy stories in British fiction; whilst factually Colonel F. M. Bailey's *Mission to Tashkent* would be hard to surpass, certainly in its Central Asian setting. Russians on the other hand have always had spies in their midst almost as part of their way of life: they have no need or inclination to read about them. A corollary of that is that they quite naturally expect other countries to employ spy networks to the same extent as themselves. They see spies under the bed where the West might see Reds.

Another misconception of ideas exists as between the words

133

'information' and 'intelligence'. The general British conception of intelligence in the particular sense under discussion here is that it is the collection of information, especially military information, about another country which that country wishes to keep secret. Russia however tends towards a much wider view of a spy's duties as covering all kinds of information about another country or person, with no particular object in view but just in case it may be useful one day.

The relatively modern use of the word 'agent' as meaning 'spy' has also led to confusion. Originally it simply implied a 'representative': as the Concise Oxford English Dictionary puts it, 'one who does the actual work, especially one who represents a person or firm in business'. That was the sense in which it was used by the East India Company, and by the Crown when it took over from the Company, for its representatives in Indian States and frontier districts. Outside India it was used during the British occupations of Afghanistan, whilst Ney Elias at Mashhad in Iran held a dual post as Agent to the Viceroy, in the latter's capacity of Governor General of India, and as Consul General responsible to the Foreign Office in London. Agents were graded First or Second Class. It would be of little reward to trace the first use of the term 'secret agent' in India; it was certainly used by Lord Northbrook in 1876, although as will be seen lower down he was not using it in the sense of a trained or professional spy, nor was he applying it to the Agents of the Political Service; in fact he too was under a misconception. In Russia it appears that the change from 'spy' to 'agent' is also of recent origin, probably since the Revolution. Unfortunately where Central Asia is concerned Soviet historians writing about the nineteenth century believe, or affect to believe, that all the Company's Agents were spies, which is a complete misinterpretation of the facts.

Kim did not help matters. It was not published till 1901 when the conflict was nearly over but its readers, whether British or Russian, can be forgiven if they thought it was at least based on truth. Kipling's Ethnographical Department, in which the delightful character Hurree Chunder Mookerjee appears, never existed although it has been said that the picture of Hurree Babu was based on a member of the Survey Department of India, Sarat Chandra Das. Mahbub Ali, the resourceful Afghan horse coper, was another who existed only in Kipling's fertile imagination.

Although there is no evidence to support it, the character of Kim himself might, like the babu, have just possibly been drawn from life. Kipling could well have read Mountstuart Elphinstone's *An Account of the Kingdom of Cabool*. It was written when he was Agent at Poona and in it Elphinstone told how he came across a ragged outcast son of an English soldier and a Bengali mother called Durie, who had travelled through Afghanistan disguised as a Muslim and he gave Elphinstone valuable information about that too little known country. He was a wanderer somewhat comparable with Giovanni, and having refused Elphinstone's offer of a job in his office, he set out for Baghdad, apparently his Mecca, and disappeared for good.

So what are we to make of the early British travellers in Central Asia in the light of Russian charges that they were spies and political saboteurs? Broadly speaking they were acting on their own initiative and they went there with two objects mainly in mind. One was to pick up as much belated information as they could, geographical, ethnical and political, of an unknown region. Most but not all of them carried credentials from the Company or later the Government of India, and where they adopted disguise it was from personal predilection or for greater safety in travel rather than to worm out secrets. The second object of all the early journeys was to try to persuade the khanates to recognize British rather than Russian influence as paramount. Although they had no official briefing, they followed the Company's traditional policy of developing trade links which would lead to that end; that at least was the intention. It may be remarked in retrospect that it is hard to see what scope there was for any worthwhile increase in trade; Indian traders were customarily to be found in all the oases of Central Asia and their goods were shoddy compared with Russia's. The modern Soviet suggestion that the industrial revolution in Britain would have resulted in goods at competitive prices reaching Central Asia was baseless and in any case there was no official backing for it in India; indeed it was opposed as likely to damage the Indian economy.

The ultimate objective behind all these efforts was, as always, the defence of India, and that included the contributions of Abbott and Shakespear in releasing the Russian slaves from Khiva. Throughout the early days it was the policy of the Company to try not to become involved beyond its borders. The adventurer William

Moorcroft, whom the Russians regard as a spy, was forbidden to negotiate any treaty with Bukhara, and his earlier so-called treaty with Ladakh was disclaimed. Weapons which were what the khanates really hoped the British would supply were always refused and that policy was adhered to notably by Lord Lawrence and his successor Lord Mayo: under them all the explorers could ever offer was the friendly support of the great British raj.

Two minor mysteries of these early days remain unresolved. The first was that before he left on his last journey Moorcroft had twice written to the Governor General asking to join the 'Intelligence Service'. Sir Charles Metcalfe, refusing both requests, wrote on the second occasion that 'It is not thought proper that the reduction of the Intelligence Establishments should be delayed'. The use of the plural is confirmation that there was no central organisation. Evidently, however, there were some kind of local intelligence organisations and a likely solution will be offered lower down. A different sort of mystery concerns Shakespear. When he left Khiva with his slaves he unwisely omitted to destroy some of his papers. These were found by the Russians over twenty years later when they captured Khiva and they were also seen by J. A. MacGahan, the American journalist who was present. They consisted of drafts of his dispatches to Todd and, rather strangely, of a copy of a letter from Palmerston to the Ambassador at St. Petersburg telling him that Britain might consider a Russian advance on Khiva as a *casus belli*. That information must surely have been passed on by Nesselrode to Perovskiy so by that time it was scarcely secret, but why was he carrying it? In his dispatches he went fully into his negotiations with the Khan concerning friendly British support, the release of Stoddart and the threat of an invasion force to that end. There seems to have been nothing else that he could have discussed; he certainly had no power to offer arms, and the invasion force never evolved beyond MacNaghten's wild imagination. The evidence of Shakespear's papers was quite enough for Khalfin to name him in his book as a spy along with Abbott.

Khalfin also names two other spies, the already mentioned Captain R. Burslem and Lieutenant Sturt, who in 1840 spent two months surveying passes over the western Hindu Kush and beyond. He deduces from the former's book that, 'in their travels these two often encountered British "agents" – Indian Muslims on their way back with all sorts of information on the situation in the khanates. Some of them had graduated at a special "intelligence school" ("the Pundits") run by "Captain Dalgetty" in India'. Burslem did not in fact refer to encountering any British agents. What he actually wrote was, 'Another traveller came across us this day who had resided for some years at Kokan and furnished us with some account of the nature of the Chinese garrison at that fort ... My informant had been in the service of the Kokanese and was now on his way back to Hindoostan; in military notions he must have been of the famous Captain Dugald Dalgetty's school, for I afterwards met him as a non-commissioned Officer in Shah Seujah's Goorkah Battalion'. It will be noticed that Burslem did not use the word 'Intelligence' in mentioning Dalgetty's school. To judge by a footnote to his book Khalfin found it in a hitherto untranslated Russian book, *Turkestan* by I. V. Mushketov (St. Petersburg 1906): 'After Dalgetty Major Walker and Captain Montgomery (*sic*) were Directors of this "School". It was given the name of Trigonometric Survey of India'.

Khalfin's zeal in tracking down British agents has led him amusingly astray. In the first place Montgomerie was the director of the Survey Department of India. Its work will be discussed lower down, but it was certainly not a school for spies. Dalgetty was a mystery to the present writer for his name did not appear in the annual *Indian Register*, but readers of Sir Walter Scott's novels came to the rescue. Dugald Dalgetty was a seventeenth century soldier of fortune in Scott's novel *A Legend of Montrose*, which was so popular at the time Burslem wrote his book that all his readers would have recognized him. Of his Dalgetty, Scott wrote in a foreword that he might change his service as he would his shirt. Thus Burslem was simply saying that the N.C.O. whom he met was, like Dalgetty, a mercenary soldier. Scott based his Dalgetty on a real life character, one Sir James Turner.[1]

Strangely enough there was in Central Asia at this time an American Scot called Alexander Gardiner who was just such another soldier of fortune. He had gone to Russia on a mining exploit in the Caspian region but when that failed he actually joined the Russian army for a time. From there he went to Afghanistan, fighting in the internecine wars of the day until he journeyed from the Caspian to Kashgar. If his story is to be

---

[1] See *Dictionary of National Biography.*

believed (and it was accepted by the best contemporary authorities) he would have been the first westerner to make the journey. Thereafter he joined the Sikh Army of Ranjit Singh, though he seems not to have campaigned against the British. Many times wounded he had retired before the Indian Government ever heard of him, to live in Kashmir as a pensioner of the Kashmir government, until he was over 90.[1] No doubt he delighted in telling his story and in giving what political information he could to the Indian government in his later years. One Tsarist historian, Terent'yev, excusably misrepresents Gardiner as an English Colonel: he wrote, 'In this way the agents of the English stand sentry the outlets to the mountain passes'. Incidently he may have been the first to draw attention to the use Russia might make of the Chitral passes in a flanking attack on Afghanistan directed through Jalalabad.

Whilst both Britain, or to put it more specifically the Indian government, and Russia were equally suspicious of each other's missions and envoys operating in Central Asia, the fact of the matter was that until Russia subjugated the khanates India had just as much right to send parties there to collect information and try to keep them on her side as had the Russians doing likewise. Equally, until Britain finally settled her relations with a unified Afghanistan, and Russia accepted the country as being within the British sphere of influence, there was nothing which could truthfully be called *sub rosa* about the Russian negotiators and envoys whom Russia sent there. Of course Tsarist historians claimed, and Soviet historians still claim, that whilst their men were engaged in legitimate enterprise the British were always engaged in spying, but that is only to be expected. The one Russian we know of who might be classed as a spy was Valikhanov in Kashgar, yet his was a unique case.

Spying within Russia or India was a different matter. The men sent by the Punjab government under Lawrence's instructions to Bukhara, Badakhshan and Khodzhent were emphatically spies when on Russian subjugated territory. We know of no others till 1918 when Colonel Bailey, who set out for Tashkent as a member of an official Government mission, turned himself into a spy of his

---

[1] *Soldier and Traveller. Memories of Alexander Gardiner.* H. Pearse London 1908
When Men and Mountains Meet. John Keay. London 1977

own volition and for his own safety. That he was not recalled was
due to lack of any means of communication on the part of the
Indian government. As for Afghanistan, of course Russia had
agents in Kabul, Herat and elsewhere, just as India had newswriters, and just as both countries had in Iran. But in the former
country at least they would not have been 'white' Russians, simply
because, for the same reason as for the British, foreigners were
distrusted and usually murdered. So Russian agents there would
have been Central Asians of one race or another, perhaps with a
Russian passport, but in any event more or less equivalent to the
British Indian newswriters, except that they were probably trained
for the work.

The only known Russian agent to visit India was Dr. Pashino
(the name is not Russian) who went there fairly openly in 1875. He
consorted with all the Russophile and anti-British elements he
could find, but they were disappointingly few. He marvelled at the
small number of British compared with Indian administrators, the
work on schools and hospitals and the number of popularly elected
representatives. He did not fail to note the paucity of the army
compared with Turkestan. His report cannot have pleased the Tsar.

From discussing espionage the next step is to examine the
various organizations in the Indian government whose work it was
to collect information of all kinds beyond India's frontiers, which
was needed to help secure India's defence. One myth, Kipling's
Ethnographical Department, has already been destroyed. Another
one, popular alike with Russian historians and with British readers
of *Kim* which was basic to the story, must now be exposed too. That
superb organization, which watched every move of the 'dread
power of the North' beyond the passes into India and frustrated all
her emissaries, never existed. There never was in the Indian
government any organization comparable with the C.I.A., the
K.G.B. or the S.I.S.

Kipling never claimed any factual basis for his work of fiction,
but a more recent and apparently responsible source has furthered
Khalfin's theme. In 1926 W. H. C. Davis read a paper at the Royal
Academy, London entitled *The Great Game (1800–1844)*. In it he
discussed the work of the early travellers and explorers, laying
much emphasis on their intelligence role. He said that 'The history
of the intelligence service on and beyond the north-west frontier
would be a most curious and instructive chapter if it could be

written from the archives'. He went on to discuss the work of some of the Indian travellers amongst them Izzat Ullah who reconnoitred the road to Bukhara and accompanied Moorcroft, and Mohun Lal who accompanied Burnes. He calls them their agents, but assistants would have been more accurate. He suggests that the names of others were suppressed for political reasons; but even if they were it is doubtful whether their necessarily worm's-eye reports were of any great political value. They would however be useful for finding itineraries. The Europeans of the intelligence service were, he said, less picturesque and he included in them all the early explorers mentioned in Chapter 5. In describing their work he said 'They were invited to trace the ramifications of Russian diplomacy, to fathom the designs of Russian generals'. He continued, 'The story is a tangled one, because the intelligence work of the Indian Government was not controlled from a single centre....' So far so good, but he then went on, *There were at least four official seminaries in which the intelligence officer might learn his business; these were Bombay, Cutch, Lukhiana, Tehran'.*[1]

His use of the words 'intelligence service' suggests a coordinated body on the frontier but there was no such thing; moreover a careful search, not only of the official archives but of the relevant Davis papers in the Bodleian Library, has revealed no evidence for his 'seminaries'. Two were primarily listening posts. If Davis had confined himself to calling them rival schools of policy (a phrase he used immediately after) he would have been nearer the mark. In spite of being the Editor of the *Dictionary of National Biography*, he seems to have indulged a taste for mystery. It was perhaps inevitable that somebody, not necessarily a Soviet historian, would read more into these seminaries than perhaps even Davis intended. A subsequent writer has described McNeill at Tehran, Wade at Lukhiana and Pottinger at Kutch as 'spy-masters' with rival policies who sent out agents who knew their masters' theories and looked for information to support them. That is scarcely a compliment to men like Burnes and Rawlinson: and who would call Colonel Stoddart a spy any more than Colonel Butenov?

After the days of the early 'politicals' the development on sounder lines of the Political Service was firmly taken in hand and aspiring entrants, who might come either from the army or the

---

[1] Present author's italics.

Indian Civil Service, had to be nominated and pass an examination. The consequence was that by the '70s its members were a fully experienced band of men. Ambitious they often were, but there was no room for mere adventurers. Examples of the first fruits were the brothers Lawrence. In the middle period there emerged frontier makers like the too little-known Ney Elias, Jacob, Sandeman and Napier. They were followed by the brothers Yate and, perhaps still the best known to-day, Francis Younghusband. In between missions beyond India's frontiers (when they were officially described for pay and allowances as being 'on special service') they were accredited as the Viceroy's representatives at the capitals of India's Princely states. They were stationed at all the hill states on India's northern frontiers. When British relations with Afghanistan under Abdur Rahman were finally established it was the Viceroy who nominated a member of the Political Service as his representative; so too at a later date at Lhasa, the capital of Tibet. It was mentioned above that the Political Service (it was administered by the Indian government's Foreign Department), had the normal duty of providing the government with political information. In that respect its members were acting precisely as ambassadors do in western countries. There was perhaps one difference. Although the 'politicals' did not intervene in a State's internal administration, they were responsible for advising the ruler on his external relations.

In the countries surrounding India's frontiers there was never any secret intelligence of a military kind to be acquired. What the government needed to know was mainly political – which tribes might be plotting to overthrow some ruler and what might be the effect on the border tribes. These matters were always of particular importance to the Punjab Provincial government, and later to the North-West Frontier Province, because the border tribes who often straddled the North-West frontier, were both warlike and highly volatile. Ever since the days of Mountstuart Elphinstone who began it, Indian 'Newswriters' who were traders living in the more important towns, had been appointed to send periodical letters telling what was going on. They were presumably paid by the Agent concerned from some fund at his disposal and that is the most likely origin of the Intelligence Establishments referred to by Sir Charles Metcalfe in his letter to Moorcroft.[1] Their reports

---

[1] Research by Dr G. J. Alder has since found confirmation of this interpretation.

varied in reliability, some were no better than mere gossip writers retailing bazaar stories. An exceptional case in the 'thirties was Charles Masson, a deserter from the Company's army, then living in Kabul. In the 'nineties the newswriter at Kabul was a hospital orderly and he was apt to retail with relish the gruesome fates which the Amir meted out to offenders. Thus in one month he reported that six people had been thrown down the Dark Well, three of them women of the Amir's own household who had unfortunately become pregnant. All these reports from the North-West frontier were duly forwarded to the Foreign Department and were printed in a *Monthly Memorandum of Information regarding the course of affairs on the North West frontier.* It seems to have been nobody's duty to evaluate these reports and their value in general is perhaps best inferred from the sub-heading to each memorandum which ran, 'Statements of fact [sic] made in this memorandum are based upon reports, newsletters or hearsay'. As late as 1925 the Minister at Kabul complained that his own information was being duplicated in these memoranda and that his reports were much more reliable.

Besides the appointed newswriters, Political Officers on the outposts regularly met Indian traders returning from trading expeditions (those spoken of by Ignat'yev at Bukhara would be in that category). Sometimes they would have paid the traders for their information, depending on their reliability, but these occasional informants were certainly not trained spies. In the exceptional case of the Indians sent by the Punjab government to obtain the information required by Lord Lawrence, these had all been volunteers without previous experience; one was a civil servant whose particular interest was the history of the tribes of Central Asia; another was a goldsmith; a third was a member of a literary society. The episode is further proof in itself that no central intelligence organisation existed.

Political Officers on the North-West frontier prided themselves on their rapport with tribal leaders, whether within or beyond the border, and as a rule, they were very well aware of political shifts and likely repercussions. In general, it could be said that every Political Officer whether in the Hill States, Tehran or Mashhad ran a local information or intelligence service which Russians might call a spy network, but it was a very informal and parochial affair. Indeed some considered it was too parochial. Lord Salisbury when at the India Office, complained to the Viceroy, Northbrook, that too little intelligence about Central Asia was coming from India. Northbrook replied that he had clamped down on the publication of the adventures of 'secret agents', before being checked by the Foreign Department. He said he had no desire to curtail exploration but the information they published could be politically detrimental. He said the Russians had made use of articles in the *Daily News* and the *Pall Mall Budget*. It cannot be inferred from his letter that he was thinking of professional spies – it would be unthinkable for a genuine spy to write for the Press, at any rate until he defected.

Salisbury repeated his complaint to Northbrook's successor, Lord Lytton, who thought the horizon of the frontier Political Officers was too limited, as perhaps it was. Lytton organized an intelligence service there under Major Cavagnari who was later murdered in Kabul. His innovation was strongly opposed by the Political Service and by the Punjab government. Both preferred open diplomatic relations with the trans-border tribes to any underground methods. As for getting information from within Russian occupied territory, after the unique case of Lawrence's enterprise that was never envisaged until Ney Elias went to Mashhad as Consul General in 1891. Rumours of Russian troop movements on the Afghan border with the object of attacking Afghanistan through Herat were then rife in Iran and Elias selected three relatively reliable agents to go into Transcaspia, whose reports he could cross-check. Their reports never confirmed the rumours, which in any case Elias had not believed. The Russians intercepted one report and nearly caught the agent himself.

From the period begun by the tentative Clarendon-Gorchakov Agreement on spheres of influence until the Anglo-Russian Pamirs Agreement of 1895 the attention of the Indian government was concentrated on Afghanistan and India's immediate defences. Hence it tended to see less need for information about Russia in Central Asia and less still after the Anglo-Russian Convention ten years later. But in 1875 two independent British travellers were able to reach Central Asia. Major Herbert Wood of the Royal Engineers accompanied the Grand Duke Constantine's expedition organized under the auspices of the Imperial Russian Geographical Society and led by the geographer, Khanykov, to examine the Amu

Dar'ya. In the same year the dashing cavalry officer Captain Fred Burnaby received grudging Russian permission to visit Khiva. Both men published accounts of their journeys.[1] But it was not till 1888 that the Viceroy, then Lord Lansdowne, lifted the ban on big game shooting beyond India's northern frontier. That gave a chance to adventurous travellers, soldiers like Lord Dunmore and Ralph Cobbold, to combine their favourite sport with the collection of political information. The latter went too far and was actually detained for three weeks in Rushan in the Pamir by local Russian troops. They too wrote books about their adventures, but because they were untrained their political and geographical information was unreliable. For a last proof of how little the Indian government tried to keep abreast of affairs in Russian Central Asia we may cite once more its despatch of Colonel Bailey to Tashkent in 1918, although a Central Intelligence Bureau had been established in 1904–05.

If in retrospect the Indian government can be accused of laxity in acquiring and analysing political information in Central Asia it must be repeated that it had no direct relations with Russia. Viceroys could and did correspond with the Ambassador at St. Petersburg but policy matters were, as always, the responsibility of the Foreign Office in London; hence Central Asia tended to be somewhat of a no man's land between the two.

The other department of the Indian government which Russians have always suspected of being a cover for espionage was the Survey Department. It was formed from the previous Topographical Department and, like its predecessor, was responsible for the survey and mapping of India. In the early days only British surveyors were employed on the work, usually officers of the Engineers. Some of its members did indeed go beyond India's existing borders. Thus Lieutenant John Wood of the Company's Navy surveyed the Indus in 1833. In 1837 accompanied by Dr. Lord he travelled into Badakhshan and surveyed the upper reaches of the Amu Dar'ya from its source, which he located as Lake Zorkul, as far as Ishkahim. Others such as Lieutenant Sturt surveyed passes over the Hindu Kush. These men were of course all fully trained surveyors. The early Political Officers were given

---

[1] J. H. Wood, *The Shores of Lake Aral,* London 1876.
   F. Burnaby, *A Ride to Khiva,* London 1877.

some elementary topographical training including the use of the sextant; Burnes carried one and so too did Shakespear, though the latter could not use his at Khiva because of the Khan's suspicion of figures on paper. They could carry out a road survey as they travelled and could note the features of the country from a military point of view, but they were scarcely map makers.

In the 1860s in the course of the Great Trigonometrical Survey the then Director of the Department, Colonel T. G. Montgomerie, extended its scope to include countries adjacent to India, with the ultimate intention of covering all those between British and Russian territory. At the same time he decided that the Survey should include information on other subjects, such as ethnography and the flora and fauna. British officers would have been bound to attract suspicion in these primitive regions and would probably have been murdered, so Montgomerie recruited and trained a team of Indian surveyors who were called the 'Pundits'. Even they had to conceal their identity from suspicious tribes. They were known only by pseudonyms and for the same reason they adopted a variety of disguises so as to travel unobtrusively. Many of these Pundits were so dedicated to their work that they performed incredible journeys whilst enduring great hardship. Some were murdered, others returned permanently broken in health. A——— K——— the most famous of them was away for three years. At one time he subsisted as a mere shepherd in Tibet, but with his calculations safely hidden in his Buddhist prayer-wheel. The Pundits had no military or political training and, as their reports show, the activities of Russia were quite outside their scope. Two were sent to Badakhshan and Kashgar and they also reached Rushan and Shughnan, small states in the Pamir lying athwart the Amu Dar'ya, but none was ever sent to the three major Central Asian khanates. It is easy to see how their work has attracted Russian suspicions, nevertheless these suspicions were quite unjustified. The Indian government itself was partly to blame; it was very secretive about its maps, which greatly annoyed the Royal Geographical Society. The Russian Imperial Geographical Society on the other hand regularly published the handiwork of its surveying missions. To judge by Ignat'yev's map buying exploit when he was military attaché in London the Russian army appreciated the military importance of maps of foreign countries long before the British army did.

Readers of *Kim* may have been misled by the mysterious Colonel Creighton into thinking that the army in India was concerned with espionage, but nothing could be farther from the truth. The British Army was the last in Europe to form an Intelligence Department and the Army in India only followed suit in 1879. It consisted of three officers, an Indian interpreter and three clerks and was looked on with some scorn by the Political Service. Its sphere included Central Asia, but excluded territory annexed or subjugated by Russia. The latter was the concern of the Intelligence Department at the Horse Guards (subsequently the War Office) by whom it was thought of so little significance that it was grouped with a number of minor countries – including Polynesia. The first concern of the Indian army's Intelligence Department was a wider distribution of maps, which hitherto had been confined to higher formations. It had never been deemed necessary for regiments to have them. Subsequently it undertook the distribution of military pamphlets and such other information as the army at home received from the military attachés at the European capitals including St. Petersburg. It was only in the 1860s that the India Office employed John and Robert Michell to translate articles printed in Russian newspapers and periodicals and not until 1876 was it recommended that their translations should be circulated to the Foreign Office and to the Government of India.

Whereas the collapse of British policy in Afghanistan after the First Afghan War ended any further investigation in Western Turkestan until Lawrence sent his posse of spies fifteen years later, the failure of Perovskiy's Khivan compaign had no such effect. Russia continued her missions of exploration, investigation and intrigue both before and after the subjugation of the three khanates. As to Afghanistan no doubt she relied, as the British did, on information from traders but Lobanov-Rostovsky says that the 1878 mission sent to Kabul by von Kaufmann left agents behind when it withdrew. We have very full proof of Russian activities in the 1890s both in the Afghan province of Herat and in the province of Khorasan in Iran, from the despatches of Elias at Mashhad; activities of which perhaps even Soviet historians have no knowledge. Russian agents were organised by the Consul General at Mashhad, Vlasov, styled by diplomatic courtesy as M. de Vlasov. He had been there since 1888 and he had made good use of his time, as Ney Elias found when he got there in 1891. Strategically Khorasan was important to Russia because if she ever saw fit to attack Afghanistan it lay on the Afghan flank. It also lay on the route to the Indian Ocean where she longed for ports. For similar reasons Russia was then showing considerable interest in Sistan further south. Consequently there was always much intrigue in Mashhad and unusual spice was added because both Vlasov and his secretary had British wives. Moreover the former's step-daughter married the British surgeon. One of these ladies once unwittingly disclosed a plot by Vlasov who was trying to incite a riot by spreading the unfounded rumour of a bread shortage. Over coffee she told a British official that some days earlier Russians had been advised to lay in a stock of flour. Elias took the necessary steps to dispel the rumour and avert the riot. The government of Khorasan was a very corrupt affair and Vlasov had his agents and paid informers very well placed indeed.

One of the first discoveries Elias made was that Vlasov had bribed officials of the Iran telegraph, which was British laid and owned, to give him copies of all telegrams passing to India. A little later the Hon. H. D. Napier on a mission to Sistan found that one of his own servants was in Russian pay. Rather more sinister was the episode in which two obscure Persians were alleged to have been murdered on their way to Herat though no bodies were ever produced. Mashhad officials charged three of Elias's Turkmen bodyguard with their murder. Elias was able to provide a complete alibi for them but it took him a little time to find the real reason behind the absurd charge. He reported subsequently that had good grounds for believing that the murdered men were carrying a large sum of money to Vlasov's official agent at Jam for the purpose of sending a spy to Herat. Only later did he learn that Vlasov had been reading his letters to the Mashhad authorities and drafting their replies. Several times previously Elias had frustrated Vlasov's attempts to send spies to Herat, by ascertaining their names and warning the Governor. This was entirely in accordance with British treaty relations with Afghanistan whereby Britain controlled the Amir's relations with foreign states, just as Russia did in the case of Bukhara. Herat was a fertile ground for Russian intrigue because it was the Amir's most dissident province and indeed he had earlier had to quell a rebellion there; consequently Vlasov never desisted in his efforts to infiltrate spies. On a later occasion when Elias had established what seems to have been effective counter-espionage measures he was able not only to tell the Governor of Herat the name of one of Vlasov's intended spies but even the salary the Russians had offered him. There was also the occasion when Elias intercepted a report from one of Vlasov's men showing that he had been intriguing against the C. in C. of the Iranian army stationed at Mashhad and had got the unfortunate general arrested. He was old and frail and Elias quickly achieved his release. Elias was very fortunate in that he was trusted and greatly respected by Mashhad officials who often consulted him, whereas the Russians were both distrusted and heartily detested.

Rather like Petrovskiy, the Russian Consul General at Kashgar whom we shall meet in the next chapter, Vlasov seems to have regarded all British officials as intriguers and interlopers while their own devious activities were always pure as driven snow – by their own standards. Regard for the truth has never been a characteristic of Russian diplomatists.

Vlasov continually denounced Elias's Turkmen bodyguard as spies and even tried to bribe them to spy for him. Unluckily for them their families lived in Russian Transcaspia and they too were subjected to harassment. Elias succeeded in getting his men naturalized as British subjects, which relieved the pressure on them though not on their families.

One last example of Russian espionage in Herat may be cited. This concerned the Governor General of Transcaspia, General Kuropatkin. One of Vlasov's junior officials complained urgently to the British Consulate General that the Governor of Herat had wrongfully arrested an innocent Russian Turkmen. As it happened the Governor had already reported the arrest to the Consulate and it had just been established that in fact he was a Russian national sent by Kuropatkin; the official was somewhat disconcerted at finding the Consul General knew his Russian name. The Governor was advised to send the man back under escort and put him across the border, which he did. Yet until it was done General Kuropatkin continued personally to press for the release of the alleged Turkmen without any apparent embarrassment or regard for the truth.

There is no doubt that Elias, during his time at Mashhad, established an efficient local intelligence service of his own. In spite of his distaste for the work he nevertheless had to counter the constant Russian activity and he seems to have succeeded very well with no help from India or Britain. But it all took place in a relatively limited area where Russia was then concentrating a great deal on the harassment of Britain, through Iran. The general picture of British and Indian intelligence activity in Central Asia is one of neglect and of a too parochial vision. It is far indeed from the imagination of most recent British writers and from the allegations of Soviet historians. The former pander to the British taste for reading about spies. The latter's inventions are at best only partially explicable by the differing interpretation of the words 'information' and 'intelligence'. The greater part is attributable to the Russian officials' characteristics of suspicion and aptitude for intrigue, and to the adaptation of historical facts for the purposes of propaganda.

The subject of espionage cannot be left without reference to the related one of leakages of secret information from British and Indian government departments. Very clearly security in both London and Calcutta was extremely lax. Thus Charles Marvin, half-Russian and a clerk in the India Office, scored a journalistic coup when he sold to *The Globe* the agreements reached at the Congress of Berlin, which published them the day before they were due to be announced by Disraeli. Marvin subsequently went to Russia for six years and, as a journalist, interviewed General Skobelev after his expedition against Geok Tepe before returning to Britain. Rawlinson, like MacGregor, incurred official wrath for his use of confidential information in his book. In 1890 most of the papers of the Army's Intelligence Branch were stolen by a N.C.O. and next year there was a scandal in London concerning Cabinet papers and secret telegrams. Writing shortly afterwards, Francis Younghusband was convinced by the familiarity of Petrovskiy, the Russian Consul General at Kashgar, with Elias's reports that the Russians had got hold of some of them. It seems possible that they even had the highly secret report of his 1885–86 Pamir journey, of which only 30 copies were printed. During the Pamir crisis of 1891, there was a leakage of information to the Russian Embassy in London where Baron de Staal was Ambassador. The first Official Secrets Act had only been enacted in 1889, but it would have taken more than that to deter Russian intelligence operations. British laxity in the light of such activities is difficult to believe, yet it was a fact and indeed a tendency which Russia has never been slow to exploit.

In St. Petersburg on the other hand, in 1859 we find the U.S. Minister at St. Petersburg complaining to his State Department in Washington that the Russian secret service was opening his despatches, and that when he went to see the Foreign Minister, Prince Gorchakov obviously knew their contents. The American Minister is not likely to have been the only sufferer. Security in the Russian capital was obviously very tight. Apart from officially inspired leakages, only one unofficial one is on record. In the same year Sir John Crompton, the British Ambassador, had been told to find out all he could about Russian policy in China and Central Asia. After explaining how difficult it was to get any he lamented the recent sudden flight from Russia of 'a gentleman to whom my predecessors and myself were... indebted for the communication of some interesting facts'. In her book Mrs R. K. I. Quested speculates that he may have been the man who revealed the Russian army and navy estimates to Crompton, which showed the weakness of the services.

CHAPTER ELEVEN

Kashgar and Ili [1]

It is customary to look at events in Kashgaria and Ili from about 1865 onwards through the Indian end of a telescope, but in fact the Russian and Chinese Empires, because of their common frontier, were far more deeply involved. The physical barriers of the Himalaya and the Karakoram ranges effectively limited both Britain and India to diplomatic activity. These barriers, and the reluctance of Viceroys such as Northbrook to allow British explorers to go beyond them, also meant that India had far too little knowledge of the peoples, politics and the terrain of Eastern Turkestan. Until Robert Shaw and George Hayward defied the official veto and went to Kashgar in 1868, the latest information was based on the reports of the three German Schlagintweit brothers who travelled there in the 1850s, but since then there had been momentous political events.

Long before Russia's expansion, indeed even before her unification, China with her deep sense of history, had regarded Eastern Turkestan as of particular concern to her. Successive dynasties always feared the incursion of barbarian horsemen from the western region and her historical aim was one of 'Grand Unification' which would bring it under her full and permanent control as a colony. Emperor Ch'ien-lung of the Manchu (Ch'ing) dynasty nearly achieved the task and in 1768 it was named Sinkiang – the New Territory. But like others before him his successors weakened, and by the beginning of the nineteenth century they were faced with Muslim revolts in China proper which, thanks to weak and corrupt rule, in due course spread to Sinkiang. Chinese Muslims

---

1 In writing this chapter I must acknowledge my debt to Immanuel C. Y. Hsü whose valuable book, *The Ili Crisis* was not available when I discussed the subject in my biography of Ney Elias.

had always been more militant than indigenous Han Chinese and were never fully sinicised. The Taiping rebellion of 1855 led to another in Yunnan which was followed by similar uprisings in Kansu and Shensi. The unrest spread westwards and in 1865 Muslim Tungans had captured most of Sinkiang north of the Tien-shan, known as Dzungaria. This disaster occurred when Russian expansion in Western Turkestan was about to result in the capture of Tashkent and the subjugation of Bukhara and Kokand – the last-named once regarded by China as an outpost. China now had to face, not only the task of recovering Dzungaria, but the threat that a land-hungry Russia would move in first from her newly-established base. To make her troubles still worse, by 1865 Yakub Beg was putting himself in firm control over Kashgaria, the southern half of Sinkiang. Thus the prospects were far more serious than the traditional threat of mounted barbarian nomads, who had always been ejected when the dynasty in power felt itself strong enough. This time there might well be the permanent loss of the dominion, or the equally unpleasant alternative of war with a Western power. Fortunately for China Russia too had her difficulties and uncertainties which gradually emerged during the next decade. It was also lucky for her that Britain, for her own very good reasons, was actively interested in promoting a peaceful diplomatic solution between the two Empires. Not that Britain derived any benefits from her activity; indeed when Russia and China ultimately agreed to terms, Britain found herself at a considerable disadvantage in Kashgar both diplomatically and commercially vis-à-vis Russia.

Russia had had long experience of China's western frontiers and these Muslim uprisings were of considerable concern to her, partly because she had a large restless Muslim population on her own side of the frontier and partly because of the various treaties, notably those of Peking and Tarbagatai, which already allowed of consular representation in certain cities of Sinkiang, and favourable terms of trade. It was very disconcerting that losing factions on the rival Chinese side could cross into Russia and spread disaffection amongst her Muslim population, as well as raid her caravans and pillage her villages. At the same time Russia saw the possibility of profit. To the north-west of Dzungaria along the Russian border lay the Chinese prefecture of Ili, and the Ili river valley, on the old Silk Road to the West, was the most fertile region in the whole of

Siankiang, even more fertile than the Kashgar oasis to the south. If not the Russian government, von Kaufmann himself was quick enough to see that the chance might occur for the permanent Russian occupation of Ili, but he had to proceed warily and wait on events: it would be diplomatically unwise to antagonize China. Meanwhile although no common frontier in Sinkiang had yet been agreed, he had already occupied territory within striking distance of Ili.

Firmly established in Kashgar as he was by 1865 Yakub Beg had so far only limited control over a small part of Dzungaria, but he was now a force to be reckoned with and by Britain as well as Russia, although Valikhanov's report may have left the latter with some doubts about his stability. He had imposed peace and a certain amount of justice where before there had been uprisings and the inevitable corruption resulting from weak Chinese rule. Kashgaris themselves welcomed the change. Mainly of Turkic origin, they were used to being governed and they did not much mind by whom provided that taxes were fair and that they could therefore trade profitably; less nationalist than their fellow Muslims to the north they were in the main peaceful traders. Yakub was anti-Russian (he had already fought Russian troops in Kokand) and Russia saw the danger that he might foment Muslim unrest in Russian Turkestan. She did not want to offend Peking, but on the other hand she feared lest Kashgar fall under British influence. So for the time being Russia held her hand. Britain, however, relying on the apparent stability of Yakub's rule, saw the advantages of making Kashgar a buffer state between all three Empires. Shaw's reports after his visits there in 1868 and 1869 in which he eulogized Yakub and his Kashgari subjects ('just like Englishmen if they were not such liars') saw great opportunities for trade with India. The old Company tradition that the expansion of trade would induce khanates, amirates and the like to accept British influence as paramount died hard. As has already been observed, what the latter really wanted but never got was arms with which to carry on their local feuds; except for Yakub Beg, and later for Afghanistan and Chitral as allies, the Government of India was careful never to supply them, although there was undoubtedly some private gun-running to Kashgar. John Keay, author of *When Men and Mountains Meet*, an absorbing account of the early travellers and explorers in the Himalaya, found evidence that

Alexander Gardiner tried to import 20,000 muskets to Kashgar on behalf of Yakub Beg, and it is supported by that of G. J. Alder, but the Indian government stopped the deal fearing that the consignment might in fact be intended for the Maharajah of Kashmir. The old warrior certainly had good contacts in Eastern Turkestan. Shaw also held the belief that it would be possible for a modern army to traverse the Karakoram and descend on India's northern frontier and that too was given credence. Shaw, a tea planter by profession, was a very cultivated man who carried his Herodotus with him and likened the local women to Rubens' portraits; but he was basically just an enthusiastic and impressionistic traveller. His companion on his 1868 journey was George Hayward an army subaltern and a surveyor who on this occasion was sponsored by the Royal Geographical Society. Neither man was capable of assessing the confused politics of Chinese Turkestan.

Shaw's reports naturally did not impress Lord Lawrence who did not fear a Russian presence there and had no wish to get politically involved. But they had an effect on Lord Mayo who saw an advantage in including Kashgar in his ring of friendly states surrounding India. As for the possibility of a Russian diversionary threat, the army took it seriously and its feasibility was hotly debated for the next few years. A Mongol army of 5,000 men had once successfully descended on Kashmir, though it had lost four fifths of its force on the way back. There were those who believed a modern army could do better. In 1870 Mayo sent an envoy to Kashgar, the well-qualified professional Indian Civil Servant, Douglas Forsyth. He left Leh the capital of Kadakh accompanied by Shaw, whom Yakub had asked for, and a doctor. They spent a fortnight at Yarkand and returned safely, but having failed to meet Yakub they accomplished little beyond gleaning information of the history and conditions of Chinese Turkestan and an over-optimistic idea of the prospects of trade. It may be that Yakub avoided a meeting because of his fear of Russia.

By this time Thomas Wade, the first and on the whole remarkably successful British Minister at Peking, was urging the Tsungli Yamen (the Ministry for External Affairs) to recognize Yakub's independence. With too little understanding of China's inexhaustible patience he did not think she could ever recover Sinkiang, although the Regent, Prince Kung, assured him that Sinkiang differed from other tributary states, and that it would be done. Wade did not cease his urgings however, because he was assured – wrongly as it transpired – by Li Hung-chang the grand old soldier statesman who, with General Gordon as his assistant, had put down the Taiping rebellion, that it was not worth the trouble of recovery. But Wade had to be careful because, against the strategic advantages of Sinkiang as an independent buffer state, he had to weigh the risk of offending China and thus damaging Britain's rich and increasing trade with her. Added to the complete disruption of Russian trade with Chinese Turkestan, the activities of Shaw and Forsyth greatly annoyed von Kaufmann as well as General Kolpakovskiy, the Governor of the Oblast of Semirech'ye. It was not only the possibility of Kashgar itself falling under British influence, but they anticipated that the next step would be active British support of Yakub Beg in an attempt to capture the capital Ili; and the Ili valley was potentially of greater economic importance to Russia than was Kashgar. So to frustrate such a chain of events Russia began to cultivate her own relations with Yakub.

It is not difficult to see why the Ili valley was so coveted. In addition to its agricultural fertility it was rich in minerals and by 1856 Ili's exports to Russia were worth over one million pounds sterling per annum. Its products were of course worth a great deal more to China. That explains why Ch'ien-lung set up a military governorship at the town of Ili commanding the whole of Sinkiang. Although Muslim, the indigenous tribes were a heterogeneous collection and to control them the Chinese stationed troops of outside origin. These were mainly Manchus, but included some 3,000 Chinese, altogether making a garrison of about 16,000 along the northern Tien-shan route. Moreover only officials of the highest integrity were sent there. But after Ch'ien-lung's reign the officials and the army became increasingly lax – the only interest of the former being their own gain – with no concern for the indigenous population. Hence the risings, first of the Taranchis (now known as Uygurs) in 1857 and then the Tungans in 1864. Against these fanatical insurgents the ill-trained and ill-equipped garrison had no chance. In 1864 the Governor appealed to Peking for 40,000 troops but got none. In turn the Tsungli Yamen sought help from Russia but got only vague promises. The rebels beseiged Ili[1] and it

---

[1] Ili (subsequently for a time called New Kuldja), lay west of modern Kuldja (I-ning).

ultimately fell with fearful carnage. Gradually the whole valley was laid waste. The Russian orientalist, W. Radlov, who had known it before the rebellion wrote a graphic description of the scenes of death and desolation when he returned later.

Von Kaufmann was very correct in dealing with China and he held his hand until 1870. Then after a fruitless mission of conciliation by Baron Kaulbars of the Russian General Staff, and having informed St. Petersburg, he sent a force to occupy the strategic Muzart Davan pass across the Tien-shan, so as to prevent an invasion by Yakub Beg and hence any British interference. Next year General Kolpakovskiy moved into Ili and announced that he had occupied the valley 'in perpetuity'. (The wording was toned down to 'recovered from the rebels' when Peking was informed.) Although the British Foreign Office heard of the occupation in August 1871, Wade in Peking did not learn of it until the end of the year. Knowing so little about Ili the Foreign Office asked him whether it had any significance for India. Wade replied that he thought it was too far off to matter, but he himself knew little enough about Ili.

This is the appropriate moment to introduce in more detail the man already referred to more than once, who in twenty odd years had perhaps the greatest practical experience of all the professionals of his day, Ney Elias. By inclination he was a scientific explorer. His first notable contribution had been a survey in 1868 of 500 miles of the new course of one of China's great rivers, the Yellow River (Huang Ho) which, about twenty five years earlier, had overflowed its embankments and formed a new outlet into the Yellow Sea (Huang Hai) causing floods and utter devastation in a huge area of the countryside. In 1872 he was about to undertake, alone and unsponsored, an exploratory survey of western Mongolia starting from Peking and hoping to reach India. It was probably Wade therefore who suggested that he should include Ili on his route. After a hazardous journey he reached Kobdo (Hovd), but the rebellion had made it far too risky to travel on to Ili and India so he continued a further 2,000 miles across Siberia, camping out in mid-winter till he reached the railway at Gorkiy. His journey of 2,300 miles, across Mongolia which he surveyed meticulously up to and even beyond the Russian border, earned him lasting recognition as a leading authority on the history and politics of Central Asia. Thereafter he joined the Indian government's Political

Service and was next employed on the ill-fated Burma-Yunnan
mission when Augustus Margary was murdered. Elias spoke
Chinese; he was a careful planner with excellent judgment and
there were those who said he should have led that expedition. His
next hope was to carry out a survey of Tibet, at a time when his
great Russian counterpart, Colonel Przhevalskiy, was trying to go
there for political as well as exploratory reasons. In the event
neither man did and it was twenty years before Elias was able to
explore again. Although he always felt frustrated as an explorer
– he might have felt more at home in the Survey Department
– nevertheless his diplomatic skill and judgment were to have even
greater and more lasting effects on India's northern defences, as
well as on the Burma-Siam border, than his explorations. There
will be more references hereafter to his work, which he carried out
under the constant handicap of increasingly serious tropical
diseases. He was a regular correspondent of *The Times* for twenty
five years. During his years in Central Asia he came to know many
of the tribes: they trusted him and he travelled everywhere in
safety.

To the world Russia announced that she had taken over Ili from
the rebels until China was ready to re-occupy it, but of course in
the hope and expectation that she never would. After his visit there
Schuyler showed it as Russian on his map. Yakub Beg's rule was
now seen by Russia to be an advantage. The longer he was in
power the less likely it was that China could win back Ili; so in 1872
Baron Kaulbars negotiated a commercial treaty with him. Yakub
Beg was now indulging in the usual practice in Central Asia of
treating with both his potential supporters at the same time and
keeping his options open: he was also receiving help from Turkey.
This was a custom the British did not, and never could, understand.
In 1873 in spite of his liberal policy of not getting involved,
Northbrook, following Mayo, sent Forsyth on his second mission to
Yarkand this time with almost plenipotentiary powers. It was a
huge party of 300 with 550 baggage animals and it included two
British surveyors, Gordon and Trotter, and two Indian surveyors
all from the Survey Department as well as a present of some
thousand old-fashioned muskets, with an escort of the Guides.
Such a large party was intended as a prestige symbol but it was a
mistake which was to be repeated more than once elsewhere. The
sparse economy could not support all these mouths without local

hardship and ill-feeling, and it took Ladakh four years to recover. That, incidentally, should have proved how impossible it would have been to supply and maintain a fighting force from India. However, following Kaulbars he too concluded a commercial treaty which included the right to establish a consulate, although ultimately Yakub Beg never ratified it and it came to naught.

The surveyors did good pioneer survey work. Gordon in particular was another of the real professionals. His important survey of some of the passes from the Pamir into the small hill states of Hunza and Chitral suggested that they might be feasible as military routes. His findings, coupled with the recognition that added to Kokand, Kashgar could be a valuable supply base on the flank of a Russian advance from the Pamir, certainly alarmed the Government of India. The consequence was to hasten a flurry of political and military defensive preparations towards meeting the threat. Gordon was the first British explorer of the too little known Pamir since Wood, although Russian missions and explorers had been increasingly active there for some years. Forsyth's two Indian surveyors travelled on to the northern loop of the Syr Dar'ya where they made discoveries about the small states of Shughnan and Rushan which were ignored at the time but were later to create a serious frontier problem. After the hardships his mission suffered in crossing the Karakoram, Forsyth revised his notion that the route from Kashgar was militarily feasible, but it did not end the debate. This mission marked, although quite unintentionally, a change from the long policy of 'masterly inactivity' towards Central Asia and was really the beginning of a new stage of the 'forward policy'. It is interesting that it should have happened so far from the main field of rivalry and during a Liberal government. Nevertheless, Forsyth's main recommendation was that Britain and Russia should negotiate a friendly agreement to recognise Chinese Turkestan as neutral territory. After his first mission he had been sent to St. Petersburg to try and arrange a commercial treaty there. However all discussions with Russia about any neutral zone were subsequently shelved because of von Kaufmann's expedition against Khiva in 1873. In Chinese Turkestan it could be said that the honours between Russia and Britain at that time were about even, with Yakub Beg supported by the British in Kashgar and Russia in full occuption of Ili. But situations were apt to change quickly in Central Asia and Chinese Turkestan was no exception.

The step that began the change went unnoticed by both Britain and Russia. China, summoning unsuspected reserves of strength, began the long task of quelling the Muslim rebellion. After first putting down two separate rebellions, the Taiping and the Nienfei, the next stage was the recovery of the province of Yunnan, which Muslims there (known locally as Panthays) had occupied for 18 years. It was accomplished with much savagery by a provincial scholar landlord with no previous military experience. With military resources thus released a start was made in 1868 in Shensi. The general entrusted with this formidable task was another patriot and scholar Tso Tsung-t'ang who had already distinguished himself against the Nienfei. He and his predecessor in Yunnan were the fore-runners of the warlords of the twentieth century. Tso Tsung-t'ang proved himself to be a brilliant strategist and leader and in the following year he recovered all of Shensi. Next year he turned his attention to Kansu with the result that by 1873 he had restored imperial government throughout the dissident provinces. There was then a pause while much wrangling went on at the Imperial Court. Japan was threatening Formosa at that time and Li Hung-chang whose main responsibility was for maritime defence argued that this had priority over the recovery of Sinkiang. That would explain why in all honesty he told Wade that the province was not worth recovery. Tso submitted a state paper in which he argued that the Western powers were interested only in ports and profits from trade, whereas Russia was expanding territorially and against her Sinkiang was the first line of defence. The argument was resolved in Tso's favour when he was appointed Imperial Commissioner in charge of military affairs in Sinkiang. This was the first non-Manchu appointment to a top post in Sinkiang since its original conquest in 1759.

Tso had many problems concerning the raising and supply of his army. He recruited them mainly from Hunan which traditionally supplied the best Han-Chinese soldiers. He decided to attack first in Dzungaria north of the Tien-shan and to turn his attentions to Yakub Beg afterwards. He began his long march in March 1876. In August he captured Urumchi. The town of Manas fell in November and its capture marked the complete pacification of Dzungaria – not however without a great deal of ruthless slaughter. It is said that although he had been given modern rifles he left them in armouries in Kansu, fearing that if the campaign failed he might have to account for them. Consequently he relied on swords, spears and bows, with which his troops were doubtless better equipped than the insurgents, besides being better led. That winter he rested his men, who literally 'cultivated their gardens' and planted vegetables against the spring campaign. Yakub Beg had been quick to read the signs and he sent an emissary to London to seek mediation and through Forsyth he offered to become a tributary of China. In June 1877 Lord Derby at the Foreign Office authorised Wade to offer British mediation but Tso Tsung-t'ang argued successfully that the offer was made chiefly because of British fears concerning Russia, and that Ili could not be recovered till Kashgaria had fallen. In any case, although neither the Foreign Office nor Wade knew it, the British offer came too late. Tso had begun his campaign in the spring of 1877 and after the capture of two towns Yakub's resistance was broken. Yakub himself died suddenly in May, some said by poison. All Kashgaria was recovered in the remarkably short time of ninety five days. Contrary to the example of Dzungaria there was no slaughter. A prosperous Kashgaria would be unlikely to make common cause with a scorched earth Dzungaria. The return of China was actually welcomed with relief by the Kashgari population and the way was now clear for China to negotiate with Russia for the return of Ili.

Shaw had returned from Kashgar without his appointment as Consul being ratified.[1] As it happened that was just as well but the news of Yakub Beg's death did not reach London till July. It had been reported to Ney Elias, then the Viceroy's Joint Commissioner at Leh the capital of Ladakh, by one of the Turkish officers lent by the Sultan of Turkey to train Yakub Beg's army. Elias had been sent to this lonely outpost in Ladakh in 1877 by the Viceroy, Lord Lytton, 'for the express purpose of watching events in Kashgar' which naturally included Russian moves. Leh was a rather inadequate listening-post: reliable news was hard to come by and it took him two years to piece together the story of Tso Tsung-t'ang's triumphant campaign, and even that was before Wade knew it all.

Here was an outstanding example of India's chronic lack of political information and any efficient means of obtaining it. But the Russians too were taken unawares. Never having expected to

---

[1] Having been accepted into the Political Service he was thoughtlessly posted to Burma. The sudden change to an unhealthy climate was too much and he died a few weeks later.

have to negotiate for the return of Ili they now stalled. The fact was that neither Britain nor Russia had ever understood either China's special concern for Sinkiang or her historical sense of patience (the case of Taiwan is a modern example). Wade himself was misled by Li Hung-chang, whose main concern was elsewhere. But with eyes always focused on Russia neither the British nor the Indian governments would have listened to Wade; the latter in particular invariably ignored him just as it consistently ignored the importance of the third Empire. For years the only Chinese speaker in the Political Department was Ney Elias. It would have been a wise diplomatic move, even in merely good-neighbourly terms to have congratulated China on the recovery of her lost 'colony'. The chance did offer itself, and indeed China saw Elias's first unofficial visit to Yarkand in that light, but when later it could have been made officially with likely beneficial effects on future relations with China and hence Sinkiang, the next Viceroy, Lord Ripon, chose not to take it. From then on China discouraged not only British representation at Kashgar but Indian trade too. The trade proved to be worth little but official British representation could have been worth a lot to both Empires.

China's first step towards the recovery of Ili from Russia was the despatch of a mission in 1878 led by Ch'ung-hou. Ignoring advice to travel overland to St. Petersburg and consult Tso Tsung-t'ang on the way, Ch'ung-hou went by sea and he had no notion of the Ili situation when he reached the capital. Russia was however fully prepared, although there had been earlier internal dissensions. The Tsar considered the return of Ili to be a debt of honour. Milyutin, the War Minister, wanted to retain it and was prepared to fight for it. On the other hand, von Kaufmann had had to send away some of his few good officers and men for the war against Turkey and his preference, therefore, was for a negotiated return of Ili but at a very high price. The delegation which met Ch'ung-hou was led by Milyutin. Prince Gorchakov, the nominal Foreign Minister, was deemed to have failed at the Congress of Berlin and he was represented by his deputy Giers (properly Girs, he was of Swedish origin). During the discussions both Gorchakov and the Tsar were away at Livadia and this hampered the negotiations, though it suited Russia's delaying tactics. In the intervals plenty of pressure was brought to bear on Ch'ung-hou, interspersed with lavish entertainment. Whilst agreeing to return Ili the Russian delegation did not disclose all its compensation demands at once. The clauses in the final draft treaty allowed Russia to retain several hundred square *li* of territory which included the Muzart Davan and the Torugart, both of them strategic passes across the Tien-shan. They were of particular importance to China as being the keys to the control of Kashgaria from Ili. The Muzart was important to Russia too because it also led in to Kokand. Under the treaty China was to accept Russian consulates in seven towns in Dzungaria and to allow Russian merchandise to be free of duties in Mongolia and on both sides of the Tien-shan. Finally China was to agree to pay Russia 5 million roubles for her expenses whilst occupying Ili. Ch'ung-hou had been given exceptional powers and he was in a hurry to go home. He signed the Treaty at Livadia in October 1879 without further authority. When it heard the terms the Tsungli Yamen was aghast, but the treaty could not then be re-negotiated. Russia was correspondingly elated. Tso Tsung-t'ang was particularly infuriated, as well he might be. He argued against ratification and made a strong case for a new diplomatic approach, with war if that failed. On the other hand Li Hung-chang took a pacific line. Memorials poured in to the Imperial court. The most impressive of them by a hitherto unknown young scholar, Chang Chih-tung, was not only drafted with logic but with great literary skill, which was regarded by the old order as important as its arguments, and he strongly supported Tso Tsung-t'ang.

Apart from recommending the execution of Ch'ung-hou the main points were as follows. Russia's duplicity and treachery should be exposed to the world through the foreign press, thus setting one barbarian against another in the classic manner. Her exhaustion after the Russo-Turkish war meant that she was in no position to fight China. The restitution of Ili should be postponed pending further diplomacy. Lastly China should look to her defences in Sinkiang, Western China, Manchuria (which was too far off for Russia to penetrate for any sustained period), whilst Li Hung-chang built up the fleet. The Tsungli Yamen did not at all want war but was forced to bow to all the memorials supporting the young scholar's recommendations. However, partly to strengthen her relations with the West, and in response to foreign appeals, notably by Queen Victoria through Thomas Wade, Ch'ung-hou was pardoned. A new envoy, Marquis Tseng Chi-tse, the Minister in London and Paris, was chosen to go to St. Petersburg to re-negotiate the Treaty of Livadia. Meanwhile Tso continued his preparations for war and China began to buy foreign arms and ships. She also sought foreign aid in training the army. Wade was still against a war, which he thought China would lose, nevertheless he considered that Western support should be given lest China break up altogether, with consequent heavy loss to British trade. The British Foreign Minister, Lord Salisbury, ever careful not to commit himself too far, said Britain could not officially supply personnel for a war against Russia, but he saw no objections to individual arrangements being made. General Gordon was summoned back to China, but he was so out of touch with events and his inherent instability had become so marked (the trusted Inspector General of Chinese Maritime Customs, Robert Hart, commented that he seemed to be 'not all there', and Wade said he was 'no longer perfectly sound') that his presence was mainly symbolical of Chinese determination; a point not lost on Russia. His confusing advice, though appreciated, went unheeded and he duly departed.

In April 1880 Tso Tsung-t'ang submitted a progress report. He said he would not begin the war, but he would invade Ili first and then if necessary fight on Russian soil. He believed resolute action would strengthen Tseng's negotiations and he judged that Russia was so financially weak that she would not lightly begin another war. He advanced his headquarters to Hami, significantly taking his coffin with him. That was customary for elderly Chinese but it had the added advantage here that it proved he would not desert his men and would see the job through to the end. Meanwhile Russia too was making preparations, news of which alarmed the Tsungli Yamen. She sent reinforcements to Ili and added twenty three ships to her Far East fleet. Tso soothed the officials by pointing to the length of the frontier. If Russia did invade in one direction he could invade in another. Von Kaufmann's military preparations did not greatly impress the British military attaché at St. Petersburg. He told Lord Dufferin, the British Ambassador, that if the Chinese were in earnest then Russia must be relying more on her fleet. It was undoubtedly lucky for China that Japan decided not to become involved, but Li Hung-chang, pursuing his peaceful role and with some personal animosity against Tso, rightly pointed out that it would not do to rely on hopes of active Western intervention; indeed the British and French Ministers were still working for peace, and only the German von Brandt wanted war. Nevertheless war seemed near and everything depended on the St. Petersburg negotiations.

Marquis Tseng took on his mission with extremely natural misgivings; he not only expected to have to pay the extreme penalty in the event of failure but he also feared he might be refused entry to Russia. Before he left London for St. Petersburg he was careful to ask for the support and advice of the British Ambassador there. He was accompanied by Halliday Macartney, who had served the Chinese ever since the Taiping rebellion, and was at this time Secretary to the Minister in London. Unlike Li, Tseng was no pacifist and he correctly saw that there could be no peace in the Western Region until Ili had been returned and that that must be immediate. He argued that the three issues to be solved were boundaries, trade and compensation. To gain the first and essential point he was prepared to bargain on trade and to conciliate on compensation. Tseng was quick to appreciate Russia's weaknesses. Diplomatically she faced China without a single friend in the West, and only three years after being forced to re-negotiate the treaty of San Stefano at the Congress of Berlin. Furthermore Britain was re-establishing control over Afghanistan. Ili was a relatively minor issue for Russia compared with the Near East but still more than symbolically important. She had also serious military and domestic difficulties. Not only was she in such financial straits that she could not afford another war, but there was considerable internal unrest and there had been crop failures. Her intelligence sources may have exaggerated the strength of the Chinese army facing her, but she had only been able to reinforce her own garrison on the frontier by about 5000, and troop movements were slow over such great distances. She also feared an attack on her Amur river frontier.

The opening session between the two delegations was held in August 1880 and afforded a nice demonstration of the strongly contrasting characteristics of the two countries. Giers began the proceedings by asking aggressively 'How is it possible to negotiate with a people who cut off the heads of their Ambassadors?' Anticipating such a thrust, Tseng replied humbly, almost apologetically, that this view was understood and that Ch'ung-hou had already been pardoned in order to protect Russian honour. Thereafter they got down to business in which Dufferin, in touch with both parties, sometimes acted behind the scenes as a mediator, and the Tsar gave his assent to the re-negotiation of the Livadia treaty. The Russians wanted to transfer the talks to Peking, where Wade was unfortunately still harking to Li Hung-chang and was pressing China to ratify the Livadia treaty. It must be acknowledged that Wade's part throughout, though well-meant, did him no credit. He was reprimanded by Lord Granville, the newly appointed Foreign Minister, and the negotiations were continued at St. Petersburg as China had insisted. Russia had procedural difficulties in arriving at a united policy. Milyutin the War Minister was in the chair but Giers was away and his deputy knew nothing about China. Von Kaufmann's advice was sought but his demands were too severe to be of any use. When Giers eventually returned in October he wanted a quick settlement of the 'cursed' Chinese affair.

The agreed result, which Lord Granville urged Peking to accept, was that Russia would return all of Ili, thus including the important Muzart pass – except a small strip reserved for Tungan refugees. The boundaries laid down in the Livadia treaty were to be ignored and new ones, including the Kashgaria boundary, were to be agreed by a joint commission. Russia's favourable trading terms were retained but new consulates were reduced to two, though with the promise of five more as trade increased. Thus the most contentious issues were peacefully resolved. The problem of compensation was finally settled by China's agreement to pay the heavy sum of nine million roubles for Russia's 'occupation' costs. The resulting Treaty of St. Petersburg was signed in 1881 and ratified by both countries in the following year. Having feared worse Russia was pleased, but the honours went to China. Marquis Tseng Chi-tse was congratulated on all sides for his brilliant performance and in China his rank was raised. Confronted with firm opposition, Russia had backed down for the third time in five years.

* * * * *

Mayo's 'ring of friendly states' policy could never have succeeded in respect of Chinese Turkestan, whose natural lines of communication lay eastwards and westwards. From the south caravans to Yarkand from Leh, the most advanced trade centre from India, commonly took a month or more to traverse the Karakoram. In the winter months snow closed the passes altogether. India's only long term hope lay in British support of China, by whatever means lay in her power, in maintaining her hold on Sinkiang. Two factors operated against such a policy. One was that China rarely wanted any western support except, as we have seen, when threatened by Russia. On a subsequent occasion when she saw herself threatened by France from Indo-China, Lord Ripon unwisely ignored Chinese overtures. The other factor operating against better Chinese-Indian cooperation was that relations between Wade in Peking and the Indian government were always strained and often non-existent. Both parties could claim some justification – given the chance Wade, as the expert, wanted to hold all the reins, whereas the Government of India preferred to ignore both Wade and China as far as possible.

If China had lost control of Sinkiang for a second time, there is little doubt that Russia would have moved back into Ili and would certainly never have left again. With Ili as a base and with control of the Muzart pass she would quickly have moved southwards into Kashgar. Her fear that India could get there first and hold it in force can now be seen to be groundless. From there and from the Pamir Russia could have reached Kashmir: then indeed the three empires would have met. Ney Elias early foresaw that threat and ultimately devised the means to avert it, which the Governments of India and Britain adopted – but that was nearly ten years later. Altogether it was fortunate indeed for India that China was able to hold Sinkiang.

Meanwhile it may be asked why Ili, so far distant from India, was of any importance to Britain. Leaving aside the obvious predicament she would have had to face if there had been war between China and Russia, the answer lies in the trade agreements embodied in the St. Petersburg treaty. They presented vexatious problems which dogged her relations with Russia insofar as they affected the Game, and with China too, for years to come. To explain them we may start at 1880 when Elias put forward his plan for his second, and this time official visit, to Yarkand and Kashgar. In general he proposed to collect information which might lead to increasing commercial activities, observe any activities of Russia towards Kashgar and lastly to travel on to Badakhshan. This last object was important in his eyes because no British officials had been there since Lieutenant Wood and Dr. Lord; Russian missions on the other hand were active along the middle reaches of the Syr Dar'ya in addition to the Pamir. But the Viceroy vetoed his last objective as being politically too risky and he confined Elias's instructions to discussing the improvement of trade relations with the Chinese. Unfortunately his credentials went somewhat awry. The one he carried with him was signed only by a minor official and not by the Viceroy himself whilst the all-important Chinese passport which Wade had obtained from the Tsungli Yamen never reached the Amban of Kashgar. (The Amban was the approximate equivalent of a British Resident in an Indian State, but in practice he had great prestige and hence more power.) He was again welcomed by the Amban of Yarkand but when he reached Kashgar, though greeted 'very civilly' by the Amban there, he could make no progress in the subsequent talks on trade. The Amban affected not to know that there was any trade between India and Kashgar (at one time there were about a thousand Indian traders in Sinkiang) and Elias realised that if the trade clauses of the Livadia treaty were ratified, China would immediately raise her tariffs against India. That of course was exactly what happened as a result of the St. Petersburg treaty. In their political discussions the Amban showed much bitterness against Russia and Elias was at pains to point out that Britain and China could usefully help each other by exchanging information. But in concrete terms the mission was a failure and Elias made a dignified withdrawal.

Once the St. Petersburg treaty was signed India's relations with Kashgar worsened still more. Petrovskiy the Russian Consul General appointed to Kashgar in 1882 quickly made his presence felt. He was a cultured man and well-versed in European affairs: he could be polite and affable but for the most part he was brusque and overweaning, often behaving as if he himself was the governor of Sinkiang. Indeed it is fairly certain that it was just what he hoped one day to be. The Chinese soon had reason to fear him for like so many Russian consular officials he was an arch intriguer. His presence may well explain the change in Chinese policy which led to the refusal to negotiate with Elias four years later although the excuse then was that Kashgar was not a 'treaty port' in the terms of the 1860 Treaty of Peking, and that meant no consular representation in Sinkiang. Unofficially the Chinese said one consul was more than enough and they did not want to risk another like Petrovskiy.

Successive Joint Commissioners at Leh did what they could to foster trade, but it was little enough and it duly declined. Whilst Elias was at Leh the principal trade goods were percussion caps and *charass*, which was the local word for cannabis. Worse still Leh was not nearly such a good listening-post for events in Central Asia as Kashgar would have been.

The inconsistency of viceregal policies which changed regularly every four years was remarkable. Lytton, though a strong proponent of the revived 'forward policy' towards Afghanistan, had never much liked it towards Kashgar, where he had inherited it from an otherwise non-interventionist Northbrook. After Lytton, Lord Ripon pursued a policy of non-involvement by India in any relations with China or elsewhere and he refused to press even for a consul. Although also a Liberal, Lord Dufferin who took office in 1880 was to adopt a much stronger and more positive policy on frontier and trans-frontier problems than his predecessor. Russia had already occupied Merv and Russian survey parties had been reported in Badakhshan, Balkh, Chitral and Hunza as well as in the Pamirs. The Penjdeh 'incident' in 1885 had been seen as a serious crisis in Anglo-Russian affairs. By then Elias had for years been urging the need for a British exploratory mission in the Pamirs and Badakhshan, and at last in 1886 he was chosen to undertake it. But first he was to go to Kashgar on his third visit, as before to try to negotiate a trade agreement. The British Chargé d'Affaires in Peking, in asking for his passport, was told to point out to the Tsungli Yamen that Britain wanted similar treatment for British Indian traders in Sinkiang to that accorded to the Russians and for a British Resident at Yarkand to supervise them. The Chargé was also to point out that this officer would be able to furnish information about affairs beyond the Chinese border. But the Chargé (who may not have pressed very hard) could only get a passport which entitled Elias to go as a traveller 'for pleasure and instruction', and it omitted any mention of his official status. He was thus, in Chinese eyes, in no position to negotiate. The consequence was that the Amban at Yarkand adopted the Peking line, which though favourable three months earlier thanks to British support of Marquis Tseng at St. Petersburg, had now changed completely. So Elias did not even go on to Kashgar which he knew would be fruitless; instead he cut his losses and proceeded on the second part of his mission to the Pamir. At the time there was a school of thought in India which envisaged either a military alliance with China against Russia or Chinese troops under British leadership. Having seen the deplorable standard of the Chinese garrison in Sinkiang Elias firmly disposed of any such fanciful notions in his report.

It was four years before India again took any positive action there. In 1890 under the instructions of Lord Lansdowne young George Macartney was posted to Kashgar, although officially unrecognised by China. Macartney was the son of Sir Halliday Macartney and his Manchu wife and he was bi-lingual. He also had the Chinese characteristics of imperturbability and patience, and at Kashgar he needed them. Together with Ney Elias he had been a member of the Sikkim expedition in 1888. He spent the next twenty eight years observing closely and reporting with accuracy and foresight both Chinese and Russian moves in Central Asia. His first test came when Britain annexed Hunza, the turbulent state on India's northern border, on which Russia was casting covetous eyes from the Pamir. Until 1903 he had to put up with the machinations and vagaries of Petrovskiy who always regarded him as an interloper. For a period of two years after a pretended infringement of protocol, Petrovskiy refused even to speak to him. Then there were insurrections in Sinkiang, corrupt officials, harassment of Indian traders and all kinds of annoyances and frustration to occupy him. Imperturbably he survived them all; almost more remarkably his English wife patiently put up with them too. The Indian government kept him languishing in his unofficial role until 1911 when at last he was appointed Consul General. In his last year of service the Bolshevik revolution broke out and his final action was his visit to Tashkent with F. M. Bailey, on the orders of the Indian government, to find out what was happening. Finding chaos he wisely returned whilst Bailey chose to remain. By that time, although a legacy of suspicion lingered on, the main issues had long been resolved; but George Macartney worthily upheld the latter day standard of the best 'politicals'.[1]

---

[1] The story of his life has been told by C. P. Skrine and Pamela Nightingale in *Macartney at Kashgar* (1973).

CHAPTER TWELVE

Forward Again

The story of Kashgar has chronologically outrun events in the main field to which we now return. The Khivan campaign had widespread repercussions and one which has escaped due notice was von Brunnow's reaction. Like other Baltic Germans he had served two Tsars faithfully and well, but over nearly 40 years he had become almost more a referee than a participant. Latterly he had observed the rising power of the Conservative party in Britain and that it was becoming increasingly irritated by Liberal supineness in the face of Russia's latest gains. He was so disturbed at the effect the campaign against Khiva would have on British opinion that he took the extreme step of writing direct to the Tsar, which he was entitled to do, but it naturally annoyed Gorchakov. One consequence was the despatch of Count Shuvalov to allay British fears. Von Brunnow was highly pleased with the assurance conveyed by Shuvalov from the Tsar that the expedition was purely punitive and that no permanent occupation was intended. But the episode came at the end of von Brunnow's long term of office, for he was succeeded by Shuvalov in 1874. His pacifying influence was a great loss to both countries. He died in the following year.

The campaign also stiffened India's determination not to let Afghanistan become part of any neutral territory. Gorchakov was offended, or affected to be, by that decision, but it was undoubtedly the right one from India's defensive point of view. It was on this decision that Rawlinson scored his first real success in stipulating that the Amu Dar'ya must form the Afghan frontier, the line which was followed by Mayo and subsequently adopted by the British government. In any case the neutral territory plan so favoured at the outset by Gorchakov had become another casualty of the Khivan campaign.

In Britain the affair marked the end of Gladstone's Liberal regime, just as von Brunnow had foreseen. A Conservative government under Disraeli as Prime Minister, with Lord Derby succeeding Granville at the Foreign Office, was elected in 1874. The Liberal Northbrook remained in office as Viceroy of India until 1876 when he resigned and was succeeded by Disraeli's nominee the Earl of Lytton. These events marked the end of the 'masterly inactivity' policy and the beginning of a new stage of a forward policy. From Russia's point of view the timing of the Khivan campaign, even though it could no longer have been postponed, had certainly been unfortunate in arousing another wave of Russophobia in Britain. However, if for the time being it postponed any further expansion in Central Asia it certainly did not end it. Gorchakov had nevertheless been forced to make one great, if reluctant, concession to Britain. As a result of the four years of negotiations from 1869-1873 Russia formally agreed to recognise the northern and north-western frontiers of Afghanistan and accepted that Afghanistan itself was outside her sphere of influence. That included the recognition of Badakhshan and Wakhan as Afghan possessions, whilst the actual boundaries remained still unknown.

Michell's translations from Russian newspapers make interesting reading at this time, because the Russian press, being of course government controlled and inspired, could often be taken as official thinking. These suggest that it was neither enmity against Great Britain nor envy of the treasures of India that led her into Central Asia, but solicitude for Russia's own safety. That can be accepted as a genuine aspect of Russia's own insecurity. Only if there was war with England through European misunderstanding would Russia try to take advantage of her stronger position in Central Asia to damage the influence of England in the East. Nevertheless although the papers do not say so, the fact was that every southward move by Russia, besides bringing a stable boundary nearer, brought her into a better position to make a diversionary move threatening India if there was war in the Near East, as the Russo-Turkish war was to prove. The point was well made in so many words by the historian Terent'yev.

According to Gregorian in his excellent history, *The Emergence of Modern Afghanistan,* Gorchakov made one more attempt after the virtual breakdown of the 1873 Agreement. He proposed an

Anglo-Russian agreement on freedom of action whilst respecting each other's interests and thus avoiding a collision. Each side had Bukhara and Afghanistan respectively in mind but this was not really breaking new ground; since 1839 each side had repeatedly given each other such assurances. Terent'yev says that on one occasion specifically, Russia had actually warned Bukhara not to go to war with Afghanistan and to keep to the right bank of the Amu Dar'ya. Similarly Britain had warned Sher Ali not to go to war with Bukhara. But such an agreement would have been worth nothing unless and until the future of Afghanistan was firmly settled, and that entailed settling the Herat question as well as her frontiers. It was a matter which deeply concerned Russia who still feared Herat as a British stepping stone towards supremacy in Central Asia, whilst Britain took precisely the opposite view. Moreover Iran might still one day try to recover it.

With the arrival in power of Disraeli and his romantic notions of Empire and with Russia flushed with her successes in reducing the khanates to a state of vassalage, a new era of aggressive foreign politics was ushered in. To take Russia first, Milyutin at the War Department was advocating an aggressive policy. He argued that Britain could menace Central Asia through her support of Turkey and he feared too the possible destruction of Afghanistan's recent independence. He was anxious lest Britain should advance towards the Caspian via Herat. Russian strategists would have preferred Herat to be in the hands of Iran, and like their British military counterparts would still have preferred the Hindu Kush and not the Amu Dar'ya to be the frontier, although it is true that rivers make bad boundaries; but Afghanistan was an exception for reasons which Rawlinson for one had clearly shown. Some extremists even argued that in the event of war in the Near East, Russia should conclude an alliance with Afghanistan and march on India, but in the light of Lord Lawrence's minute such a plan can hardly be taken seriously, and other Russian strategists opposed it as being far too venturesome.

With war clouds looming up in the Near East both countries were at this time looking beyond the relatively limited horizon of Central Asia. Disraeli thought that if there was war over Constantinople, Russia would have to be attacked from Asia and driven back from Central Asia and the Caspian. That might look well on paper though surely it could never have been regarded as feasible.

But though no strategist Disraeli did accomplish a master stroke in 1875 when he purchased a major share for Britain in the Suez Canal which had been opened in 1869, thus materially shortening Britain's strategic sea communications with India. (In spite of that it is interesting to note that in 1878 heavy guns were installed at Cape Town against a possible threat by a Russian fleet.)

Telegraphically Britain had been connected with India since 1870. Officials at both ends doubtless had mixed feelings at receiving daily, even hourly, cables instead of the weekly 'bag' by sea, but the practical benefits were incalculable. There was notably more control by the British government over the vagaries of Viceroys although it still meant that the Government, through the India and Foreign Offices, could give instructions without being fully aware of the picture from the Indian point of view. One grievous example will appear in this chapter.

Disraeli had installed Lord Salisbury at the India Office, and he was to be concerned with Afghanistan, and later when Foreign Minister, with Central Asia for many years to come. It is difficult to sum up his policy about either of them whichever office he held. Although he did not approve of Disraeli's romantic and expansionist notions of the British Empire which so appealed to Queen Victoria, he nevertheless thought Gladstone and Derby had been too weak towards Russia. He had some characteristics in common with Gladstone; a deep sense of religion was one. He certainly could not have forgotten that Gorchakov had abrogated the Black Sea clauses of the Treaty of Paris of 1870. But especially after his encounter with Ignat'yev at Constantinople he was more Russophobe than either of them. Although still more open-minded, yet he was certainly not an expansionist. He was determined that Russia should not have unrestricted access to the Eastern Mediterranean, but his policy for Afghanistan was less sure; his thoughts were screened, as it were by his huge beard, and it may be they were more pragmatic than he would admit. If asked what his general political philosophy was he might have answered 'What we have we hold', and that, to take one example, meant agreement with Disraeli in supporting the Ottoman Empire. It also meant taking a more forward policy towards Afghanistan and Central Asia.

Northbrook had resigned, partly because of a difference of opinion with the India Office over cotton duties but also because

Salisbury, fearing British strategic weakness in Afghanistan, had proposed that Britain should install a permanent British representative at Kabul. Northbrook had doubtless not forgotten the urgent representations of both Dost Muhammad and Sher Ali never to put British officials into Afghanistan. Salisbury may never have heard of their requests or else he no longer realised their significance; at any rate when Lytton was installed in 1876, Salisbury renewed his instruction to the new Viceroy. Lytton was the son of the poet and perhaps he remembered his father's lines:

> 'Beneath the rule of men entirely great
> The pen is mightier than the sword'

It has been suggested that he wanted to live down his poetic inheritance, and if not prove his father's lines wrong, then at least to prove himself a thrusting statesman. If so it cannot be said that in the exalted post of Viceroy he achieved his purpose. In his biography of Salisbury, A. L. Kennedy had commented that 'people who knew the East would agree that at least an astute understanding of tortuosity was an asset there'. That asset applied no more to Lytton than to Salisbury: but the two men were at least in general agreement that Russia must be stopped as far from India as possible and that meant keeping Afghanistan under British influence.

Meanwhile further trouble was looming ahead in Afghanistan. Relations between von Kaufmann and Sher Ali had begun in 1870 with a letter from von Kaufmann in very correct terms which said that he recognized Afghanistan as being an Indian protectorate and that as Britain and Russia had friendly relations, Sher Ali need not fear Russia. He enclosed a copy in English for the benefit of the Indian government, which drafted Sher Ali's reply for him. In 1872 he wrote again and the Amir told Northbrook that von Kaufmann wanted regular correspondence with the Kabul government. Von Kaufmann called the Amir his 'neighbour' although Bukhara and Khiva then intervened. Alarmed at impending events the Amir asked India for more help in establishing and retaining his frontiers. The Viceroy, relying on Gorchakov's assurance to Clarendon of 1869, told Sher Ali he had nothing to fear; but von Kaufmann flouted this assurance by continuing the correspondence through his agent at Tashkent.

The Anglo-Afghan agreement of 1859 had guaranteed the

integrity of Afghanistan against Iran, Russia or Bukhara. Now alarmed by the fall of Khiva in 1873 Sher Ali sent an envoy to India asking for money, arms and troops if necessary to repel unprovoked aggression by Russia. It was on this last point, when the Duke of Argyll, who was at the India Office under the Gladstone administration, rejected his request that Northbrook resigned. Britain had previously also refused to arbitrate on a frontier matter between Afghanistan and Iran. These events were the turning point in Sher Ali's relations with Britain. Sandwiched between the two great powers, liking neither – Afghans were strongly xenophobic – he turned to Russia from whom he hoped to get better terms: that was simply the usual Central Asian procedure of horse-trading. In 1875 a Russian envoy arrived at Kabul and subsequent envoys had secret talks with the Amir. It must be conceded that von Kaufmann played a very skilful diplomatic hand, designed to allay Sher Ali's fear of Russia whilst luring him towards her, yet at the same time doing nothing to offend Britain too strongly. By 1878 he had established considerable influence in Afghanistan. He was much more subtle at dealing with oriental potentates than Lytton or Salisbury with their heavy handed methods, and only the skill of the Lawrence brothers was comparable.

By this time all eyes were turned on the Near East and the Russo-Turkish war of 1877-78. Gorchakov had been warned that British interests in Suez, the Persian Gulf, Constantinople and the Straits were vital and he promised to respect them, having obviously no desire to take on Britain and France as well as Turkey. But whilst the war was on Lytton was repeatedly reporting Russian advances in Central Asia and urging military counteraction. There is no doubt that Russia was using her stronger position there to exploit British fears and create a diversion. She publicized her plans for a march on India which according to Lobanov-Rostovsky would consist of three columns. The plans and some troop movements certainly alarmed India, just as they were intended to, but it is impossible to believe they could have been serious. Indeed, as Schuyler pointed out, Russia's administrative difficulties in Turkestan alone would have made them difficult for years to come. In any case the distances from European Russia, the bad communications and the intervening deserts would have made them logistically impossible. The only way into India was the classic one through Iran and Afghanistan, and that was not envisaged in the publicized plans.

By about 1874 Sher Ali had written off Britain as an ally, thus abrogating the 1859 treaty. He felt he could no longer rely on her against Russia. A couple of years later it could equally be said that von Kaufmann, whether with or without Gorchakov's tacit approval, had come to regard the 1873 Agreement as a dead letter and he continued to send envoys to Kabul. Just before the Treaty of Berlin was signed General Stoletov had been dispatched by von Kaufmann to Kabul with a draft treaty of friendship. Neither von Kaufmann, nor St. Petersburg, could flout the Berlin treaty and Stoletov was ordered to withhold the draft. Britain knew of his departure and in retaliation sent a Political Officer, Neville Chamberlain, whom Sher Ali refused to receive. At that time India's only representative at Kabul was an Indian who tended to follow Sher Ali's advice. Britain had of course protested at Stoletov's activities and had received the usual bland, reassuring replies. Part of the Russian case was that the Tekke tribes south-east of the Caspian were being harassed by Turkmen from across the Afghan frontier and that these tribes had to be pursued and punished. It was a somewhat specious excuse but that state of affairs could not be allowed to continue. By 1878 there was no question but that Afghanistan had fallen under Russian influence, and India was in ignorance of the state of affairs there.

Lytton had had many conversations in London including one with Shuvalov before he left to take up his post. He had come to the conclusion that Britain's need was a 'strong peaceful bulwark in Afghanistan, and to increase its prosperity'. The Russian government 'whose real policy had not been and cannot as yet be openly disavowed, would gladly disarm the Amir and absorb his dominions, either by sharing them with Britain or alone. The Amir was falling into a trap and becoming a tool'. Disraeli endorsed these views privately through Lord Salisbury (who became Foreign Minister in 1878, with Lord Cranbrook at the India Office) so as not to embarrass the Viceroy's Council which had hitherto been Northbrook's.

At Calcutta Lytton was met with some antagonism from the old masterly inactivity adherents. The Amir's line of reasoning appeared to be that so long as he refused intercourse with both Britain and Russia, they would both seek his friendship and

Afghanistan would prosper; but this argument had probably been suggested by Stoletov who was still at Kabul: however it sufficed for Sher Ali to refuse to receive Chamberlain. His refusal, conveyed privately, was partly because he could not guarantee Chamberlain's safety and partly because to refuse him openly would be a breach of friendship. Lastly he could not conceal such a mission from the Russians; but they were too strong for him to refuse them too.

By this time Lytton was thoroughly alarmed. He argued that if Russia attacked Afghanistan it could only be with the further object of attacking India. He said the object must not be war for the defence of India, but security of the Indian frontier so as to prevent war, and he then asked Sher Ali to reconsider his refusal. At the same time von Kaufmann sent the Amir another letter describing the taking of Kokand, which was intended to impress Sher Ali with his own weakness. Britain again protested and Lytton asked Salisbury to consider Russian reactions if India had opened the same friendly relations with Bukhara or Khiva.

At length the Indian Agent at Kabul was sent to Calcutta to explain the Amir's views and fears of India. The Agent took back to Kabul certain very definite proposals. They included an alliance, assistance in men, money and arms in the event of unprovoked aggression, and a yearly subsidy. (This last may have been included because Mayo had never given the Amir the £100,000 promised him by Lawrence.) It was basically a renewal of the 1859 treaty, but the Viceroy also stipulated a British Agent on the frontier. The Amir sent no reply because the Russo-Turkish War had broken out which he expected would lead to war between Britain and Russia, and in which case he would sell himself to the highest bidder.

Meanwhile Lytton concluded the treaty with Kelat which he saw as the most open road of attack on India from the Caspian and Afghanistan. It was of course well in advance of the Indus-Sutlej line of defence, favoured hitherto by the masterly inactivity school, and certainly of much greater strategic value. The Russian government had the chance to contrast this action with her own annexations against which Britain invariably protested, but it seems to have ignored that point. The semi-official *St. Petersburg Gazette*, more concerned just then with Turkey, only commented that this was a blow by Lytton against Afghan neutrality.

At the end of 1877 Sher Ali agreed with reluctance to reopen negotiations. He had apparently thought the treaty had been intended to cover all his affairs, internal as well as external, whereas it was only meant to cover the latter; but he still refused the new clarifying treaty that was offered him. Lytton now considered there were only two alternatives open. One was a forced or negotiated settlement with Afghanistan under British influence; the other was to break up Afghanistan and conquer what India needed to defend her frontier, notably Kandahar and Herat. The issues really differed little from those which led to the First Afghan War. Meanwhile it did not help to make a decision any easier that Sher Ali was becoming unpopular as a ruler, and there were rumours that he was preparing a Jehad or holy war against Britain because of Kelat, though he had also denounced Russia too. Affairs in Afghanistan were becoming very confused.

The Stoletov and other missions had given Lytton the best possible excuse for sending one of his own. The Russians, as was not and still is not, unusual, had over-played their hand. Lytton had sent an ultimatum which Sher Ali ignored, and he thereupon decided on action, though not without weighty objections at home. Lord Lawrence for one voiced his apprehensions; as quoted by Gregorian he wrote to *The Times* in September 1878 'What are we to gain by going to war with the Amir? Can we de-throne him without turning the mass of his fellow-countrymen against us? Can we follow the policy of 1838–39 without, in all probability, incurring similar results? ... Are not moral considerations also very strong against such a war? Have not the Afghans the right to resist our forcing a mission on them, bearing in mind to what such missions often lead, and what Burnes' mission in 1836 did actually bring upon them?' But, alas for Britain and India, Lawrence's wisdom, so consistently sound as it had proved to be, no longer carried any weight. If he had been in office the chances are that there would have been no war.

The Russian blunder, the refusal of the Amir to receive Chamberlain, and the failure to reply to his ultimatum, had put Lytton in a favourable position. He sent three forces across the passes into Afghanistan, the one to Kurram being commanded by General Roberts V.C. Sher Ali promptly retired in favour of his son Yakub – a weak young man – and withdrew into Russian territory. Negotiations were opened, and in 1879 under the Treaty of Gandamak, Yakub assigned certain Afghan border districts, including Kurram, to the British. He agreed to conduct his foreign relations under the Viceroy's advice and accepted a British Agent, not at Herat, as the British wanted and where he might have been safer, but at Kabul. The unfortunate Political Officer, Louis Cavagnari, was chosen for the job and Roberts recalled his misgivings as he passed through his lines on his way. He reached Kabul in July 1879 and from the first was regarded with suspicion. Three months later he was murdered and thus were confirmed the warnings of Dost Muhammad and Sher Ali. It was another blunder, this time a tragic one, on the part of Salisbury who had urged it and Lytton who carried it out. Conolly and Stoddart could not have been avenged, but Cavagnari had to be and thus was precipitated the second phase of the Second Afghan War. Roberts occupied Kabul, and Kandahar was occupied too. A British force was massacred at Maiwand and Kandahar was besieged. The latter occasioned Roberts' famous forced march from Kabul to Kandahar to relieve it. Meanwhile Yakub had abandoned his opposition and went to live in British India. A difficult situation now arose for, as Roberts remarked, although he had won a war he now had nobody to treat with. The interregnum which followed the First Afghan War might have been repeated but at this point the British had a slice of unexpected luck. Abdur Rahman had arrived from exile in Russia to claim the vacant throne: he had actually accompanied Roberts to Kandahar and had created a favourable impression by his willingness to cooperate.

There is little doubt that the Second Afghan War was as unnecessary as the First War had been. But for Abdur Rahman's timely appearance it would have been just as politically unproductive. Granted that Britain had to take steps to counter von Kaufmann's skilful finessing they need not have been such clumsy ones. Sher Ali had shown himself open to diplomacy; it was British ignorance and mistrust that led to the war. The only man to have shown up well was General Roberts, the Commander. Already the holder of the Victoria Cross and known to his men as 'Bobs' he was the greatest leader of the day. He was the first general to 'care for his men' whether British private soldier or Indian sepoy. He deployed them in open order to reduce targets and casualties, and he did much to relieve the monotony of the soldier's life in cantonments. He was a good and practical strategist too; he drove his men hard but they would have followed him anywhere because they trusted him.

But the same cannot be said for his statesmen-masters. Salisbury, egged on by Rawlinson, and Lytton himself were bent on action particularly after the Stoletov mission. The former did not want actual war (although if it ever came to war with Russia he would have preferred it in Central Asia to the Near East), but in the present case he made a grave mistake in giving Lytton such a free hand. Neither Lytton nor Salisbury had the remotest understanding of Central Asian politics. After all Sher Ali had voluntarily sent a copy of von Kaufmann's first formal letter to the Indian government, and he had been justifiably alarmed by the fall of Khiva. Then was the time to demonstrate continued Indian support by increasing his subsidy and arms supplies. If that had been done probably no more Russian envoys would have been allowed at Kabul, and his son, Yakub Khan, confirmed that view at the time. His father was, at any rate to begin with, only following the custom of all eastern rulers, whether by offering himself to the highest bidder or simply keeping in well with a possible enemy.

That was the mistake that led to the first phase of the war. The second was to insist on a British representative in Kabul in spite of the previous warnings of Dost Muhammad and now of Sher Ali himself. For that tragic blunder both Salisbury and Lytton must share the blame. There were certain other political resemblances between the First and Second Afghan Wars which will occur to the reader; one which might be overlooked was the installation in each case of a weak Amir; in the second war that was Yakub Khan.

From the beginning of his Viceroyalty Lytton had been imbued with the fear of a Russian invasion: it might be thought he had never read the views of Lord Lawrence on the subject. Apart from Afghanistan he did however make two contributions to the defence of India. The first was the treaty negotiated by Sandeman in 1879 that brought the annexation of Kelat and Baluchistan. That gained Quetta as a military base, which by controlling the Bolan pass secured the southern frontier of India, and covered the road to Kandahar. His second contribution was to the defence of the northern frontier when he enunciated the principle that India's frontier in that direction 'should be the watershed of the Indus'. The subject has been dealt with by G. J. Alder in his *British India's Northern Frontier 1865–1895.*

Looking at Russia's part in the recent events the duplicity of
Prince Gorchakov, Shuvalov and finally of von Kaufmann himself
have been obvious. If their efforts did serve to bring on the Second
Afghan War and embarrass the British, their principal object which
was to influence the results of the Congress of Berlin in her favour,
were a complete failure. The personal consequence for Gorchakov
was that he lost his post. Shuvalov retired in 1879, and von
Kaufmann died in 1882.

Meanwhile the immediate consequences of Lytton's war, even
while Abdur Rahman's claims were being considered, left Afghanistan in chaos with Roberts alone exercising some control and
Britain without a policy, except that Roberts had announced that
there would be no annexation. Lytton himself believed that the
permanent disintegration of Afghanistan must be faced and Lord
Cranbrook, now at the India Office, supported him. Both men
stood by the Gandamak treaty which would give India control over
the external relations of the separate provinces whilst guaranteeing
no further annexation by Britain or any other power. Western
Afghanistan under an Afghan governor would thus become just
another Indian tributary state, and the Indian army would be
within striking distance of both Kabul and Kandahar. The
possibility of handing over Herat to Iran was debated between the
British and Indian governments but was not pursued. It appears
that only Lytton (and perhaps Salisbury) still had a vision of
Indian supremacy in Central Asia although it is hard to believe
they could have been so out of touch with realities. Soviet
historians have of course made the most of it. On the immediate
practical level Lytton was faced with the task of withdrawing Lord
Roberts' force from a chaotic Afghanistan without any more
fighting but without giving any indication of weakness; and also
with trying to reach an agreement with the new claimant, Abdur
Rahman. The latter wanted an Afghanistan unified under his own
rule from Kabul and he wanted a very precise definition of the
terms Britain would demand concerning his relations with Russia;
but he was actually prepared to accept a British representative at
his capital. They had already begun discussions before the disaster
of Maiwand and the relief of Kandahar. However his terms were so
far apart from the Viceroy's that it is difficult to see how the two
men could have reached an agreement. Lytton also feared Abdur
Rahman might be in the pocket of Russia. As it turned out the fall

of the Conservative Government saved any further argument between them and Lord Lytton resigned.

The Second Afghan War had not been popular in England, and it coincided with the equally unpopular Zulu War. Gladstone saw his chance; there was a general election and it put the Liberals back in power. Lytton having resigned, the evacuation of Afghanistan, the formulation of a new policy and further discussions with Abdur Rahman were taken over by his successor, Lord Ripon.

When Lord Ripon assumed office in 1880 he soon reached an agreement with Abdur Rahman. He could scarcely do otherwise after Gladstone's pontificating electioneering speech about 'the sanctity of life in the hill villages of Afghanistan among the winter snows ... being inviolable in the eyes of Almighty God' – not that he or his hearers had the remotest idea what their lives were really like. But in any case Liberal policy was always to avoid involvement in foreign affairs. Hence Ripon promised independence for a united Afghanistan including Kandahar, subject only to the Amir's acceptance of British control over his foreign policy and that he did not undertake any unprovoked war. He promised that Britain would give the Amir full support if attacked by a foreign power, i.e. by Russia, although the extent of that full support was not precisely spelt out. And of course the Amir was promised arms and an annual subsidy. The terms were a treaty in all but title and they satisfied Abdur Rahman who was then proclaimed Amir at Kabul. Although there were subsequent crises as will appear from the next chapter, the terms stood the test and indeed were renewed by Lord Curzon in 1905.

*   *   *   *   *

The Duke of Wellington is quoted, in referring to what he called the 'business of war', as 'guessing what was at the other side of the hill'. It is instructive to apply this aphorism to the Russian expansion in Transcaspia. All guesses in Britain and India concentrated on the threat to India, if not by ultimate invasion then at least by gaining control of Afghanistan and, through her, sowing discord in India. But at that point their guessing stopped. Clearly enough Russia was happy to embarrass Britain by her moves but we also see that just as Britain feared Russian domination of Herat so Russia apparently still feared Britain might use it as a step towards ultimate supremacy in Central Asia. The fact that Lytton and possibly Disraeli were probably the last leading statesmen to entertain such a vision would scarcely have been realised in St. Petersburg. That was where Russian guessing stopped.

But Russia had always had one much wider motive which Britain never guessed. That was her need for a stable southern frontier which was suggested early in this study as being the dominating motive of her expansion. The Caucasus frontier had been settled but, besides the Afghan frontier, the one along Iran's province of Khorasan still remained open and securing it was unlikely to entail war with Britain, especially as she was fully occupied with Afghanistan. It was a hard frontier to reach in a military sense because so much of Transcaspia consists of the Karakum desert. Only south of the desert, east of the Caspian and running more or less parallel with the Khorasan border lay any appreciable oasis – that of Akhal. It was impossible to reach it from Khiva in any strength because of the intervening desert, but once Krasnovodsk and other ports on the Caspian had been developed military action became feasible. When Akhal had been subdued not only could the Iran frontier be drawn but the rich resources of Khorasan could be used to supplement the sparse economy of Transcaspia.

But it so happened that the Akhal oasis was inhabited by the only really good fighting race that Russia had yet encountered. They were the Tekke Turkmen, who were not only marauders into Khorasan but frequently attacked Russian forts on the Caspian as well. The Tekkes comprised the only settled tribe in Transcaspia and they could build good defences as well as use their cavalry. The somewhat nominal capital was the separate oasis of Merv farther east, nearer to and due north of Herat. It was another aspect of the Duke's aphorism that Britain did not realise the importance to Russia of subduing the Akhal, still less the extreme difficulty she would have in doing so. In fact it took two campaigns, of which the first was a costly defeat, before the job was done; and until it was done any major action against Afghanistan, even if it had ever been intended, was out of the question. Russia never had the limitless resources that seem usually to have been taken for granted in Britain and India, and there again the Duke's aphorism was never applied.

General Lomakin who led the expedition of 1879 had already suffered one defeat in a minor expedition, when he had been forced to retreat to Krasnovodsk, but the Tsar decided to give him another chance when the commander designate died unexpectedly just after setting out. On his second expedition Lomakin commanded a big force of some 15,000 troops with a supply train of about 20,000 camels and pack ponies, but owing to faulty administration only about half that number reached the Akhal oasis and then, faced with much greater numbers of Tekkes, they were forced into a disorderly retreat to their base of Chikishlyar on the Caspian, mainly because of lack of supplies and water. An interesting side issue was that when the Foreign Office in London learned of the projected campaign it believed that it was directed against Merv, and because that would have brought Russia so much nearer Herat, Lord Salisbury protested. In fact it was directed against an oasis considerably nearer the Caspian, and St. Petersburg then denied any intentions of advancing to Merv. It was at this time that the expression 'Mervousness' became current in England.

The disaster, which showed Russian military administration at its worst, had to be avenged and the commander chosen to lead the force next year was General Skobelev, a man of a very different stamp to Lomakin. This time the administrative preparations were adequate. It took Skobelev five months to collect enough supplies mainly from Khorasan, for what, compared with an invasion of Afghanistan, was a relatively minor campaign. When he reached Akhal he laid siege to Geok Tepe the principal town and fortress in the oasis. Its fall was inevitable but there followed a massacre, appalling in British eyes, in which women and children were not spared. There had been a similar massacre at Khiva, but this one was on a far greater scale, and there were violent British protests. Charles Marvin interviewed Skobelev who spoke up for his policy. According to Marvin he said 'We killed nearly 20,000 Turcomans at Geok Tepe. The survivors will not soon forget the lesson'. In his official report Skobelev had said 8,000 Tekkes of both sexes were killed *after* the assault. Skobelev confirmed the figure to Marvin and added 'I had them counted'. He said 'I hold it as a principle that the duration of peace is in direct proportion to the slaughter you inflict upon the enemy. The harder you hit them the longer they will be quiet afterwards'. He also compared his action with that of General Roberts at Kabul where the latter carried out some public executions: he said these would only make the Afghans hate the British. After hitting them hard Skobelev claimed it was then time to be humane.

It is interesting to compare his policy with that of the British on the north-west frontier of India. There, as was remarked earlier, punitive expeditions were frequent but they were lenient, although in the long run they were costly in lives as well as money. It is a fact that after Geok Tepe the Tekke tribe never gave trouble again. It was said at the time that because of the violence of British public opinion the Tsar recalled Skobelev. It is true that Russia was, and perhaps still is, sensitive to Western opinion, but if he was recalled it is more likely that it was as he claimed, because he had completed his assigned task.

Transcaspia had already become a province separate from the Caucasus in 1874. In 1881 Russia formally annexed Akhal and that finally settled her frontier with Iran. Merv, in spite of earlier Russian protestations, was quickly occupied by General Alikhanov and in 1883 was also annexed. It was claimed that because of the fear that if it was occupied Britain would occupy Herat, Alikhanov acted against orders. If he did it was another example of the independence of Russian generals, as well as of Russian duplicity. However Britain could only protest again at the *fait accompli*, whilst the Rawlinson school with its concern for actual mileages loudly pointed to the narrowing gap between Russia and Herat. No doubt Russia was pleased to have got so much closer to Britain's Achilles heel, but in a strategic view Merv was still on a less favourable line of approach than Sarakhs on the Khorasan-Russian border. It is a useful exercise to compare this latest Russian annexation with Britain's annexation of Baluchistan only a few years earlier.

During the whole period of the struggle for supremacy in Central Asia there are constant examples of moves and counter-moves sometimes intentional, at others fortuitous. For example Burnaby's journey to Khiva was followed in 1880 by a foraging mission undertaken by General Grodekov. He travelled from Samarkand through Khorasan to Mashhad and Herat. It was the result of his mission that was to enable Skobelev to collect enough supplies to carry out his expedition. If it had taken five months to collect enough supplies for this minor campaign, that makes a Russian invasion of Afghanistan even more unthinkable. About the same time a certain Captain Butler went to Akhal from Khorasan in Iran and advised the Tekke on their defences at Geok Tepe. Neither of these journeys seems to have been secret and both men talked about them subsequently. According to Marvin, who had a high opinion of the Russian Government's Topographical Department and the ready availability of their maps, a map based on Grodekov's survey was soon on Russian bookstalls.

The building of railways marked another stage of developments in Central Asia. In India, General Roberts (he became Commander-in-Chief in India in 1885) was amongst the first to stress the need for road and rail development on the frontier. The extension of a branch line from the Indus valley railway towards the frontier had reached Sibi in 1879, but work on the extension to Quetta and up to the frontier itself was postponed not for strategic but for administrative reasons until 1884. India was fortunate for in this region there was a good supply of local coal.

Russia began to build the Transcaspian railway also in 1879. From the Caspian it reached Kizyl-Arvat in 1881 and the Amu Dar'ya in 1885. From Merv a branch line was built to Kushka near the Afghan border in 1898. In India much strategic importance was attached to this railway. Curzon who travelled on the line and wrote about it in his book published in 1889 *Russia in Central Asia* thought Russia might want to extend it to Penjdeh. He believed the Transcaspian railway had changed the focal point from Turkestan to the south. But India and Curzon were almost certainly wrong for two very good reasons. One is that it is not good strategy to build a railway so close to and parallel with a frontier – the Russians are now rectifying that early mistake on the Trans-Siberian railway. The other reason is that there was no coal available locally; not only the railway engines but even steam boats on the Caspian had to burn the local shrub called saxaul – a kind of brittle briar. No army could be transported, still less supplied, with only such poor fuel available. When Elias was subsequently Consul General at Mashhad, a Japanese colonel who had travelled there by both railways said that all Russian rail development was being concentrated on the Trans-Siberian, whilst the Transcaspian railway was being neglected. Although it is looking ahead somewhat that put the latter in its true perspective.

Meanwhile to return to Afghanistan, the decade which had begun so hopefully with the Clarendon-Gorchakov discussions concerning a neutral zone in 1870 had ended with a very different picture emerging of Afghanistan as an independent buffer state under British influence, whilst of the three Khanates of Western Turkestan two had become vassals of Russia, whilst the third, Kokand, had been completely absorbed.

CHAPTER THIRTEEN

The Buffer State Solution – Afghanistan

Abdur Rahman, a nephew of Sher Ali, was to become the greatest Central Asian character to emerge during the whole period under review. In political acumen and astuteness he was far ahead of the Khans and Amirs of Bukhara and elsewhere such as Russia had hitherto to deal with. He was probably ahead even of his grandfather, Dost Muhammad, who after all was the first man in that period to unite Afghanistan although he was given no chance to prove himself thereafter. It would be fruitless to wonder how long British and Russian rivalry might have continued, still less what the upshot might have been, but for Abdur Rahman. In his shapeless clothes and Russian boots he resembled a bear, and he could be bear-like in other ways too as the Indian government was to discover. Often enough he had cause for provocation from within as well as without, but there was a look of greatness about him. He may not have been the British ideal of an ally; for instance besides making use of the traditional Dark Well for punishment he was prone to devise other peculiarly unpleasant tortures for miscreants; yet on the other hand he had an English governess for his children. But what mattered most was that having finally thrown in his lot with India he remained staunch and thereby contributed more than any single man to the ending of the Game.

Lytton had regarded Amir Abdur Rahman with some suspicion when he arrived to claim his throne, as well he might. For the Amir had been a contender for his uncle's seat, but had fled to Bukhara in 1869 when Sher Ali succeeded, and had spent the next ten years in Russian asylum. Russia moved him from Bukhara to Samarkand with a small entourage, where he was allowed to remain on condition that he took no part in Afghan politics. Stephen Wheeler, the Amir's biographer, quoting General Skobelev, says that in 1871

Abdur Rahman asked the Governor of Zaravshan for help to seize his throne and promised friendship with Russia if he did. That is not unlikely, although Abdur Rahman himself said that he behaved during all these years as if he was just dull and that he did not even disclose that he had learned Russian – but it may be doubted whether he fooled the Russians to that extent. On the other hand we may be certain that he maintained good contacts in Kabul and knew very well what was going on there. With typically oriental disregard of time he was in no hurry to declare himself though he was already about forty. Disliking both Britain and Russia he described himself as being between two millstones. When he did declare himself in favour of an alliance with Britain it was because that was where his prospects of relatively independent survival seemed brighter. He had seen what Russia had done with the khanates of Turkestan. Nevertheless it was extremely lucky both for Afghanistan and India that Lytton departed when he did, for Lytton, following the Rawlinson school, still wanted to annex Kandahar and, if not actually to occupy Herat, then perhaps to hand the province over to Iran. Abdr Rahman would never have accepted those terms; he was determined on an Afghanistan united as it had been under his grandfather and again under Sher Ali. It was most fortunate that Ripon became Viceroy at that crucial moment, still more so that as a Liberal he had a more flexible approach and wanted no more annexations.

The fact that, during all the ten years Abdur Rahman had spent in Turkestan, von Kaufmann made no attempt to build him up as a potential Russian ally when the time was ripe, may be taken as one more sign that Russia had no intention of invading Afghanistan. The first chance had offered itself many years earlier when Russia withdrew and disowned the Vitkevich mission which had promised well. The second offered itself when Stoletov went to Kabul carrying a draft treaty with Sher Ali in his pocket. But again the mission was promptly recalled by von Kaufmann and although Stoletov did visit Kabul subsequently there were no offers of arms nor apparently any secret promises. When Abdur Rahman set out for Kabul in 1880 to claim his throne, he was given a small subsidy, an escort of a hundred men and a few arms as a parting present. No doubt von Kaufmann's successor hoped that Abdur Rahman would leave with friendly feelings which might one day be turned to account; but there was no secret treaty nor even any secret understanding. Of course it may never have been expected that the Amir would be able to hold Herat, that province over which Russia and Britain alike wanted to exercise control: but the Amir did hold it. He held it in spite of an insurrection led by his cousin the Governor of Herat (who fled to Russia where he was carefully nursed), and in spite of all the later efforts on the part of General Kuropatkin, Governor of Transcaspia, to stir up trouble there. These were referred to previously in Chapter 10 describing Ney Elias's experiences.

Ripon's liberal policy of non-intervention in foreign affairs was a mistake when he neglected China at a time when she was in need of British support. It also spoilt Elias's chances of developing good relations with Kashgar from his fastness at Leh and again in 1885 when he set out on his last epic journey, but that neglect was not vital. On the other hand the same policy reaped a rich reward in Afghanistan. Ripon was only too glad to do a deal with Abdur Rahman whereby he extricated India from any further responsibility for Kandahar and Herat, thus avoiding any further annexations; but with the important proviso that Abdur Rahman accepted India's condition that his foreign affairs were controlled by the Indian government. That meant that he could have no separate contacts with either Iran or Russia. But Abdur Rahman drove a hard bargain in return. He demanded and got, not only big subsidies and plenty of arms but a guarantee of active support against any foreign invasion. Incidentally it ended the mainly military arguments in India as well as Russia for a coterminous Hindu Kush frontier. The bargain was agreed by an extension of the Gandamak treaty and it was an important step further than his predecessors had achieved.

Although Rawlinson has been belaboured in these pages for his obstinate adherence to the forward policy and his conviction that Russia intended to seize Herat and ultimately to invade India, he must be given due credit for two contributions to India's defence, in which the worth of his geographical and historical knowledge considerably exceeded that of his political prognostications. The first was his strong recommendation that Badakhshan must not be detached from Kabul. Secondly it was Rawlinson who originally defined the Amu Dar'ya, with its northern reach the R. Panjah, as Afghanistan's northern frontier. Largely through ignorance of the precise ethnic and geographical facts, both contributions were yet to cause much friction and indeed two serious crises between Britain and Russia during the next dozen years. That was despite the fact that after 1878 Russia had ceased to have any influence in Afghanistan, and in practice could only intrigue in Herat and the Pamir. The Afghan boundary was only finally agreed in 1895, when it was ultimately based on the original Anglo-Russian Agreement of 1873, which itself derived mainly from Rawlinson's memorandum of 1869 to Lord Mayo.

Abdur Rahman ruled his united country with great firmness and with very decided ideas on what should be done. He was frequently disturbed by rebellions which he put down ruthlessly. He was against modernization such as railways; but he accepted a British representative at Kabul which he probably thought would strengthen his hand against possible invasion. The treaty itself referred to 'unprovoked attack' but it was imprecise as to what help he would actually be given in such an event and judging by past experience he probably did not expect much other than war material. Russia, of course, protested that British actions in Afghanistan were in contravention of the 1873 Agreement recognising her independence. But Britain had plenty of grounds for complaint against Russia for her activities in the Pamir and in the Afghan tributary states of Rushan and Shughnan. According to Stephen Wheeler, Britain lodged eleven protests with St. Petersburg during this period. Naturally the Russian annexation of Merv had been one such occasion, for it had perturbed Abdur Rahman as well as India, and Ripon took the precaution of reminding him that his friendship lay with Britain and not with Russia though he also increased his subsidy.

Looking at the previous years from the Russian view point, Michell, in his *Russian Abstracts* derived from Russian periodicals, deduced that Russia still had no long-term policy for Central Asia. He believed that she actually wanted to refrain from further expansion, but that circumstances forced it on her. British criticism of her actions greatly affected her policy, but she genuinely feared that British influence in Afghanistan would render insecure her position in Central Asia. Here we see the other side of the coin for it was precisely the fear of Russian activities which made Britain determined to maintain influence over Afghanistan. Just as Britain saw danger in the Russian missions, so Russia saw similar danger in British travellers, even such amateurs as Burnaby. But it must be said that from 1874 Russian missions had been far more active, and their objects particularly in the Pamir were by no means confined to exploration.

It was perhaps as inevitable that Britain should acquire and retain influence over Afghanistan as part of her Indian defence policy as that Russia should gain control over Western Turkestan. Both countries had come to recognize that fact and the difference between them was mainly a matter of degree, which ought to be settled diplomatically. But before that final stage could be reached there was one outstanding problem which could only be settled in the field. That problem was still Afghanistan's northern frontier. With Abdur Rahman firmly installed, his frontier had to be established once and for all, and the time was the more favourable because Russia knew that Gladstone's Liberal Government would prefer to negotiate a peaceful settlement. The Viceroy's fiery military advisers such as General Roberts and his Quartermaster General, McGregor, who still wanted military occupation of Afghanistan, were out of favour, and all Indian troops had been withdrawn.

The frontier settlement was no easy matter because neither country really knew the extent of the Amir's possessions. Russia still upheld the claims of Bukhara to Badakhshan, and to Darwaz in the northern loop of the Amu Dar'ya, and she doubted the Amir's claims to Shughnan, Rushan and Wakhan farther east. The Amir was emphatic that both historically and *de facto* they were his rightful possessions. He quoted the medieval historian Mirza Haidar Ali, author of the *Tarikh-i-Rashidi*[1], to support his historical claims and in 1883 he put Afghan troops into Shughnan and Rushan. (That action followed an insurrection by Shughnan against him in 1882, said to have been staged by Dr. Regel's Russian mission: Dr. Regel claimed that Shughnan was a tributary of Kokand.) The Amir also installed an Afghan Governor of Wakhan. Russia claimed that Abdur Rahman was acting contrary to the Anglo-Russian Agreement of 1873. Clearly there was a lot of work to be done in the field to clear up all the existing uncertainties and in the process even more were disclosed.

In 1884 after the Russian annexation of Merv, a start was made

---

[1] This work was subsequently translated by Denison Ross, with an Introduction and annotations by Ney Elias.

towards settling the Herat frontier. Britain and Russia agreed to set up a joint Afghan Boundary Commission, with the Amir's somewhat reluctant agreement, but with his own representatives on it. India sent a huge party with a military escort of 500 men under General Lumsden with the object not only of demarcating the frontier but of carrying out a very complete survey of the Herat province. These two objects should never have been combined – the ornithologists and mineralogists were quite unnecessary appendages. The economy of Herat could not support 1300 men and 2000 animals and the Commission soon became unpopular, not only locally but with the Amir himself both because of the time it took and because Herat was his most dissident province. The Commission was actually in the field for two years. Moreover, because of Russia's continued concern with Herat the Russian delegates tried to obstruct the frontier work and they also indulged in intrigues against Britain and the Amir. So far as its terms of reference concerned the frontier, the Commission was intended to demarcate it from the Iran border to the confluence of the River Kokcha with the Amu Dar'ya, but by the winter of 1885 it had got no farther east than Bala Murghab – under 200 miles from its starting point – with the Russian delegates disputing every demarcation point along the route.

In the spring of 1885 Russian troops began to be assembled at Penjdeh (now in Kaganovicha) opposite the Afghan province of Maimana to carry out what was essentially a minor border adjustment in Russia's favour. Such actions had frequently been undertaken on the Iran border without incurring any foreign criticism, but the setting and the consequences on this occasion were very different and gave rise to a serious débâcle which quickly became known as the 'Penjdeh incident', as it has been called by all historians and writers on the period.

The Amir regarded Penjdeh as his territory and Britain accepted it as such. If Russia pressed on with the occupation and was opposed by the Afghan troops that the Amir had assembled there, that could be regarded as a case of unprovoked aggression against which Britain had promised all aid to the Amir, albeit not in very precise terms. Hence the telegraph lines between London and St. Petersburg became very hot indeed. St. Petersburg was very well aware of the British guarantee to the Amir, but although it claimed that the Russian commander had been warned against extreme action there is at least some doubt about whether he received the warning or if he acted in spite of it. The fact was that the incident arose just when Gladstone's government was under heavy criticism at home for mishandling the war in Egypt and for failing to relieve Gordon in Khartoum; Russia may have judged that Britain would not support the Amir to the point of declaring war against her. There were two other factors which may not have been sheer coincidences. One was that General Lumsden's Commission was encamped only a few miles south of Penjdeh. The other was that Lord Dufferin had just succeeded Ripon as Viceroy and he had invited the Amir to a durbar. The whole affair blew up just as the Amir reached India.

Dufferin was another Liberal and was not disposed to believe Russia had designs on India. He had had experience of Russia as Ambassador at St. Petersburg during the negotiations leading to the Sino-Russian Treaty of St. Petersburg, but he did not fail to see the risks involved in the buffer state policy which might still bring on the war it was hoped to avoid. On the other hand he also did not fail to note that Penjdeh was even nearer Herat than was Merv. His Foreign Secretary at the time was Mortimer Durand, a young man of only thirty six who might be described as an ambitious hot-head and inclined to dramatization. The latter doubtless did not fail to stress to his Viceroy the position of Merv.

Russian and Afghan troops had been facing each other for some months at Penjdeh and General Lumsden's camp was only a few miles in the rear at the time. Lumsden was only administratively under the Indian government; diplomatically he received his orders from Lord Granville, the Foreign Secretary in London. The latest despatch seems to have advised him that Giers had informed the Foreign Secretary that the Russian troops under General Komarov would not attack unless the Afghans advanced, and indeed that he had been ordered by the Tsar to withdraw. Hence Lumsden was presumably playing for time when he told the Afghan commander that he did not think the Russians would attack him and that therefore he should not withdraw. The Afghan commander with his weak force was in a quandary. Before the Amir left for India he had told him to stand his ground but that he should also take the advice of Lumsden. But meanwhile Russian troops began to bait the Afghans; according to *The Times* and *The Pioneer* correspondents they were even pulling the Afghans' beards and provoking them to attack. Lumsden remained at his base camp some miles back. Colonel West Ridgeway, a Political Officer who was Lumsden's second-in-command, was forward and he advised the Afghan commander to withdraw; but he did not, probably partly because he feared the Amir's wrath if he did, and partly because of the way his men, all good Muslims, were being insulted. At the last minute two members of the Commission tried to talk the Russians out of it during a lunch, but in reply they read out an ultimatum from the Tsar to the Afghan commander ordering him to withdraw, or he would be attacked. That was not at all what Lumsden had been led by the Foreign Secretary to expect. At last, provoked beyond endurance, the Afghan troops retaliated and that gave the Russian troops the chance they wanted – they attacked. With their old muzzle loaders the Afghans stood no chance and they suffered heavy casualties before withdrawing. The two British members of the Commission (Captain Yate who was also a Press correspondent, and Dr. Owen) observed the engagement, which took place on the 30th March 1885. At the crucial moment the telegraph line to London was cut at Mashhad – there is no need to guess by whom.

Press correspondents with the Commission were somewhat muzzled. *The Pioneer's* despatch was dated the 2nd April but it was not till the 9th April that a despatch from Rawal Pindi to *The Times* was able to report a brief description from General Lumsden of the engagement. On the following day a St. Petersburg newspaper carried the official report of General Komarov that 'in consequence of the aggressive and openly hostile action of the Afghans he was compelled to attack their fortified position on both banks of the R. Kushk'. It reported that having defeated them he had then returned and reoccupied his former position.

We may never know by how far he and Giers were in connivance, whether Giers deceived Granville or whether Komarov actively flouted Giers. Certainly the event was nicely timed whilst the Viceroy and the Amir were still in durbar, and peace or war seemed to depend on whether the Amir would demand active British support to recover Penjdeh. As it turned out the Amir was quite unperturbed. His revenues from Penjdeh had been falling and the tribesmen were a troublesome lot, so he willingly relinquished his claim, thus opening the way towards a settlement by diplomacy. A report from Paris dated the 8th April to *The Times* said it was generally believed that war would be avoided if the Viceroy and the Amir could reach an agreement. Other continental papers took the opposite view but they were wrong. Giers told the British Ambassador that it had been a 'regrettable incident'; but in the diplomatic world the tongue is so often in the cheek. A fortnight later the Amir returned to Kabul, highly delighted with his reception by the Viceroy.

But although that had avoided immediate war there were considerable repercussions which continued for months. Of the immediate ones, Lumsden was 'recalled' to London and Ridgeway took command of the Commission. Some of Durand's heated personal correspondence is very revealing. In May he wrote to a colleague 'The insolence of the Russians has been intolerable. – We are playing the only game left to us'. To Ridgeway in the same month he wrote 'We must do our best to play the present game', and he wrote in the same terms to the Editor of the *Civil and Military Gazette*. In July he wrote to Sir Charles Grant in London, perhaps a trifle unfairly, 'The Penjdeh disaster was much due to Lumsden's vacillation, he blew hot and cold'. Earlier, in September 1884 he had written to Sir Alfred Lyall, an Indian Civil Servant who later wrote a biography of Lord Dufferin, 'Lord Granville has lately shown some glimmering sense of the importance of the affair and even at intervals some resolution towards Russia, but ignorance at home is dark'. His views in this last letter were perhaps a forecast of the wider repercussions to come.

Uncharacteristically, but stung by public criticisms of his procrastination over the Sudan, and now faced by the Penjdeh crisis, Gladstone had called up the army reserves (the Indian Army had already been mobilized, and British troops there reinforced), and sought a war credit. The sequel was a General Election. The incident had thoroughly aroused public opinion not only against Russia but against Gladstone's government too. The Liberal party fell and a Conservative government took over with Salisbury as both Prime Minister and Foreign Secretary. That was an unexpected blow to the Russian government which hitherto had always known where it was with Gladstone's policy of non-intervention and that it could act accordingly. Dufferin, however, remained as Viceroy and Salisbury expressed his satisfaction with his handling of the Penjdeh affair. With no shortage of alarmists round him, Dufferin who knew Russia from his ambassadorial days, never expected war and kept clam. Although he told Lord Cross at the India Office in 1886 that he thought Britain was then in a worse position vis-à-vis Russia than in 1880, yet in 1887 he wrote to him 'The longer we can keep Russia the other side of the present boundary the better, for every year our relations with Afghanistan are improving'. Supporters of Rawlinson of course still saw Penjdeh as another step on the Russian road to Herat.

Salisbury was always more concerned about the Near East than Central Asia, and during the Gladstone régime Russia had again been active there. The Bulgars had revolted against Turkey. Russia wanted Bulgaria to remain disunited, the opposite of her case before the Berlin Treaty. Salisbury now opted for a united Bulgaria, thus abrogating his Berlin Treaty. His biographer, A. L. Kennedy, commented 'Both governments illustrated the unhappy rule of European politics that when the observance of Treaty clauses contradicts immediate self-interest, it is almost always the observance that gives way'.

It was the third time since the middle of the century that Britain had confronted Russia over Turkey. Salisbury behaved as if he wanted to defy Russia to attack. Robert Morier had just been appointed Ambassador at St. Petersburg and according to his biographer, Agatha Ramm, Salisbury told him 'We must lead her into all the expense we can, in the conviction that with her the limit of taxation has been almost reached and that only a few steps further must push her into revolution'. Morier however differed and considered Britain should look to peace instead of war. The consequence was that thereafter he was always regarded as a better spokesman for Russia in London than for Britain in St. Petersburg. Between London and St. Petersburg there was another round of bluff and counter-bluff. If it ever came to war Salisbury seems always to have thought Russia was invulnerable in the Near East and that it would have to be fought in Central Asia, which confirms his lack of understanding of the region. But once again there was no war, and once again we may recall Palmerston's dictum of fifty years before.

But if the Amir was happy when he went back to Kabul after the durbar, Dufferin was voicing his disquiet a year later to Lord Cross then at the India Office. Commenting bitterly on the Amir's uncooperative behaviour he complained of his sorry treatment of Ridgeway's Boundary Commission, in contrast with the money and arms with which Britain was supplying him and even the subsidies being paid to his rivals to keep them quiet. It was a trifle unfair because Ridgeway was, as we shall see, bringing some of the scurvy treatment on himself. More importantly Dufferin said he proposed reminding the Amir that Herat would have fallen into Russian hands if Britain had not threatened war and that if he was unwilling to follow Britain's recommendations she would have to recover a free hand. He would tell him that if Russia renewed her aggressive attempts it would mean war and British action towards Afghanistan would then depend on his conduct and not on any specific agreement like that of 1880. That was strong meat from a Liberal who moreover had always believed that relations between Britain and Russia concerning the Afghan frontier could be settled diplomatically. In a letter from Cross to Dufferin the former said he thought the Foreign Office paid too much attention to the actual wording of the 1873 Agreement.

The fact was that Dufferin believed Ripon's agreement with Abdur Rahman had gone too far and he wanted an excuse to get out of it. That agreement had promised not only unity but that military help for him, although carefully unspecified, would be forthcoming in the event of an unprovoked attack. The latter, in the sense e.g. of sending troops to Badakhshan, was an impossibility. Hence Dufferin actually preferred the Lytton policy of a divided Afghanistan: he may have had in mind the words of Ridgeway who considered Britain could not hold the Afghan frontier and told him the only frontier she could defend would be the Hindu Kush down to Kandahar, 'and if Russia is to get the rest it means Herat, Balkh, Maimana – in fact all Afghan Turkestan'. That of course had always been the view of the Commander-in-Chief, Lord Roberts. Yet, specifically in the case of Badakhshan, Dufferin ought by that time to have read the despatch of Ney Elias to the Foreign Office in London, whose views on its military value to Russia will appear in the next chapter. The impression gleaned from the records is that in fact he did not read it: it was left to his successor, Lord Lansdowne, to read and act on it when he assumed the Viceroyalty at the beginning of 1890.

After Penjdeh, negotiations with Russia rumbled on for three years. In her turn Britain now accused Russia of violating the Anglo-Russian agreement that the latter would not advance into territory the Viceroy claimed was Afghan. Salisbury had taken over the Foreign Office in 1887 and he distrusted Sir Robert Morier at St. Petersburg because he thought he was too Russophile and prone to détente. He told him 'Be very careful not to give Russia any points in the game'; i.e. the game of Afghan border demarcation. Astonishingly, however, Salisbury still wanted to keep open the possibility of extending British influence among the Turkmens so that they would look to Britain rather than Russia: that was part of his Fabian policy. He told Morier he did not think Russia would invade through the unsettled Penjdeh line, but he feared the Amir might be violent if Britain forced him to concede to Russia too much Afghan-claimed territory.

On the Russian side the Tsar was in a predicament because his military party were threatening to carry out another 'incident', and he needed the support of the army to keep him on his throne. But Morier told him firmly that the British public would not stand for another incident. The upshot was that Russia backed down once more and reduced her demands. Consequently, in July 1887, Morier got his agreement. But it left in abeyance and still to be faced the seemingly intractable problems of Shughnan, Rushan, Wakhan and Darwaz.

CHAPTER FOURTEEN

The Last Crisis and the Final Settlement of 1895

In 1884 when the Afghan Boundary Commission was already in the field, Lord Dufferin decided to send out two more missions. Although a Liberal he was distinctly more concerned with foreign policy as it affected the defence of India than his predecessor; he realized that India's northern frontier from Afghanistan eastwards was in a deplorable state of flux of which there were distinct signs that Russia was going to try to take further advantage. The activities of the Regel and Kostenko missions in the western and eastern Pamir were significant, as were Przhevalskiy's explorations towards Tibet. Indeed Colonel Kostenko had shown in his map and his report that the Pamir was a no-man's-land and hence ripe for the taking. Ney Elias had already pointed the situation out in a memorandum dated 1882, probably after reading Kostenko's report. He had commented that all the territory south and east of the Chinese district of Sarikol as well as Badakhshan, Shughnan and Wakhan were entirely open to the Russians 'if it suited their convenience or ambition...and that the time when the British red line and the Russian green one shall meet on the map of Central Asia seems within measurable distance'. If that had happened we have only to recall the Russian harassment of Herat to realize how she would have intrigued amongst the Indian hill states on the other side of her border.

The missions had two distinct tasks. One was to ensure that the hill states along the Indus watershed, as previously defined by Lytton, and along the Hindu Kush as far as Afghanistan were brought fully under the influence of India. The other had a much wider task. In general it was to clear up the ambiguities of the 1873 Agreement by ascertaining the precise situation along Afghanistan's eastern border, of which the Amir himself was in some ignorance. The British knew practically nothing and only the well-equipped Russian Kostenko mission of 1883 had done any recent work. Kashmir with its tributary state Ladakh had already concluded a treaty with India, but there were other states to be considered, all covering possibly important passes from the north.

The next two immediately important hill states to be reconnoitred were Chitral and Hunza. The latter was a small state east of Chitral which under a very wily Mir was giving trouble not only to Ladakh and other hill states but to China too. The Mir's principal source of revenue was the robbery of Kirgiz caravans, including those trading to Sinkiang, and there were strong hints that, goaded by their complaints, China might assume control and if not China then Russia. The Mir said he acknowledged the 'King' of China as his overlord and he paid an annual tribute of gold dust to Peking but to be on the safe side he also paid tribute to Ladakh, Kashmir, Chitral and Afghanistan, besides professing friendship with India: recently however he had been making overtures to Russia too. He was obviously going to need firm handling and ultimately he got it – not from China who must have decided he was not worth the trouble, but from India. But the most important hill state, because it commanded the passes into Wakhan and Badakhshan, was Chitral.

In 1885 a Chitral mission was despatched under Colonel Lockhart, an Indian army officer with no experience at all of the hill tribes. He was given no Political Officer to advise him though he had an army Intelligence Officer and two good men from the Survey Department. The mission was, like the Afghan Boundary Commission, far too big for a mountainous country, only a little larger than Wales, to support. It consisted of 300 men, over 300 animals and carried a load of 200 rifles as a present for the Mehtar. Broadly Lockhart's instructions were to establish good relations with the Mehtar and to reconnoitre all the passes leading into Chitral from the north over the Hindu Kush. He was to try to penetrate the primitive and little known state of Kafiristan, though with great caution, but he was not to cross the Afghan border. So far so good, but a totally unnecessary instruction at this early stage was to carry out a complete survey of the country including the flora and fauna, which would mean a lengthy stay.

Although without definite instructions to do so Lockhart intended to include a visit to Hunza in the spring of 1886. The Indian government had been very concerned about Hunza for some time and when Elias reached Yarkand in 1885 he reported to India that he was very reliably informed that the Mir would attack the Chitral mission if it went there; China having told him to 'keep the English out'. In fact the information was correct: the Mir had been sent two guns from China to help him, but they became stuck in a snow drift. The Mir was afraid to attack without them and in the event Lockhart, who seems not to have had Elias's warning passed on to him, had crossed the Kilik Pass out of Hunza before the guns were extricated. But meanwhile at Chitral, with no experience to guide him, Lockhart seems to have accepted at face value the Mehtar's assurances of friendship and that he regarded his territory as British, notwithstanding reliable reports that he had been intriguing with Russia. He apparently did not know that the Mehtar paid regular tribute to Afghanistan. By the end of October 1885 the surveyors had finished their work. Lockhart had concluded that the Baroghil and other passes were at best only feasible for small raiding parties, and he recommended an agreement with the Mehtar that he should raise a militia to guard them, backed by a British military base at Gilgit. He then retired to Gilgit for the winter, intending to return again in the following spring. But already the Mehtar had had enough of the mission and had begun to withhold supplies. Moreover Abdur Rahman had heard of his visit to Kafiristan which he regarded as his territory and had complained to the Indian government. Lockhart was beginning to make himself unpopular, but there was worse to come.

The account of the other mission, Ney Elias's across the Pamir and into Badakhshan, can be taken from the point where he abandoned as fruitless the first part of his instructions, namely to restore relations with Kashgar. By inclination a lone explorer and from practical experience a believer in small missions, his party numbered only 26. He had rather unwisely refused the Viceroy's offer of a doctor, but he had a Persian munshi (interpreter) and an Indian medical assistant. The prospect of a winter crossing of the Pamir might have daunted many and Elias had only recently returned from a year's sick leave. But he had made his winter crossing of Western Mongolia and much of Siberia in mid-winter and he was not to be put off from undertaking a mission he had pressed for unavailingly five years earlier, and for which he was

uniquely suited not only by experience but because he was known
to so many local rulers and their subjects. Like Lord Lawrence he
had an intuitive understanding of their ways and they respected
and trusted him. Elias had an international reputation as a reliable
explorer and his expeditions were always news, but this one was
considered so confidential that it was not reported till it was over
and even then only in a two line despatch in *The Times.*

After the inability to fulfil his Kashgar instructions the only
remaining one was 'To explore the Afghan districts on the Upper
Oxus' for which he had been given further guidance namely '... to
ascertain as nearly as possible the recognized boundaries of these
districts (Wakhan and Shughnan) and the Russian and Chinese
possessions on and near the upper waters of the Oxus. It is possible
that the Afghan Boundary Commission may delimit the frontiers of
Afghanistan in this direction.... You will of course endeavour to
gain the goodwill of the rulers and people... and to discover their
feelings towards the Amir'.

He set out from Yarkand on 1st October 1885, following for a
short distance the maps of Hayward and Trotter and thereafter he
had to map his own route without a guide. He chose one which he
believed was that described by the fifth century Chinese explorer
Hsüan Tsang. His principal object while making his crossing was to
discover the western limit of Chinese-claimed territory in this
sparsely populated region inhabited by a variety of races and
tribes, and the eastern limit of Afghan territory. He found the local
mullahs gave useful information, otherwise it was mainly a matter
of determining to which country the tribes paid the most tribute.
Elias also gave himself the secondary task of making détours, in
some cases involving considerable distances, to survey as many
passes as possible to determine their feasibility for military
purposes. This latter task he continued throughout the whole
journey.

As regards the westernmost limit of Chinese claimed territory he
found there was a void between Lake Rang Kul southward through
the Taghdumbash Pamir to Sarikol which China would find it hard
to claim if Russia moved in first. Farther west both China and
Russia recognized the River Aksu (or Murghab) as their boundary
with Afghan Shughnan and Rushan, but there were no military
posts on either side to guard it. As it was impossible to follow the
bed of the Aksu down to its confluence with the upper Amu Dar'ya

(the Panjah) he traversed the Alichur Pamir to the Neza Tash Pass, joining the Aksu (locally called the Gund just there), lower down. There he was met by an escort of 40 Afghans sent on the Amir's orders. On his route across the Pamir the only important passes he had failed to visit, owing to the weather and lack of time, were the Kizyl Art, which he was satisfied from local enquiry marked the Sino-Russian border, and the Koitezak. At Bar Panjah, by the Amir's instructions he was greeted effusively by the local Governor who gave him a good Turkmen horse which he accepted on behalf of the Viceroy. The Amir's goodwill further showed itself when supplies destined to meet him in Wakhan whence he had been expected, were brought back by a messenger. He had prudently armed himself with an imposing passport provided by the Aga Khan, who had many Ismaili adherents in these parts, but on the Amir's instructions he was treated as an honoured guest wherever he travelled in Afghan territory.

From Shughnan, taking advantage of fine November weather he followed the Ab-i-Panjah upstream and satisfied himself that this river, and not the Pamir Murghab as had been reported by Forsyth's Indian surveyors and claimed by some Russians, was the main feeder of the Amu Dar'ya. He was not likely to be wrong on that score for in 1868 he had surveyed the new course of the Huang Ho (the Yellow River) in China and had a good knowledge of river hydrography. His only problem was that his escort refused to let him discuss their political leanings with Shughnani mullahs. He ended his survey at Ishkashim, the westernmost point reached by Lieut. Wood in 1838, and then travelled back north to Rushan, where he reconnoitred more passes. Altogether, after leaving Sinkiang he had reconnoitred more than forty passes, none of them in his judgement of any military importance. Rushan was another state which, to be on the safe side, paid tribute to several states, Bukhara, Kokand and Kashgar. It may have been on the point of turning over to Russia following the Regel mission when Abdur Rahman put down an insurrection there in 1883; since then it had been in a sorry state because he had forbidden its principal trade which was slavery.

From Rushan he travelled on to Darwaz but before he could complete his survey there the terrible weather conditions forced him to abandon it, hoping to return in the spring, and to travel to Faizabad which he reached in mid-December and thence to

Khanabad, the capital of Badakhshan. He was handsomely greeted by the Governor who he was sure was serving the Amir faithfully but found the Badakhshanis detested their Afghan rulers and he thought they might even prefer 'foreign' i.e. Russian rule. Although neither the miserable people nor their poor territory would be of any military value to Russia, on the other hand he did not consider that Britain could possibly give any direct military help there to the Amir. These two opinions were of considerable military importance. Westwards from Badakhshan Elias met with some initial mistrust of his intentions which he largely allayed, although it increased noticeably later on when it was learned locally that Lockhart's and Ridgeway's missions were on their way there. In Kataghan, another primitive province south of Badakhshan, the principal trade was in horses and sheep. He noted particularly the good quality of the former which were of the breed Moorcroft had set out to bring back to India. The best showed good shape and stood up to 15 hands. They were of the same breed that had outstripped the Cossack cavalry at Khiva on their Don horses. Centuries earlier, as remarked in the Introduction, they had been in demand by the great conquerors such as Chingis Khan and they had also probably contributed to the breeding of the English thoroughbred, through the Byerley Turk for one. But since those days they had been falling greatly in numbers and perhaps to some extent in quality, like their owners.

At Tashkurghan (now Khulm) severe illness overtook him. He applied to the Indian government and to Ridgeway for medical assistance but got no help from either. The former did not answer, and the Commission's only doctor had much sickness on his hands. Elias had another trouble because he had been told to expect further instructions when he reached Badakhshan. He had then had only one mail in two months, and repeated requests to the Indian government for his further instructions were completely ignored. Ill and neglected he struggled 300 miles through Maimana to the Boundary Commission's camp at Bala Murghab, in a litter provided by the Governor of Badakhshan. But even then his troubles were by no means over; the doctor took the view that he was simply hypochondriac and Ridgeway would only offer to enrol him as another surveyor; an offer which Elias promptly declined. About that time and probably fearing he might die, he sent a long despatch for forwarding to the Foreign Office, under whose political control he was whilst in Afghanistan. As it embodied nearly all the points made in his final report they may conveniently be dealt with here.

Undoubtedly his most important and far-reaching recommendation was that in order to frustrate Russian ambitions to occupy the Pamir and thus gain direct contact with the hill states, China and Afghanistan must be persuaded to close up their respective territories to their common frontier, thus 'leaving to Russia only the possibility of violating it by an open act of aggression or war'. He said that in making this recommendation he was well aware of the political complications involved.

His next most important point was his confirmation that Rushan and Shughnan, although historically and *de facto* claimed by the Amir, both straddled the Panjah, and its upper reaches known as the Ab-i-Panjah. Moreover Rushan in particular was ethnically linked with Bukhara. These findings severely dented the basis of the 1873 Agreement which he believed might have to be abrogated and a new Agreement drawn up. His last discovery was that though Darwaz was similarly *de facto*, and in accordance with the 1873 Agreement, under Afghan rule, the people there also belonged ethnically to Bukhara which was another most unsatisfactory situation: Darwaz had only been conquered by Afghanistan in 1876. Finally he did not believe that either Badakhshan or Maimana, the next province to the west, could be of any military importance to Russia. What emerged from these recommendations and discoveries will be discussed lower down. It should perhaps be added in parenthesis that Elias had never believed Russia had designs on India.

After a month at Bala Murghab, anxious to get away from Ridgeway, lacking any further instructions from Durand, and feeling somewhat better, Elias set out for Badakhshan on his way back to India. This time he travelled alone without any Afghan escort. As Ridgeway had said his Commission was following a fortnight later to survey Badakhshan, Darwaz and Wakhan, there was no work left for Elias to do, but he had sent some very scornful letters to Durand concerning the Commission's work, its 'horde of surveyors' and its increasing unpopularity. The two men disliked each other intensely and his letters were not calculated to improve matters. On his way he received a letter from Lockhart, who, after leaving Hunza, had disobeyed his orders and crossed into Wakhan which was definitely Afghan territory. He now asked Elias to help him with supplies as his party were nearly starving. The fact was that by this time Ridgeway and Lockhart had so infuriated the Amir that both missions were being denied supplies and Lockhart's mail was being withheld. The Amir told the Viceroy that he had given Elias 'all the honours', that he still trusted him and he demanded that the other two missions should be withdrawn. There was also a row between Ridgeway and Lockhart, the former claiming that Lockhart was infringing on his work and supplies and should withdraw. There was yet another row between Ridgeway and Durand, the former complaining that his Commission was being neglected: this time Durand had to apologise 'in sack cloth and ashes'. Lockhart had either forgotten or was never told that Elias was in the field and had earlier asked the Indian government who the reported lone British traveller was. Now he asked Elias to meet him at Zebak and travel with him back to Chitral. One meeting with Lockhart decided Elias that he would travel alone, but his request to the Indian government to forward his credentials to the Mehtar was ignored and so on arrival he had no status.

Whilst agreeing with Lockhart that the main northern pass, the Baroghil, was suitable only for small raiding parties he was in total disagreement with him about the Mehtar's trustworthiness. He said he might once have been shrewd but was now senile – he fell asleep three times during Elias's second interview and had to be prodded awake by his vizier. Elias strongly disagreed with Lockhart's suggestion as to the value of the proposed militia and also with his plan for Gilgit as a suitable base, for which he said only the Punjab was suitable. Whether on his recommendation or not the Punjab was ultimately chosen. Finally on the Mehtar's death there was much disorder and a military expedition under Younghusband had to be sent up to restore the situation, lest Russia took advantage of it. The troubles there also showed how little trust could be placed in any Chitral militia.

But perhaps the final blow to Elias came when he heard far too late, that Ridgeway had withdrawn without telling him. The home Government had ordered him to withdraw at least a month earlier, but he had ignored that order. The Salisbury government had fallen in 1886 and a new Liberal government under Lord Rosebery was now in power. Thus Wakhan which Elias had been instructed to explore was never surveyed, for Lockhart had not done it either.

It was a disconsolate Elias who was summoned to return urgently to Simla, which he reached after being away for 20 months. But when he got there all the acknowledgement he got was a perfunctory letter of thanks from Durand, and not even an interview with Dufferin. His report was neglected and he went home on a year's sick leave.

Early in his Viceroyalty Dufferin had written that he had a low opinion of the Indian Civil Service with the exception of Durand, 'the most solid man in India'. But having previously been Governor General of Canada he had become very much the *grand seigneur*, and was surrounded by 'toadies' not excluding Durand. Sir Olaf Caroe, the last but one Foreign Secretary before Independence in 1947, commenting in a letter to this author on Elias's unacknowledged achievement as the real architect of the corridor policy, wrote that he 'did most of the peripheral work around India for which Viceroys down, not excluding Foreign Secretaries, took the credit'. That attitude was common, but no doubt Caroe would exclude the next Viceroy, Lord Lansdowne, at any rate as far as Elias was concerned, for he consulted him and accepted him as one of his acknowledged advisers. He personally chose him as Commissioner of the successful Burma-Siam Boundary Commission.

Nothing can exculpate Durand and his Foreign Department for their total inability to coordinate the work of the three missions. Lockhart and Ridgeway were both knighted; the former ultimately became Commander-in-Chief in India and the latter Governor of Ceylon.[1] After the Boundary Commission, Ridgeway was sent to St. Petersburg where in a few months a protocol was drawn up delimiting a further 200 miles of the Amir's northern border – the same distance as had been achieved in two years of actual demarcation. At St. Petersburg in 1887 Ridgeway displayed a good deal more tact than he had with the Amir. Morier, the British Ambassador, reported that he had made a favourable impression with the Tsar, and he added that Giers had been conciliatory. The part played by Morier, who was always working towards détente and entente, was probably valuable too. A year later Elias was

---

[1] Ridgeway became godfather to West Ridgeway Bandaranaike, later the Prime Minister of Sri Lanka.

According to the *Dictionary of National Biography*, Lockhart had handled his mission 'with firmness and tact'.

awarded a C.I.E.: having always, perhaps quixotically, told Durand he wanted no decorations, he returned it. In the furore which followed the Press both in India and Britain strongly supported Elias. Kipling who had been in India in those days was another who later refused all honours – perhaps he too was nauseated by the lobbying he had seen there and written about.

Although Elias's report was subsequently adopted, as was proved in a Memorandum dated 1891 by Steuart Bayley, there is a gap in the archives concerning the actual date. Durand, who always wanted all the credit for himself, was then at home on a year's sick leave, so it must have been Lord Lansdowne who acted on it. It was to fall to Francis Younghusband to follow Elias, for whom he had unbounded admiration, in carrying out the next stages of the policy of which he had been the architect.

Abdur Rahman was strongly opposed to any further delimitation of his frontier but there were other reasons why no immediate action had been taken on Elias's report. Lord Rosebery's Liberal Government was far more concerned with Home Rule for Ireland, the subject that had brought down the Conservatives, than becoming entangled once again with Russia over the Afghan frontier and India's northern border problems. That no doubt was why it had ordered the withdrawal of the Boundary Commission, whilst Elias's findings and recommendations only indicated further problems ahead. Finally Dufferin was about to retire and rest on his laurels after going to Burma to receive the submission of Upper Burma – Britain's last Indian annexation.

Meanwhile however there was much for the Indian government to do towards bringing the hill states under the firm control of India in accordance with Lytton's policy. For the next few years the man most involved was Captain Francis Younghusband. He was only in his twenties but he had just sprung to fame through his pioneer journey from Peking to India. He consulted Elias – who whilst scorning mere travellers, was always helpful to genuine explorers – as to what he should do next, but in any case the government had marked him down and for the next few years kept him constantly on the move. His first mission was to Hunza in 1890 where it had now become clear that the Mir was treating with Russia. He had two tasks, of which the first was to examine the hitherto un-reconnoitred passes east of the Baroghil. The second was to oust Captain Gromchevskiy then reported to be negotiating

an agreement with the Mir and subsequently intending to visit
Ladakh for the same purpose. The two men met in Hunza and
Younghusband found Gromchevskiy personally very likeable; but
neither had any illusions about each other's intentions. It was
Younghusband who scored, by a ruse which cut off his rival's
supplies. Gromchevskiy had to retire or else starve and sensibly
chose the former.

As to Hunza itself, in spite of possible Chinese reactions a
military operation brought it under control two years later, thus
filling another gap in the northern defences. Sikkim had already
been brought in in 1888 after another military expedition, following which both Durand and Elias had conducted the preliminary
treaty negotiations. (Elias had then only just returned to India after
another year's sick leave recuperating from his Pamir journey.
After Sikkim it was Durand's turn; he was stricken by what was
probably a coronary thrombosis and spent the next year in
England.) Both these military operations had been undertaken
while Lord Lansdowne was Viceroy and a Conservative Government had returned to power with Salisbury – never prone to give
Russia too much rope – as Foreign Secretary once more.

Younghusband had been appointed Political Agent to Hunza
but he was not allowed to remain there for long because Elias's
Report was brought to life. Russian activity in the Pamir and in
Badakhshan had increased; Russia still seemed to think India
intended to occupy the latter. Chitral was under threat and
Younghusband was chosen to follow up Elias's recommendations
in detail. Abdur Rahman had taken Elias's advice and established
a garrison in Shughnan, though he had done nothing about
Wakhan. But he refused to let Younghusband in to carry on where
Elias had left off, so Younghusband was sent with George
Macartney to Kashgar to follow Elias's footsteps from there. He too
failed at Kashgar but he left Macartney there as was described in
Chapter Nine. Passing along the Alichur Pamir (the Pamirs were
eight high valleys between impassable mountain ranges), he
remarked that Elias had 'travelled in this as in almost every other
part of Asia'. There he found an Afghan military post which was
inside the Aksu boundary claimed by China. Whilst he was there a
clash occurred between Afghan and Chinese troops and Younghusband, without asking for orders, unwisely requested the Afghans to withdraw. When he heard of it the Amir made a strong

protest to India and the Indian government had to apologise to him.

Younghusband's presence in the Pamir brought a rival Russian party with a military escort under Colonel Yanov (following Elias, Younghusband had only a small party and no escort). The two men met for a sociable, if correct, evening dinner, but at midnight Yanov sent a message saying he had been instructed by the Governor General of Turkestan to annex the Pamir and ordering Younghusband back to Yarkand the next day. He had to go but found his way to Gilgit instead of returning to Yarkand. This episode created what was to be the last crisis in the long struggle and Britain protested vehemently.

Although it received less publicity in Britain than had Penjdeh, its implications were possibly even more important. The map presented by Yanov showed as Russian annexed territory the whole Pamir including Shughnan and Rushan as well as Darwaz. Moreover a Russian party had crossed the Baroghil pass into Chitral and had entered Wakhan too. These moves were obviously designed to bring Russia up to the northern foothills of the Hindu Kush, with the ultimate consequence of a coterminous frontier which it was essential British policy to prevent; Chitral, Hunza and even Kashmir too were under threat. The problem for Britain and India was how to counteract these Russian moves without sending a force across the Hindu Kush. There were differences of opinion between Lansdowne and Salisbury on the necessary action. The latter would rather have had a quarrel with Russia than a breach with the Amir on his hands. Morier was a man who looked 'at the other side of the hill' and he knew from talks with the Russian Finance Minister, Vyshnegradskiy, that Russia could not afford a war. According to Agatha Ramm in her biography, he told Morier 'We Russians have a talent for doing things so that we go in the opposite direction to that in which we wish to go and then we are surprised at the results'. Vyshnegradskiy was determined to prevent war. Morier then began to negotiate with the Foreign Minister, Giers, taking a stronger line than Salisbury. He requested the withdrawal of the Yanov claim, and the renewal of negotiations for a permanent settlement. At about this time Salisbury lost office and Rosebery came to power. Morier seized on the opportunity and told Giers that if the Yanov claim was not withdrawn, he would be recalled and war might result. That was enough for Giers, for he too must have known Russia's financial state; he withdrew the Yanov claim and declared it illegal. This was the sixth occasion, according to this narrative, on which Russia faced with determined resistance had backed down. It seems even to have been a Russian characteristic. It must have been a severe blow to the Russian military clique. Although Morier was an eccentric diplomat and had always been distrusted by the Foreign Office his efforts to improve relations with Russia probably did help towards a final settlement.

Even before this episode there had been two unexpected developments. The Amir had decided he could not afford to exercise control over the unruly states of Shughnan and Rushan and he withdrew his garrisons across the river. At the same time China withdrew her own troops and abandoned her claim to the Aksu border. Morier urged the Chinese Minister to persuade the Chinese government to change its mind, but without success. That left the gap as wide open as before – but fortunately for India there was still Wakhan. Younghusband was then in Chitral commanding the expedition which finally brought that hill state firmly under India. The natural result of the Yanov disclaimer was a renewed request from Russia to settle the Afghan border by diplomatic means based on the 1873 Agreement. As a first step Durand was despatched to Kabul in 1893 with the object of trying to persuade the Amir to abandon his claim to Rushan and Shughnan beyond the Amu Dar'ya provided Russia could be persuaded to abandon Bukharan claims to Darwaz on the Afghan side of the river. If the Amir agreed to that and would also agree to hold firmly on to Wakhan, India would increase his subsidy. The Amir grumbled at having to hold Wakhan but he accepted the terms. He was probably not too reluctant to abandon the parts of Shughnan and Rushan beyond the river, provided he retained Darwaz on the near side – which he did. The final terms were embodied in the Durand Agreement. Thus Elias's neutral belt plan held, although truncated, with the 'red and green lines' kept apart by the narrow strip of Wakhan, which today is still a part of Afghanistan, meeting China at its eastern end. The ethnic problem presented by Darwaz, Shughnan and Rushan straddling the Amu Dar'ya was settled diplomatically by each country renouncing its trans-Panjah claims and by an exchange of populations. The way was now open to a final settlement of Afghanistan's northern frontier along the Amu

Dar'ya using Rawlinson's original formula on which the 1873 Agreement had been based. The end of the long struggle was in sight. There remained to be settled the Pamir boundary east of Lake Zorkul which had not been discussed in the 1873 Agreement over twenty years earlier. That was most amicably resolved by the Joint Pamirs Boundary Commission in 1895. It left Russia in full possession of all the Pamir, except for the Taghdumbash which was the subject of a later agreement between Afghanistan and China. In an unwonted spirit of conviviality between Russia and Britain the Commission named one of the border mountains, Mount Concord.

*   *   *   *   *

Most of the deductions have been made in the course of this study, but the most important conclusions deserve to be finally stated. The first of them is that Russia never had either the will or the ability to invade India. Whatever the hot-headed soldiers on both sides might threaten or expect, it was always the statesmen who prevented a major war. The second conclusion is that contrary to Russian fears, India never had the military capacity to move into Central Asia. What she did hope and failed to get was commercial influence. She failed because the Khans were only interested in arms for fighting Russia or against each other and it was never the Company's policy to supply them. Trade not war was the Company's role. Perhaps that was why there was such an abysmal lack of study of logistics.

As for Afghanistan Russia had not the desire or the military capability to move in there either. The decision to keep out was made easier, firstly by her own first failure against Khiva, and secondly by the spectacle of the British disaster. She would have had nothing to gain by a physical occupation of such a turbulent country when her main object was to establish a stable southern frontier. Of course Afghanistan remained a potential field, like Iran, for the Russian speciality of intrigue, to embarrass the British. To control Afghanistan would have entailed first of all full control of Khorasan as a supply base and that again was never a serious possibility.

Finally it should be stressed that Indian defence policy was most successful when Governors General and Viceroys maintained a policy of non-intervention in Afghan affairs. Every time the forward policy was tried it failed.

Apart from all other factors, the prime strategic one of logistics was never given due consideration. There have been plenty of examples of its importance throughout this account. Two of the most recent ones were Russia's relatively small campaigns against Geok Teke; added to which were the difficulties of maintaining even the Afghan Boundary Commission. All in all the limitations of logistics prove that the prosecution of a major war in Central Asia would have been an impossibility at any time. Of all the leaders of those days only Lord Lawrence and possibly General Milyutin, the Russian War Minister, recognized the fact.

Although the term the Great Game suited well the British viewpoint of its day, it belittles what was a deadly serious affair marked by many serious diplomatic and strategic blunders from which few emerge with credit. But the term has stuck and it is probably too late to change it. Certainly the whole period of conflict, even though it never developed into open war, deserves some name. Cricket was of course the game implied at the time, but that again is peculiarly British and scarcely fits the vast field of Central Asia. A much more descriptive analogy would be chess. Let us therefore end this study by quoting the words of the old Persian poet Omar Khayyam of Naishapur in Khorasan:

'But helpless Pieces of the Game He plays
Upon this Chequer-board of Nights and Days
Hither and thither moves, and checks, and slays,
And one by one back in the Closet lays'.

The pieces of the Chequer-board had lain forgotten in the Closet for more than seventy years. That was a long time in the turbulent history of Central Asia. We are now seeing them being brought out again in no uncertain fashion.

Epilogue

by

Geoffrey Wheeler

In one sense, the tussle between Britain and Russia during the nineteenth century for political supremacy in Central Asia must be regarded as a completely dead letter: the juxtaposition and near confrontation in Asia of two expanding European empires can hardly be expected to recur. Apart, however, from its intrinsic historical interest, the episode retains an abiding importance as the first stage in the establishment of Russia's formidable presence in Central Asia, a region abutting on a number of independent countries from which British presence and influence has now disappeared.

The so-called Great Game has been variously treated as a series of shrewd moves on both sides each prompting a reply from the other, as a chronicle of mutual misunderstandings and suspicion giving rise to barely credible military and political blunders on the British side and to Russian duplicity and bad faith as well as ruthless persistence, and as a romantic narrative of British deeds of daring. The British material on all these matters is extensive: it includes official dispatches, correspondence and speeches, private correspondence, political pamphlets, newspaper articles, and a wide range of books of travel and memoirs, many of the latter highly critical of government policy. By comparison, Tsarist Russian material is uninformative about the trend of Russian thinking: in nineteenth century Russia there was little or no freedom of speech or of the press; there was nothing resembling the Public Record Office; official comment and correspondence were never made public unless directed towards a foreign power; such memoirs as were published were politically unrevealing, and travel books were devoted to topographical and ethnographical matter. Soviet historical writing on Central Asia in the nineteenth century

215

is voluminous, but besides being even more strictly controlled, it is largely written from a propaganda angle. Some historians no doubt have access to secret Tsarist records, but their use of them is selective and must accord with current policy.

The retrospective scrutiny of British source-material reveals how unrealistic British thinking on Central Asia was, how greatly Russian military and economic resources were overrated and how much reliance was placed on uninformed and prejudiced counsel. An outstanding exception was the Viceroy, Lord Lawrence's, memorandum of 1867 now published in full, apparently for the first time, as an appendix to the present volume. In this he came out strongly against the 'forward policy' and advocated British non-interference in the internal affairs of Afghanistan as the best way of stabilizing the situation in Central Asia. Another rare note of realism was struck by George (later, Lord) Curzon when he wrote twenty years later in his *Russia in Central Asia*, 'in the absence of any physical obstacle, and in the presence of an enemy whose rule of life was depredation, and who understood no diplomatic logic but defeat, Russia was as much compelled to go forward as the earth is to go round the sun'.

In the event, Russia's advance did stop at the frontiers of the nearest thing in the region to what Prince Gorchakov described as 'regularly constituted states', namely Iran, Afghanistan and China. Whether she was deterred from continuing her southward advance still further by the 'forward policy' followed against the advice of Lord Lawrence can never now be known without full access to Tsarist secret archives.

The spectre of an Anglo-Russian military confrontation in Central Asia faded finally away with the signing of the Pamirs Agreement in 1895. Partly perhaps on account of the welter of baseless apprehension and the senseless warfare in which it resulted, this period of intense Anglo-Russian rivalry no longer features at all prominently in British historiography; even the region itself has long been virtually ignored in British universities. For the Soviet Russians, however, the history of what they prefer to think of as British designs on the peoples of Central Asia has remained a matter of lasting importance for reasons which it will be interesting to examine.

What might be described as the orthodox Marxist view of the

Tsarist acquisition of Central Asia was expounded by M. N. Pokrovskiy in his *Brief History of Russia* (1933); it also pervades the
first edition of the Great Soviet Encyclopaedia of which Pokrovskiy
was the historical editor until his death in 1932. This view was that
the Tsarist conquest was an 'absolute evil' and therefore not to be
distinguished from all other manifestations of colonialism, notably
that practised by Britain. A natural corollary of this was that the
resistance to the Tsarist invaders was 'heroic'. After Pokrovskiy's
death his theory began to come under criticism for reasons which
lie deep in Russian history as distinct from Marxist philosophy; it
was realized that to praise resistance to Russian power would not
only be tantamount to condoning, if not encouraging, 'bourgeois
nationalism', but would detract from the mystique of the inherent
superiority of the Russian people, which, in spite of frequent
disclaimers, the new regime was intent on perpetuating. In 1937,
Pokrovskiy's theory of the 'absolute evil' was replaced by that of the
'lesser evil', that is to say, the notion that while the Tsarist conquest
may have been ethically wrong and the subsequent administration
oppressive, it safeguarded the peoples of Central Asia from
something very much worse – British conquest and subsequent
colonization and 'enslavement'.

In 1951, the Soviet authorities had decided to abandon the
theory of the 'lesser evil'. The Tsarist acquisition and colonization
of Central Asia were now seen as positively beneficial; the term
'conquest' (zavoyevaniye) was dropped in favour of incorporation
(prisoyedineniye) which was supposed to have taken place with the
full consent of the people. This imaginary situation was contrasted
with Britain's conquest and colonization of India, a process, it is
alleged, she had every intention of extending to Central Asia.

The historical significance of the Russian acquisition and extensive colonization of Central Asia is a subject which has severely
taxed the ingenuity of Soviet historians and propagandists. They
have had to explain why this nationally distinct but economically
indispensable and strategically important territory has remained an
integral part of the Russian empire under its new name of the
Soviet Union, while the peoples of the Indian subcontinent are now
completely independent. 'Soviet historians', writes N. A. Khalfin in
the conclusion to his book *Russian Policy in Central Asia* (1960),
'are of the definite opinion that for Central Asia to have become
part of the British Empire would have been the greatest disaster for

its peoples'. Evidently the Soviet government considers that specious arguments of this kind serve to sustain the illusion, on which Soviet neo-colonial policy is based, that imperialism in South and Central Asia has been practised by Britain alone.

In the sense that Russia did what she intended to do in Central Asia and was not provoked into doing what, during the nineteenth century, she probably never had any inclination to do, namely, extend her presence into Afghanistan, she may be said to have achieved her aims. Moreover, she has not only remained in the field while Britain has left it, but during the past fifty, and more especially during the past twenty-five years, she has developed in the Central Asian republics a unique system of colonial administration and brought about a remarkable economic and cultural transformation. This, the Soviets claim, is due to the application of the enlightened principles of communism and also to the dynamic altruism of the Russian people, the 'elder brother' of the peoples of Central Asia. It is not the purpose of this Epilogue to consider the truth of these assertions, but it may be of some interest to refer briefly to certain characteristics of the Tsarist regime which greatly facilitated the Soviet take-over and subsequent revolutionary reforms. It is incidentally worth noting that these characteristics never seem to have attracted the attention of the Government of India either while the Great Game was in progress, or during the two decades preceding the revolution of 1917. The 19-volume report of the 1908–1909 Pahlen Commission of enquiry into the administration of Central Asia, and *Aziyatskaya Rossiya* (Asiatic Russia), the voluminous 1914 report of the Directorate of Land Exploitation and Agriculture, were never studied in India.

The task of conquering, pacifying and administering Central Asia was of course minuscule by comparison with the task which faced the British in India. Communications with metropolitan Russia were relatively easy; the climate, apart from a few southern localities, was not extreme and favoured colonization; the population of under ten million was broadly homogeneous and unwarlike except for a small Turkmen element in the south west, and it lacked any European training and leadership. Bearing in mind the state of affairs in European Russia as compared with Britain it was hardly surprising that the system of administration, security and culture-contact imposed on Central Asia was fundamentally different from that developed in India from 1818 onwards. To begin with, the administration of the two governorates-general of the Steppe Region and Turkestan was essentially military, executive authority down to that of the *uyezd* (county) commandants being in the hands of army officers on the active list. Since Russia herself did not adopt any form of parliamentary democracy before the beginning of the twentieth century, she naturally did not propose to introduce it into her colonial possessions. Apart from this, the Tsarist regime displayed certain positive and negative features which distinguished it from British practice, and which together paved the way for the much more arbitrary and materially progressive rule introduced by its Soviet successor. On the positive side were: the definite alignment of the frontiers with neighbouring states – Afghanistan, Iran and China; the ruthless subjection of the Turkmens of Transcaspia; and the introduction of a non-Asian population of over two million. On the negative side was the absence of three features prominent in the British administration of India: the creation of locally recruited military formations; native personnel trained in clerical and administrative duties; and the holding out of prospects of eventual self-government.

The result of this combination of positive and negative features was that when, after the revolution, the character of the new regime became evident, the Muslim peoples of Central Asia lacked the military, political and administrative ability to offer any but sporadic and uncoordinated resistance. Once this resistance had been broken down, the Soviets found a situation which favoured the remarkable political, social and economic experiment on which they were shortly to embark. The people were cowed into submission; they had no leaders; literacy stood at no more than two per cent; and there was no prospect of material or moral help either from abroad or from the non-Asian settlers in their midst who, whatever they might feel about the new regime, had no intention of making common cause with the Muslim population.

The West was slow to grasp the significance of what the new regime was trying to do in Central Asia. For at least twenty years it was widely believed that the region's economy was doomed and that Soviet rule would never survive a second world war. In the event, however, the Soviet position was strengthened rather than weakened by World War II, and from 1950 onwards the economy as well as living conditions began steadily to improve until by the 1960s productivity, education and the standard of living had in almost every respect surpassed those of the great majority of Middle Eastern and South Asian countries.

Fears that Russia still harboured some sort of sinister designs on India lingered on into the twentieth century. They were played upon to some extent by the appearance in 1901 of *Kim*. But Kipling, while painting a lurid picture of Russia's continuing machinations, showed them to be forestalled by a ubiquitous British intelligence network, which, as has been conclusively proved in the present work, was little more than a figment of his fertile imagination. From the Anglo-Russian Convention of 1907 to the revolution of 1917 the Russian menace to India was virtually forgotten; but after the Conference of Eastern Peoples held in Baku in 1920, it reappeared in a new form – that of Communism.

In his memorandum of 1867 Lord Lawrence had dwelt on the extreme improbability of Russia ever mounting an invasion of India and on the impossibility of such an invasion being successful. Sir Henry Rawlinson, a leading russophobe and advocate of the 'forward policy', was eventually constrained to concede the unlikelihood of a Russian invasion, but he continued to insist on the need for the permanent British occupation of Herat and Kandahar in order to keep Russia out of Afghanistan, whence, he maintained, she could launch a campaign of subversion in India. Fear of such a possibility, if it ever existed, was allayed by the creation with British, and apparently even Russian, support, of a united Afghanistan under the Amir Abdur Rahman. But with the foundation in 1921 of the Indian Communist Party the possibility of subversion began to assume a new reality, and it was to haunt the British government of India for the next twenty years.

The Russian Revolution of 1917 attracted the favourable attention of the Indian nationalist movement rather on account of its anti-imperialist programme than of its anti-capitalist and communist ideology, which had no appeal for the Indian Congress, or even for its offshoot the Congress Socialist Party. The Indian Communist Party was originally formed from among Indian expatriates in the Soviet Union and elsewhere, and although the Soviet government may have intended to use it as the spearhead of its penetration of the Indian nationalist movement, it was unable to fulfil this role since it never exercised any considerable influence in Indian political circles. But as a means of embarrassing the government Congress was not averse from exaggerating the communist menace, and during the period between the two world wars there were frequent scares of communist conspiracies, the existence of communist 'cells' and the like. When in 1941 the USSR entered the war on the allied side the differentiation made by the Indian Congress and the Muslim League between Soviet Russia which they admired and supported and communism which they disliked as much as imperialism became clear; and the legalization of the Indian Communist Party in 1942 met with Congress disfavour. This attitude continued after the transfer of power, Nehru taking the view that while it was right and proper to maintain close and friendly relations with her great northern neighbour, India had no use for communism.

There is now no question of 'rivalry' between the Soviet Union and the countries of South Asia. India regards Russia as its ally rather than as a potential enemy. In the West, however, and to some extent in Pakistan, Russian 'designs' on the Indian subcontinent and on the countries of the Indian Ocean basin still loom large. In the achievement of those designs communism is still expected to play an important, if not a decisive part. The exact nature of Russia's designs may be difficult to determine but they are usually thought to include the attainment of the same degree of prescriptive and proscriptive control over the whole region as was exercised by Britain at the peak of her power. Russia is still very far from exercising such control and the chances of her doing so must depend on certain factors which did not exist during the period of British expansion. The factors now thought to be favouring the further growth of Russian influence are: diplomatic relations with all the countries of the region and considerable military and economic aid projects operating in most of them; a naval presence in the Indian Ocean with shore facilities in India, South Yemen and in East Africa; overt or clandestine communist activities; and the economic, social and cultural development of Soviet Central Asia on a scale so far unequalled in the countries to which it lies adjacent; and most recently, the Russian invasion of Afghanistan. These new factors are partly, if not wholly, balanced by others: the emergence of China as a great power and as a potential challenge to Russia's position in Asia; the increasing United States' involvement in Asian affairs with a tendency towards alignment with China; and the phenomenal spread during the past fifty years of

Asian nationalism, which is now showing itself to be a much more potent force than communism.

This, broadly speaking, was the situation confronting the Soviet government in the 1970s; and, owing chiefly to the steady growth of nationalist sentiment, they could hardly have found it satisfactory. Ironically enough, it had been the Soviet policy of giving moral and material aid to nationalist regimes all over South and Southwest Asia embarked upon after the 20th Communist Party Congress of 1956 which contributed most to these regimes' present attitude. This amounts to their accepting aid from any quarter without showing the slightest inclination to conform to the wishes of the donors in respect of their sovereign rights, methods of government, administration of justice, treatment of minorities, or disposal of their natural resources. They realize that as far as the West is concerned the old method of direct military intervention is no longer seen as practicable. They do not believe, and may never have believed, what the Soviets have in the past believed, namely, that local communist parties are of themselves capable of bringing about the sort of revolution likely to promote Russian interests.

The determined Soviet attempt made in 1945–1946 to do away with Iran's independence and to draw it into the Soviet orbit had not only failed but had apparently driven Iran into the arms of the United States. The Indian government, while seeking friendly relations with the Soviet Union, would have nothing to do with communism which, in so far as it existed in India, was of the Chinese rather than the Soviet persuasion. Pakistan, while utterly rejecting communism, was on good terms with China. Since the 1950s, Soviet political and economic relations with Afghanistan had greatly improved, but the very idea of communism had not penetrated beyond the intelligentsia of a few of the larger cities.

At the time of writing (January 1981) it is not possible to determine with any degree of precision the reasons which have prompted Soviet action in Afghanistan since the coup d'état of April 1978, and still less to foresee its possible consequences. As was to be expected the warm Soviet welcome extended to the new leftist regime of Nur Muhammad Taraki was followed by a great increase in material and technological aid. As always in Afghanistan the facts have been very difficult to establish, but by the autumn of 1979 it had become obvious that the new regime enjoyed no popular support, that the increased Russian presence was widely resented and that the Afghan armed forces were unable and unwilling to maintain order. Moscow may well have decided not only that the so-called revolutionary government was of itself unlikely to contribute to Soviet interests, but that the safety of the advisory Soviet personnel was at risk.

Whatever its ultimate motive the Soviet invasion of Afghanistan in December 1979 constituted the first act of direct Soviet military intervention in the affairs of an Asian country since the retention of Soviet forces in Iran beyond March 1946 in defiance of the Tripartite Agreement of 1942. It was also the first time regular Russian forces had encroached on undisputed territory since 1838, when a small Russian force participated in the Iranian siege of Herat. It was not perhaps surprising, therefore, that the Soviet invasion at the end of 1979 was at first widely regarded as an initial step in the realization of the ambition attributed by Britain to Russia during most of the nineteenth century, that is to say, the expansion of Russian power to the Indian Ocean and the establishment of overriding influence throughout the Indian Ocean basin. That Tsarist Russia ever seriously considered the possibility of invading India by way either of Iran or of Afghanistan Colonel Morgan regards as extremely unlikely. There is, indeed, no real evidence that Tsarist Russia ever contemplated supplanting British power in India by force or by any other means. Certainly Soviet Russia, while it still headed the world communist movement, believed that 'other means' of extending its influence in Asia could be found in communism. Today, however, Asian communist parties, where they exist, are seldom under direct Soviet control; and it is noteworthy that the only country on the Asian mainland which has adopted a Soviet communist system of government and in which Soviet influence is paramount, is Mongolia,[1] where Soviet troops have been in occupation since 1921. The Soviet government may now have reached the conclusion that Soviet communism cannot be effectively established in Asian countries unless supported by a visible military presence for which material aid and thousands of advisers and technicians are no substitute.

Other possible reasons for the Russian action in Afghanistan have since been advanced. The coup of April 1978 took place at a time when American influence seemed to be firmly established in

---

[1] A possible exception to this statement is Vietnam.

Iran. The Russians may or may not have instigated the coup; but in deciding to put their whole weight behind the new government they may have had in mind a plan of outflanking the American presence in Iran by creating a similar Russian presence in Afghanistan, only to find that the coup itself carried no weight in the country as a whole. Moscow may have believed reports that the ensuing chaos was being exploited from Iran and Pakistan, and could have repercussions in the Soviet Muslim republics. Such theories add up to the possibility that Russia's unprecedented involvement in south Asian affairs is the result not of deliberate planning but of faulty intelligence and precipitate decisions, a notion unlikely to be acceptable to those still convinced of the omniscience of the Russian intelligence service and of Russian omnicompetence in the handling of Asian problems. The truth may never be known, for the Soviet government, like its Tsarist predecessor, is not in the habit of revealing, even in retrospect, the real reasons for its actions or of admitting its mistakes. One thing is certain: the consequences of this new venture will be far-reaching and will profoundly affect Russia's future political status in south and southwest Asia.

APPENDIX 1

The Khan of Khiva's Rescript

Translation of Rescript of the King of Khwárazm (Khiva), written at the beginning of Jumáda ii, A. H. 1256 [= July 31, 1840.]

Abu'l-Muzaffar Wa'l-Mansúr Abu'l-Gházi Khwárazm-sháh.

OUR WORD:

The Royal and Most High Order to the Wise Governors of the Metropolis of Khwárazm [Khiva], festive as Paradise, to its Lords and Captains, to the doughty Warriors and Chiefs of the Yemút and Chúdar (?) Tribes, to the brave Chiefs of Qázzag (Cossacks) and Quara-galpá (Black-caps) Peoples, and to all Peoples under our rule,

Know that on the first day of the month of the second Jumáda, in the year one thousand two hundred and fifty-six of the Flight of His Holiness the Prophet (may God bless and salute him), and in the year of the Mouse, it was that WE began to be on friendly and familiar terms with the Most Great Emperor, the King of the Russian domains, and to pursue peace and friendship with him.

Therefore on becoming aware of, and acquainted with, the purpose of this high command, let no one make raids into the Russian territories, nor buy Russian captives. And whosoever shall act contrary to the purport of this high command, and shall perpetrate such raids, or purchase such captives, shall be deserving of the Royal Punishment.

This Royal, most august, sacred, and sublime command received honourable issue A. H. 1256 [= A. D. 1840.]

EDWARD G. BROWNE, M.A., F.B.A.,
Adams Professor of Arabic, Cambridge.
November 14, 1920.

225

The Lawrence Minute. 1867

Nothing which I have read or heard has ever shaken my opinion that the policy which the British Government adopted in 1838–39 in invading Affghanistan, was very unwise and uncalled for. The pretext of the siege of Herat no longer remained in force; for the Persian Army had retired, baffled and discomfited from before its walls. Northern India was never more quiet, nor the Mahomedan population more contented, than at that time. I was present at Delhi when a portion of our Army, destined for Cabul, marched through the city. I can well recall the pleasure which many of the Officers expressed at forming a part of the expedition, the general enthusiasm with which the movement on Affghanistan was hailed by the English in India. I talked with some of the Native Officers and men, mostly Mahomedans, who were recruited from the District in which I was the Magistrate, for one of the newly raised corps of Cavalry, which composed part of the expedition; and was consulted by some of their relations as to the character and probable permanence of the service which was then available. But I never heard a word uttered of doubt as to our success, or of anxiety as to the movements of Russia.

On the other hand it has always appeared to me that, however confident our Officers in those days were of the sound policy which led to the expedition, the large majority of those who survived that expedition, or who have studied that question, since the War in Affghanistan, – since we have obtained a more complete knowledge of its circumstances and resources, of its Chiefs and its people, – have deprecated very strongly an advance into that country, or any very intimate interference in its affairs. It has been generally said that a large army of foreigners cannot exist in

226

Affghanistan; and that a small one could not hold its own securely. That country could not supply the food for such an army as we should require there, and therefore its supplies must come from a distance. The country can, indeed, scarcely feed its own population, however hardy and abstemious it is known to be. One, perhaps the main, cause of the constant internecine wars which prevail among the Chiefs, arises from the circumstance that they cannot subsist themselves in a suitable manner, even though they monopolize so much of the means of subsistence from the population. It is a constant struggle with them to unseat one or other as the heads of tribes and clans, or the rulers of sections of the country. For this, very terrible crimes are often perpetrated even among near kinsmen. The normal condition of the army is in a state of semi-starvation; they are habitually cheated out of a large portion of their scanty pay; and the agriculturists and mass of the people obtain the bare means of existence. A rise of the price of food, to all but the proprietors of the land, becomes a very serious misfortune; and this was one of the various causes which rendered our occupation of the country so unpopular. Ameer Dost Mohumud, when at Peshawur at the end of 1856, speaking of his resources, remarked, 'we have men and we have rocks in plenty; but we have nothing else.'

To endeavour to hold such a country firmly, to try to control such a people, is to court misfortune and calamity. The Affghan will bear poverty, insecurity of life; but he will not tolerate foreign rule. The moment he has a chance, he will rebel. His nature, his religion, the habits of his life, all tend to foster feelings of independence and hardihood.

Whether we advanced into Affghanistan as friends or as foes, would, in the end, make little difference; the final result would be the same. The Affghans do not want us; they dread our appearance in their country. The circumstances connected with the last Affghan War, have created in their hearts a deadly hatred to us as a people. And their feelings are fostered and strengthened by their Priests and Chiefs.

In 1856, during the Persian War when, by the instructions of the Government of India, I was negociating with Ameer Dost Mohumud Khan, and making the arrangements by which the British Government gave His Highness a large monthly subsidy, and a considerable number of arms and accoutrements, one of the points for which I was directed to stipulate was, that we should be allowed to have a mission composed of British Officers at Cabul. Hungering, as I may say, the Ameer was for our subsidy, he started back at the very mention of such an arrangement. He asked for time to consider the matter, and to consult his chief adherents. On the second day he sent me a message by one of his sons, that it was impossible to concede to this proposal; and when I subsequently saw him, he said that he dared not consent to it. According to my instructions, I pressed the matter, intimating that a refusal would probably lead to my breaking off negociations and withholding the subsidy. After much hesitation and evident dislike to the arrangement, the Ameer at last consented to the deputation of a mission to Candahar, on the condition that our Officers did not take the Cabul route. The Ameer either really feared, or affected to fear, for their lives if they were seen in Cabul. He frequently remarked, 'if we are to be friends, do not force British Officers on me. I have no objection to the presence of a Native Agent at Cabul.'

Our mission was some months at Candahar, during which time, and for some time afterwards, the Ameer was drawing his subsidy of £10,000 per mensem. Our Officers were all this time in a most precarious position; scarcely for a day were their lives safe, as the news of the progress of the mutiny reached Candahar. Under plea of taking care of them, from their first arrival they were surrounded by spies, and could not move a stone's throw from their residence without an escort, who watched and denounced any man who might speak to them. At last matters got so bad that they were glad to leave Candahar.

Brigadier-General H. Lumsden, who was at the head of this mission, more than once assured me, after his return, that he had better means of gaining information on Affghan and Central Asian affairs at Peshawur, than when at Candahar; for, at the former city, merchants of all these countries abound, and all will speak freely with an Officer who lays himself out for information, whereas at Candahar no one would come near him who had any regard for his life.

An opinion frequently advocated by the Press in India is that if British Officers were deputed simply as commercial agents, and not as our political representatives, they would be readily received at the different Courts of Cabul, Merve, Bokhara, Yarkund, etc. But this is wholly a delusion. There would be no security for their good treatment; no guarantee that they might not be insulted, probably murdered at any time. Unsupported by material power, and that so close at hand as to be apparent to all observers, such Officers could never be safe. They never would be in so secure a position as to be able to take an impartial and dispassionate view of affairs. They would possess little means of feeling public opinion; no opportunity of hearing the real state of affairs. They would be pressed from time to time to obtain aid of one kind or the other from the British Government; and insulted, and even maltreated, if they refused, or failed to procure it. The wealth and resources of the British Government are considered to be inexhaustible in these barbarous countries; and, in the opinion of their leading men, surely some portion of it might well be placed at the disposal of such trusty allies!

I would point to the fate of Colonel Stoddart and Captain Connolly, in Bokhara, as illustrative of the soundness of my views. I might also instance the present condition of our countrymen in Abyssinia, and the expedition that England is now undertaking into that remote country to rescue them, as evidence of the mischief which results from sending Officers to barbarous Chiefs in territories which are quite beyond our influence. If, under such circumstances, we do not stretch out our hands to assist our representatives, if we do not exert the power of Her Majesty to rescue them, if, in fact, we leave them to their fate, we are lowered in our own estimation and that of others; our prestige is overshadowed and England's power is called in question. On the other hand, if we determine on decisive action, how many lives and how much treasure must be lavished in the attempt to save them, and how possible it is that the attempt after all may fail.

I can well recall to mind the stories I have heard from the late Major D'Arcy Todd and Sir John Login of their treatment by the people of Herat. So long as they had large sums of money to scatter among them, to expend on the fortifications of the city, on anything and everything – and they certainly showed no stint in this way – the Heratees were their humble servants, ready to obey their bidding, to kiss the very dust off their feet. But from the day these supplies ceased, the tone of the people changed. It was then, 'what brings you among us? Can't you stay in your own country? What mischief are you hatching now?' And so on. Like the Lumsdens in later days at Candahar, they were only too glad to leave Herat, where their advent had been received with so much honor.

In the winter of 1853, if I recollect right, a deputation was received from the Chief of Kokan, headed by one of the Suddozai Chiefs of Cabul, sending some presents for the Governor General and asking for supplies of arms, guns, and ammunition, and, above all, for English Officers to train and discipline his soldiers, and enable them to contend successfully with the Russians. I was at Peshawur when the mission arrived, and had long conversations with the Suddozai Chief – a man of some ability and shrewdness, who had a general idea of our power and resources in India. The conclusion I came to was, that the Khan of Kokan had no army, and no adequate means of forming one; that his troops consisted of the mere militia of the country, badly armed and equipped, with no organization, under little control, and quite unable to meet the Russians in the field. In short, that it was only owing to the physical difficulties of the country, and the long distance of the Russians from their own base of operations, that Kokan had, to a certain extent, maintained its independence. I at once saw that it would, in all probability, be a fatal error sending British Officers to such a country, where it was quite impossible that they could be of the slightest service. Lord Dalhousie, however, took a different view of the matter, and instructed me to select a certain number of British Officers, with a due proportion of Native Officers, to proceed to Kokan with the mission. I remonstrated very strongly, pointing out all the objections to the plan, and expressing my conviction that it would certainly lead to the sacrifice of English lives. On this, His Lordship was good enough to accept my views; but desired that the Native Officers should be at liberty to take service with the Khan. On sending for them, however, and asking them what they really wished, not one would consent to go to Kokan. Their idea was, that where British Officers were to be sent, it was safe for them to go also; but that if the former were to be kept back, no good would come from Native Officers accepting such service.

Since then the Chiefs of Yarkund and Khotan have made similar overtures, and with like success. Indeed it is only a few months ago that the latter Chief, expatiating on the resources at his command, pressed for assistance. And now we have just heard that he and one of his sons, with many of his Chief Officers, have been murdered by the Khan of Yarkund, and the country taken possession of. Should not such evidence of the utter insecurity of those countries in Central Asia, convince the most sceptical of the folly of trusting our

Officers on such missions? Our Officers, however, are burning with impatience, and pining from inaction; and any enterprize which opens a door to distinction and preferment, is acceptable to many of them. Our merchants also are naturally eager to find new marts for their goods, and look with prejudiced eyes on the counsels of prudence and caution, however founded on experience and foresight.

The tendency in India also among the English community is to attribute such policy as I have described to parsimony, to a narrow and even mean love of economy. But such opinions are really opposed to the facts of the case. The paramount consideration, in my mind, has always been, and still is, a regard for the true interests of the State. I am convinced that we can gain nothing, but are pretty sure to lose a great deal in prestige, in honor, in the valuable lives of our Officers and Soldiers, by interfering actively in the affairs of Central Asia; and that so far from strengthening our tenure of India, we may thus shake it to its very foundations. Nor am I insensible, I admit, to the financial aspect of the question. I know well what are the wants of India; how infinite are the material requirements of this country; how limited is the accumulation of capital; how obnoxious is every description of new taxation to all classes of the people. I am, therefore, most desirous not to throw away the public money on expeditions and wars, which may be honorably avoided, and in this view I decline to be led away to engage in a course of policy which too surely ends in such results.

Lieutenant-Colonel Lumsden has brought together in his Memorandum much valuable information, and a considerable weight of authority connected with our expedition to Candahar and Cabul. He shows the difficulties of the way from Shikarpore, in Scinde, to the gates of Candahar. The heat of the climate, the scarcity of food, and the consequent privations of the army on the march; the character of the adjacent population; the condition of the troops when they arrived at Candahar, and their capacity at that time, if opposed, to have met a really resolute enemy. I recollect the account of an Officer who was present with that Army. He told me that the Cavalry Brigade of the Bengal column, which left Meerut with 1,500 sabres, all well equipped horsemen, mounted on the best class of horses which India could yield, could not have mustered 500 mounted men on the approach to Candahar, and could not have got out of their horses a canter of half a mile to have saved their own lives. The Army took three months at that city to recruit their strength, and supply their losses of animals of one kind or the other.

It may be urged that the occupation of Scinde, and the improvements and extended cultivation since then in that Province, have changed all these things. No doubt some change has taken place; but much of this must depend on the maintenance of peace and security; and how little would the resources of the country yield for the support of a large Army, its numerous camp followers, and tens of thousands of animals! The climate of the country cannot have altered, nor the character of the population, in any essential degree.

Hough, in his account of the Cabul expedition of 1838–39, tells us that in the first year of the campaign the Army lost upwards of 30,000 camels. For years afterwards the scarcity of these animals throughout Upper India and Rajpootana, was well known. The war from first to last cost some 13 millions of money; the lives of hundreds of English Officers and Soldiers; the lives of thousands of Native soldiers and camp followers. It destroyed the belief in our invincibility, and rendered our military service among the Natives of India much less popular than it had ever been before. But, above all, it created among the Affghans a hatred to our race, which a generation will fail to obliterate.

We went to Affghanistan under the assurance that a little aid from us would reinstate a fallen and exiled dynasty, which had still a strong hold on the hearts of the people. But we found, to our cost, that its representative had no real influence in the country, and no capacity for reconciling its jarring interests and rival factions; in a word, no power to maintain himself unsupported by ourselves. Hence we were compelled to continue in that country, until the incurable defects of our position, and the incompetency of our commanders, ended in the ruin of that policy and the destruction of the larger portion of the Army of occupancy.

Are we then in essentials to repeat that series of errors? Those who advocate an advance into Affghanistan, or, which is really the same thing, are in favor of measures intended to lead to that result, say that we have learnt a lesson from the errors of those days, and would for the future avoid their repetition. But whatever may have been the minor mistakes of that time, the fundamental one consisted in occupying Affghanistan at all. There was no escaping the evils which flowed from that policy.

But independent of this circumstance, which, however, should not be forgotten, I myself believe that we cannot advance a force permanently beyond our present frontier, in the direction of Candahar and Cabul, without the Affghans believing that it is intended to be the forerunner of the occupation of their country. Indeed this is the very object which those who encourage such a movement openly avow. Thus the formation of a cantonment at Quetta, a lease of the vallies of Khost and Koorum, are in view to a forward movement. The idea is that in the event of an advance by Russia, we should move on ourselves, and hold Herat and Cabul as important strategical positions. I admit at once that such is a correct description of these places. But I question whether, in the event of such movement by Russia, it would be our true interest to take the steps indicated. Possibly the day may come, when the Affghans may ask us to do so. At any rate, now, they have no apprehension of danger which would induce them to call on us for aid. A response to such a call, if ever made, may well be left to the statesmen and soldiers of the day, when a decision on such a question may be necessary. But judging from past events and present feelings, I should be decidedly opposed to such a policy.

In a political or military point of view, I do not think that we could occupy Herat and Cabul, with any real degree of security, without constructing fortifications for the preservation of our own people and to overawe the population of those cities. We should also have to hold Candahar and Jellalabad in like manner. Wherever we placed our troops, indeed, as links in the chain of communication, or for the purpose of commanding the country, we should have to construct fortifications of some kind or other.

Neither Herat nor Cabul, unless held in great strength, are positions which cannot be turned, or which may not be blockaded by an invading Army. To garrison them efficiently, and yet to have a force free to operate in the field and threaten the flanks of the invaders, with the possibility, nay the strong probability, of the people of the country turning against us in the event of a disaster, would require a considerable Army; how large, Military Officers of experience and ability can alone tell. But taking a general view of the circumstances in which the troops would be placed, I do not think that less than 30,000 men, half of whom ought at least to be British Soldiers, would be an unreasonable estimate. Let us only then consider what would be the cost of such an Army, with its followers and carriage, much of which would have to be kept up ready for field service. If the first invasion of Affghanistan was a strain on the finances of India, what would be the pressure of the second movement into that country?

The difficulties and complications which would follow from an advance beyond the passes of the mountains, forming at present the western frontier of British India, are such as no man can foresee, though any one may make a shrewd guess at them. Every particle of ammunition, all the bulk of the supplies for the troops, would have to be sent from India, and at its cost. All, or nearly all, the troops so employed would be in addition to those now garrisoning India. It has been over and over again affirmed, after careful consideration by Officers who know the country, that the force in India is barely sufficient for its security. There is little difference of opinion on this point. The troops then to hold Affghanistan must be in excess of this number, and form an additional drain on England.

The composition of such a body of Native troops for service in Affghanistan, as would give reasonable grounds for trusting to their fidelity in the event of great difficulties, would be a serious matter. Affghans in any numbers would be out of the question. Ghorkas, beyond the five regiments now on the Bengal establishment, could not be maintained; even those we now have are kept up with some difficulty. Hindostanees and Sikhs would not like such service.

I do not pretend to know what is the policy of Russia in Central Asia; what may be her views hereafter in India. But it seems to me that common sense suggests that her primary interest is to consolidate her hold on those vast regions now in her possession, in which there must be 'room and scope enough' for the exercise of all her energies and all her resources. Russia has indeed a task before her in which she may fail, and which must occupy her for generations. To attempt to advance until her power is firmly established, is to imperil all she has hitherto accomplished.

If we proceed to meet Russia in order to prevent her approach to India, we give her so much vantage ground; for we lessen the distance she has to march her armies, while we increase the interval between our own troops and their true base of operations. Instead then of advancing as the allies and supporters of the Affghans, if we should ever deem it necessary to do so, we should be the party against whom they would seek deliverance. The shoe pinches the wearer only. The side which held Affghanistan is the one against whom that people would probably join.

May not also the advance of England into, or even towards, Affghanistan, be looked on as a challenge to Russia? May it not bring on the collision we desire to avoid?

I am not myself at all certain that Russia might not prove a safer ally – a better neighbour than the Mahomedan races of Central Asia and Cabul. She would introduce civilization; she would abate the fanaticism and ferocity of Mahomedanism, which still exercises so powerful an influence on India.

But, supposing that Russia has the desire, and possesses the means of making a formidable attack on India – assuming that she can at once place her affairs in Central Asia on so secure a basis, as to justify her rulers in contending with us for supremacy in India – all of which appears to me to be very problematical, is it our true policy to go forward to meet her armies? I should say not. In that case let them undergo the long and tiresome marches which lie between the Oxus and the Indus; let them wend their way through difficult and poor countries, among a fanatic and coura-geous population, where, in many places, every mile can be converted into a defensible position; then they will come to the conflict on which the fate of India will depend, toil-worn, with an exhausted infantry, a broken-down cavalry, and a defective artillery. Our troops would have the option of meeting them either in the defiles of the mountains, or as they debouched from the passes, or at the passage of the Indus; wherever, in short, the genius of our commanders might dictate.

If, on the other hand, the invaders do not move by rapid marches, they must occupy the intervening countries on their route; they must forbear drawing any revenue from the people; they must feed their armies and camp followers from their rear; or they must turn the inhabitants against them; and, under the most favorable circumstances, they must endure much privation from want of adequate supplies.

It has been said that to allow Russia to occupy the countries adjacent to our western border, is to give her the opportunity, of which she will assuredly avail herself, of stirring up strife and hatred against us among all the mountain tribes. But will this be her true interest? And if so, will she be able to do us more harm than we can inflict on her in such a struggle? The further she extends her power, the greater area she must occupy; the more vulnerable points she must expose; the greater the danger she must incur of insurrection; and the larger must be her expenditure. The major part of the mountain country between our border and Affghanistan consists of narrow vallies and rugged hills, inhabited by races, who, though Mahomedan, are as ill-disposed to subject themselves to one master as to another. They have no desire to be ruled by the Chiefs of Cabul. There is perhaps not one of these tribes who would not earnestly seek our aid against any invader, if their leading men found themselves likely to be over-matched. Which party would be best able, under such circumstances, to win them to its side; we, or the Russians?

Further, it has been urged that the extension of Russian power to our frontier would lead to insurrection in the interior of India. I do not think that this would happen to any serious extent; perhaps it would not occur at all. Much would, of course, depend on the government of the day, and the contentment of the people. But, at the worst, our troops massed along the border, ready to meet the invaders, would have a greater influence on the discontented people of India, than the same troops locked up beyond the mountains in Affghanistan.

Or, if formidable insurrection should arise in India, with which the British and Native troops in the country could not cope, what would be the proper action of the Rulers in India? Would it not be to recall the Army beyond the passes? If, on the other hand, misfortune befel the distant force, we would have only the choice to reinforce it from India, which might be most inconvenient, or to recall it to India; and what would, in all likelihood, be the fate of that Army, encumbered with women and children and numerous camp followers, retreating before a Russian Army, and attacked on all sides by the people of the country, for the sake of plunder, if for no other motive?

Taking every view then of this great question, – the progress of Russia in Central Asia, the effect it will in course of time have on India, the arrangements which we should make to meet it, – I am firmly of opinion that our proper course is not to advance our troops beyond our present border, not to send English Officers into the different States of Central Asia; but to put our own house in order, by giving the people of India the best government in our power, by conciliating, as far as practicable, all classes, and by consolidating our resources. I am greatly in favor of opening up lines of communication of every kind, which, on full consideration, are likely to prove useful, so far as the means will permit; but I strongly deprecate additional taxation to any important extent; and I am equally averse to increasing the burden of our debt on unproductive works.

It is said that there is great force in repetition; and no doubt this is the case. People hope, by constant reiteration of the evils of non-interference in Central Asia, that the British Government may be stirred up to action. My own belief is, that there is even more power in being still and watching events, particularly under such circumstances as those of the present day. We have very good information of what goes on in Central Asia, through our own channels of communication. I do not recollect anything of importance which has occurred there, of which we have not heard in very reasonable time; and we have all which we do hear in due course confirmed, sometimes through Persia, at other times, from Europe itself.

SIMLA,
The 3rd October 1867.   JOHN LAWRENCE

Despatch by Foreign Secretary to the Ambassador at St. Petersburg. 1869

F. O. March 27, 1869

Sir,

I have lately and on more than one occasion spoken to Br Brunnow respecting Central Asia and the rapid advance of the Russian troops towards the Indian frontier. I have done so in a friendly tone, stating that I had no complaint to make on the part of H. M.'s Government who felt neither suspicion nor alarm as they had often received satisfactory assurances concerning the policy of Russia in those regions and were strong enough in India to repel all aggression, but that these feelings as H. E. must be well aware, were not generally shared either by the British or the Indian public, and it was highly desirable with reference to the friendly relations with Russia which we were so desirous to maintain that this uneasiness should be allayed. The language of Br Brunnow on such occasions has always been positive as to the desire of his Government to restrict rather than to extend the possessions of Russia southwards in Central Asia, and speaking, as he said with full knowledge of the policy of his Government he has affirmed that no onward movement disquieting to India need be apprehended.

I have expressed my opinion that abstinence from aggression would on every account promote the true interests of Russia whose territorial possessions needed no aggrandizement, and if the giving effect to this policy depended upon the Russian Government alone I should not doubt its being maintained: but I was sure, judging from our own Indian experience that such would not be the case and that Russia would find the same difficulty that England had experienced in controlling its own power when exercised at so great a distance from the seat of government as to make reference home almost a matter of impossibility – there was always some frontier to be improved, some broken engagement to be repaired, some faithless Ally to be punished, and plausible reasons were seldom wanting for the acquisition of territory which the Home Government never thought it expedient to reject and could not therefore condemn the motives or the means by which it had been acquired, such in the main had caused the extension of our Indian Empire and there was reason to apprehend that such was the course into which Russia, however unwillingly, was about to be drawn.

Unless stringent precautions were adopted we should find before long that some aspiring Russian General had entered into communication with some restless or malcontent Indian Prince, and that intrigues were rife and disturbing the Indian population on the frontier against which Government would have a right to remonstrate with Russia, and it was in order to prevent such a state of things, which might endanger the good understanding which now existed not only on this but on all other questions between England and Russia, that I earnestly recommended the recognition of some territory as neutral between the possessions of England and Russia which should be the limit of those possessions and be scrupulously respected by both Powers.

Br Brunnow appeared to think that this would be a desirable arrangement and promised to make a report of my suggestion to his Government.

H. E. called upon me this morning, and had the goodness to leave in my hands the copy herewith enclosed of a private and confidential letter from Prince Gortchakoff giving a positive assurance that Affghanistan would be considered as entirely beyond the sphere in which Russia might be called upon to exercise her influence.

In thanking Br Brunnow for this communication I assured him that the views of H.M.'s Government were in union with those of Pr Gortchakoff, but that I was not sufficiently informed on the subject at once to express an opinion as to whether Affghanistan would fulfil the conditions and circumstances of a neutral territory between the two Powers such as it seemed desirable to establish.

It is right, I should mention that a few days ago Br Brunnow informed me that an Affghan of some mark and standing had applied for protection to the Russian Minister at Tehran who had been ordered by the Emperor to refuse it as Affghanistan was beyond the limits of Russian influence.

I am etc
Clarendon

Bibliography

A. **Primary Sources**

    (i)   India Office Records
    (ii)   India Office Private Papers
    (iii)   Other Private Papers
    (iv)   Public Record Office

B. **Official Publications**

    (i)   India Office Library
    (ii)   War Office Library

C. **History**

D. **Biography and Autobiography**

E. **Travellers' Tales and Miscellaneous**

A. Primary Sources

(i) *India Office Records*

The greatest concentration of official documents on the subject is to be found amongst the Political and Secret Department records (L/P and S) and especially in the series called:

> Secret Home Correspondence (L/P and S/3, 1839–74).
> Political and Secret Home Correspondence (L/P and S/3, 1875–1911).
> Secret Letters from India (L/P and S/5, 1817–65, 1778–1865, 1866–74).
> Political and Secret Letters from India (L/P and S/7, 1875–1911).
> (*Note.* L/P and S/5 and L/7 contain the *N.W. Frontier Monthly Intelligence Bulletins on Central Asia.* These include Kashgar).
> Political and Secret Memoranda (L/P and S/18, c. 1840–1947)
> Political and Secret Library (L/P and S/20)

The following volumes or documents from the above sources are of special interest:

> L/P and S/3/75. pp. 105 et seq. Clarendon reporting to Buchanan at St. Petersburg, on his talk with Brunnow concerning a neutral zone. (See App: 3).
> L/P and S/3/75. pp. 303–305 and 311–318. Rawlinson to Mayo, 18 June 1869. Boundaries of Afghanistan etc.
> L/P and S/3/82.
> L/P and S/5/260. p. 499 et seq: Part One of Report by spies sent to Central Asia. 1865. (See Chapter 10).

L/P and S/5/260. pp. 721 et seq: October 1867. The Lawrence Minute on policy in Central Asia. (See App: 2).

L/P and S/5/274. p. 319. December 1873. Kabul Diary.

L/P and S/7/57, 58, 60.

L/P and S/18.

The following Memoranda:

    A27   Report of a Mission to Chinese Turkestan and Badakshan in 1885-86 (By Ney Elias).

    A51   Rawlinson on Rushan and Shughnan. 1884.

    A69   Table of events in Afghanistan and Central Asia from 1855 to 1877. 1885.

    A82   Note by Sir Steuart Bayley on the Pamir Question and the North-East Frontiers of India 1891.

L/P and S/20 contain R. Michell's *Russian Abstracts* (Trs: from newspapers and journals). 3 Volumes. 1865-1877. They also include reports of Valikhanov, Venukov, Ignat'yev etc.

The despatches of Abbott and Shakespear from Khiva with the covering despatch of D'Arcy Todd of July 1840 (See Chapter 5) will be found in Bombay Secret Consultations Volume 142 (Secret Correspondence No. 34 of 27 August 1840).

(ii) India Office Private Papers

MSS. EUR/C144	Northbrook
D558	Lansdowne
D727	Durand
E243	Cross
F130	Dufferin
H833-862	Hobhouse (Lord Broughton)

There is also the large Moorcroft Collection.

(iii) *Other Private Papers*

Royal Society for Asian Affairs – R. Shakespear
Royal Geographical Society – Ney Elias

(iv) *Public Record Office: Foreign Office, General Correspondence*

China (FO/11/756 and 726).   Proposed Mission to Tibet, 1875-77.

Persia (FO/60/528, 535, 546, 562, 569 and 580)   Elias's despatches from Mashhad, 1891-1896.

B. Official Publications

(i) *India Office Library*

C. VALIKHANOV, M. VENUKOV and others, The Russians in Central Asia (Trs. J. and R. Michell) (London 1865)

J. B. M. HENNESSY, Report of an Exploration in Great Tibet and Mongolia by A——— K——— etc. (India 1884)

M. VENUKOV, P. LERCH, Articles. Trs. from Russian and German Sources. 2 Vols: Govt. of India: 1863-1877

W. LOCKHART and R. C. WOODTHORPE, Confidential Report of the Gilgit Mission 1885-86 (London 1889) and Summary of the principal measures of the Viceroyalty of the Marquess of Dufferin and Ava (Calcutta 1888)

M. G. GERARD, Report of the Pamirs Boundary Commission 1896 (Calcutta 1897)

(ii) *War Office Library*

V. POTTO, Steppe Campaigns, Lectures delivered in the Junker School, Orenburg (1872) and Notes on the Khivan Expedition (1873)

C. History

* Denotes extensive Bibliography, some also listing detailed Primary Sources.

G. J. ALDER,* *British India's Northern Frontier 1865-1895,* London 1963

J. ALLAN (Ed), *Cambridge Shorter History of India,* London 1934

E. M. ALMEDINGEM, *The Romanovs,* London 1966

BALFOUR, Lady Betty, *History of Lord Lytton's Indian Administration of 1876-80,* London 1899

S. BECKER,* *Russia's Protectorates in Central Asia, Bukhara and Khiva 1865-1924,* USA 1968

C. E. D. BLACK, *A Memoir of the Indian Surveys 1875-1890,* London 1891

LEON CAHUN, *Introduction à l'Histoire de l'Asie, Turcs et Mongols,* Paris 1896

O. CAROE, *The Soviet Empire,* London 1967 and *The Pathans,* London 1958

O. EDMUND CLUBB,* *China and Russia,* USA 1971

T. C. COEN, *The Indian Political Service,* London 1971

H. W. C. DAVIS, *The Great Game in Asia 1800-1844,* Raleigh Lecture, British Academy 1926

N. ELIAS (Ed), *History of the Moghuls of Central Asia,* London 1895 (Reprinted with Introduction by D. SINOR 1972)

BRIAN GARDNER, *The East India Company,* London 1971

DAVID GILLARD, *The Struggle for Asia 1828-1914,* London 1977

R. L. GREAVES,* *Persia and the Defence of India 1884-1892,* London 1959

V. GREGORIAN,* *The Emergence of Modern Afghanistan,* Stanford Press, USA 1969

J. G. GRIFFITHS, *Afghanistan,* London 1967

G. HAMBLY et al,* *Central Asia,* London 1969

M. HOLDSWORTH, *Turkestan in the Nineteenth Century,* London 1959

I. C. Y. HSU,* *The Ili Crisis,* London 1965

J. W. KAYE, *History of the War in Afghanistan* (2 volumes), London 1857

F. KAZEMZADEH,* *Russia and Britain in Persia 1864-1914,* USA 1968

JOHN KEAY, *The Gilgit Game,* London 1979

N. A. KHALFIN,* *Russia's Policy in Central Asia* (Abridged), Central Asian Research Centre (Bibliography gives Russian sources), London 1964

A. LAMB, *Britain and Chinese Central Asia. The Road to Lhasa 1767–1905,* London 1960; *Asian Frontiers,* London 1968 and *The China-India Border,* London 1964

O. LATTIMORE, *Inner Asian Frontiers of China,* London 1940 and *Studies in Frontier History,* London 1962

LOBANOV-ROSTOVSKIY, PRINCE, A., *Russia and Asia* (2nd Ed.), USA 1951

C. M. MACGREGOR, *The Defence of India,* Simla 1884

C. MARKHAM, *Memoir on the Indian Surveys* (2nd Ed.), 1878

C. MARVIN, *The Russian Campaign against the Turkomans,* London 1880 and *The Russian Advance towards India,* London 1882

J. L. MORISON *From Alexander Burnes to Frederick Roberts,* Raleigh Lecture, British Academy 1936

MOUNTSTUART ELPHINSTONE, *An Account of the Kingdom of Caubul,* 1815

J. A. NORRIS, *The First Afghan War 1838–42,* London 1967

W. H. PARKER, *An Historical Geography of Russia,* London 1968

B. A. H. PARRITT, *The Intelligencers: A History of the Intelligence Corps.,* Printed 1972

R. A. PIERCE, *Russian Central Asia 1867–1917,* USA 1960

V. POTIEMKINE (Ed), *Histoire de la Diplomatie* (Trs. from *Istoriya Diplomatii),* Paris 1946

R. K. QUESTED, *The Expansion of Russia in East Asia 1957–1960,* Singapore 1968

H. C. RAWLINSON, *England and Russia in the East,* London 1875

Y. SEMYONOV *The Conquest of Siberia* (Trs. E. W. Dickes), London 1944

V. A. SMITH (Ed.) *Oxford History of India,* 1957, (Pt III Re-written PERCIVAL SPEAR), 1967

M. A. TERENT'YEV, *History of the Conquest of Central Asia* (Trs. H. C. Daukes), 1876

C. WEBSTER, *The Foreign Policy of Palmerston 1830–1841* (2 Vols.), London 1951

G. E. WHEELER, *Modern History of Soviet Central Asia,* London 1964

P. WOODRUFF, *The Men who ruled India* (2 Vols.), London 1954

L. WOODWARD, *Oxford History of England, The Age of Reform 1815–70,* London 1962

M. E. YAPP, *British Policy in Central Asia 1830–1843* (Unpublished Thesis), London 1959

D.   Biography and Autobiography

C. AITCHISON, *Lord Lawrence,* London 1892

R. BOSWORTH-SMITH, *Life of Lord Lawrence* (2 Vols.), London 1885

D. C. BOULGER, *Central Asian Portraits*, London 1880

BROUGHTON, Lord (JOHN CAM HOBHOUSE), *Recollections of a Long Life*, Ed. Lady Dorchester, Vols V and VI, London 1834–52

E. FORSYTH (Ed.), *Autobiography and Reminiscences of Sir Douglas Forsyth*, London 1887

P. GUEDALLA, *Palmerston*, London 1927

W. H. HANNAH, *Bobs. Kipling's General*, London 1972

W. W. HUNTER, *Life of the Earl of Mayo*, London 1876

J. W. KAYE, *Lives of Indian Officers* (2nd Ed.), 1904

A. L. KENNEDY, *Salisbury. 1830–1903*, London 1953

A. LYALL, *Life of the Marquis of Dufferin and Ava*, London 1905

J. L. MORISON, *Lawrence of Lucknow*, London 1934

GERALD MORGAN, *Ney Elias*, London 1971

H. PEARSE, *Soldier and Traveller: Memories of Alexander Gardner*, London 1908

AGATHA RAMM, *Sir Robert Morier*, London 1973

GEORGE RAWLINSON, *A Memoir of Major General Sir Henry C. Rawlinson*, London 1898

DONALD RAYFIELD, *The Dream of Lhasa: The Life of Nikolay Przhevalsky (1839–88)*, London 1976

R. RHODES JAMES, *Lord Randolph Churchill*, London 1959

ROBERTS, Lord, *Forty One Years in India*, London 1897

G. SEAVER, *Francis Younghusband*, London 1952

C. P. SKRINE and PAMELA NIGHTINGALE, *Macartney at Kashgar*, London 1973

P. SYKES, *The Rt. Honourable Sir Mortimer Durand*, London 1926

S. E. WHEELER, *The Ameer: Abdur Rahman*, London 1895

E.   Travellers' Tales and Miscellaneous

J. ABBOTT, *Journey from Heraut to Khiva, Moscow and St. Petersburg* (2 Volumes) (3rd Ed.), London 1884

F. M. BAILEY, *Mission to Tashkent*, London 1946

F. BURNABY, *A Ride to Khiva*, London 1877

A. BURNES, *Travels to Bokhara etc.* (2 Volumes), London 1835

R. BURSLEM, *A Peep into Toorkistan*, London 1846

R. P. COBBOLD, *In Innermost Asia*, London 1900

A. CONOLLY, *Journey to the North of India, Overland* (2 Volumes), 1834

G. N. CURZON, *Russia in Central Asia*, London 1889 (reprinted Cass, 1967);

Persia and the Persian Question, London 1892 (reprinted Cass, 1966), and *The Pamirs and the Source of the Oxus* (Romanes Lecture), 1907

DUNMORE, Lord, *The Pamirs,* London 1893

JOHN KEAY, *Where Men and Mountains Meet,* London 1977

RUDYARD KIPLING, *Kim,* London 1901 and *Departmental Ditties,* London 1895

E. F. KNIGHT, *Where Three Empires Meet,* London 1903

O. LATTIMORE, *The Desert Road to Turkestan,* London 1933 and *High Tartary,* London 1940

J. A. MacGAHAN, *Campaign on the Oxus,* London 1874

J. MASSEY STEWART, *Across the Russias,* London 1969

N. PRZHEVALSKIY, *From Kulja across the Tien Shan to Lob Nor,* London 1879

RICHMOND SHAKESPEAR, *A Personal Narrative of a Journey from Heraut to Ohrenbourg on the Caspian in 1840,* Blackwoods Magazine No. CCCXX Vol. LI. Edinburgh June 1842

E. SCHUYLER, *Turkestan* (2 Volumes), London 1876

R. B. SHAW, *Visits to High Tartary, Yarkand and Kashgar,* London 1871

E. TEICHMAN, *Journey to Turkestan,* London 1937

J. WOOD, *Journey to the Source of the River Oxus,* London 1872 (Reprinted with Introduction by Geoffrey E. Wheeler 1976)

A. C. YATE, *The Afghan Boundary Commission* (Privately reprinted from *The Pioneer*) n.d.

C. E. YATE, *Khorasan and Sistan,* London 1900

F. YOUNGHUSBAND, *The Heart of a Continent,* London 1896

Index of People

Index of Places

Abbottsbad, 68, 107

Ab-i-Panjah river, 55, 204, 206

Afghanistan, xv, xvi, xvii, 6, 16, 18, 19, 26, 42, 43, 47, 53, 58, 59, 60, 61, 99, 101, 103, 106, 118, 122, 127, 128, 132, 143, 168, 170–82, 187, 188–99; British policy / relations, 20–21, 23–36, 47, 76, 78, 86, 128–9, 170, 173–82, 190–99, 200, 212–13; Iranian siege of Herat, 26, 27, 28–9; and First Afghan War, 29–31, 35–6, 48, 50, 51, 57, 226; Simla Proclamation (1842), 32–3; Dost Muhammad returns to throne, 50, 78; Burnes mission to, 53–4; unification under Abdur Rahman, 54, 56, 102, 104, 105, 188–9, 191, 220; local political allegiances and, 55; British and Russian spheres of influence, 58; northern frontier defined by Rawlinson, 58, 129; antagonism between Iran and, 76; reconquest of Balkh region, 78; and of Kunduz and Badakhshan, 79; Herat comes under rule of (1863), 79, 109; Russian policy/relations, 79, 80–81, 89, 127–9, 130, 170, 171–7, 180–1, 188–200; death of Dost Muhammad creates turmoil in, 109; Amir Sher Ali Khan becomes ruler of, 112–13; territorial possessions and boundaries, 128–9, 190–91; and Anglo-Russian Agreement (1873), 129, 171, 176, 191, 200, 206; espionage, 139, 146; abrogation of Anglo-Afghan agreement, 174–5, 176; growing influence of Russia on, 175, 176; Sher Ali re-opens negotiations with British, and retires in favour of son Yakub, 178–9; Treaty of Gandamak, 178–9, 181, 190; Second Afghan War, 178–81, 182; Abdur Rahman claims throne of, 179, 181; and agreement with Britain, 182; frontier settlements, 190–91, 192–3, 198–9, 212–13; Afghan Boundary Commission, 193, 197,

200; Penjdeh Incident, 193–7; Durand Agreement (on borders), 212; Soviet invasion of, 221, 222–4; and 1978 coup d'état, 222–3; see also Badakhshan; Hindu Kush

Akhal oasis, Russian annexation of (1883), 183–5

Ak-Mechet' (now Kzyl-Orda), Russian occupation of, 87

Aksu river (Murghab), 203–4

Aleksandrovsk, 43

Alichur Pamir, 204, 210

Ambala durbar (1869), 115–16, 127

Amu-Dar'ya river (Oxus), xv, xvi, 55, 58, 65, 81, 86, 88, 100, 103, 119, 128, 129, 144, 186, 193, 203, 204, 212–13; Russian ships' navigation rights on, 42, 92, 93, 96, 119; Duke Constantine's expedition to, 143–4; as Afghanistan's northern frontier, 170, 172, 190–91, 192

Amur river/region, 3, 4, 94, 95, 96

Andaman Islands, 116

Aral Sea, 86

Astrabad, 57

Astrakhan, 5

Badakhshan, xvi, 55, 56, 57, 117, 124, 138, 144, 145, 166, 190–91, 198, 200; Russia's recognition of Afghanistan's right to, 58, 171; Afghan reconquest of (1855), 79; Rawlinson supports Afghan claims to, 103, 128–9; Russian activities and survey parties in, 168, 210; Elias's exploratory mission to, 168, 202, 205, 206; Bukhara's claims to, 192

Bala Murghab, 193, 205, 206

Balkan States, 82

Balkh, 6, 54–5, 56, 78, 87, 109, 124, 168

Baluchistan, 21, 76, 82, 113, 116; British annexation of, 180, 185

Bar Panjah, 204

Baroghil pass, 202, 207, 209, 211

Black Sea, 5, 6, 173; Russian access to, 7, 43

sion of, 79; Hindu Kush as natural
frontier of, 80–81, 100; outside
dangers to, 81-2; Lawrence's 'close
border' policy, 82; East India Company wound up, 85; and Foreign
Office becomes major policy maker
for, 85; Governor-Generals and
Viceroys selected by British Prime
Minister, 100; Iranian policy of,
101–2, 104; relations between London and Calcutta, 105; Rawlinson's
forward policy and, 102–6; Lawrence's non-interventionist policy,
106–12; and John Lawrence appointed Viceroy of, 109; Lawrence's
Minute (1867), 109–12, 216, 220,
226–37; Lord Mayo succeeds Lawrence as Viceroy, 113–14; Lord
Northbrook appointed Viceroy,
116–17; Quetta acquired by, 116;
Northbrook's embargo on British
travellers and explorers, 116–17, 131,
151; Survey Department, 131, 134,
137, 144–5; espionage, 133–50;
newswriters, 141-2; British Army
intelligence, 146; private gunrunning
to Kashgar, 153–4; Chinese Turkestan and, 151, 153–5, 157–8, 160–61,
165–9; Hunza annexed by British,
169; Lord Lytton succeeds Northbrook as Viceroy, 171, 173–4; Lord
Ripon succeeds Lytton as Viceroy,
182; railway building, 186; see also
Britain; East India Co.
Indian Ocean, 147, 221, 223
Indus river, 21, 23, 80, 102, 180, 200;
Burnes' survey of, 53, 55, 144
Iran (Persia), 6, 7, 23, 24, 37, 40, 42, 43,
46, 56, 57, 72, 99, 116, 118, 122, 175;
British policy towards, 17–19, 20, 33,
76, 101–2, 104–6; and Treaty of
Tehran, 18; Russians seize Caucasus, 18; designs on Herat by, 18, 24;
and siege of Herat, 26, 27, 28–30, 33;
Russian relations with, 40, 46–7,
101; antagonism between Afghanis-
tan and, 76; and Anglo-Russian
rivalry, 83, 89, 101, 105; Khanyov
mission to Khorasan, 89–90; Anglo-
Persian War and Treaty, 102, 105,
109; Russian frontier with, 183–5;
Soviet Union and, 222, 223; and
American presence in, 223-4; see

also Khorasan
Ishkashim, 55, 144, 204

Jalalabad, 31
Japan, 159, 163

Kabul, 24, 26, 27, 30, 34, 53, 65, 78, 109,
110, 142, 146, 174, 176–7, 228, 230,
231, 232, 233; Vitkevich mission to,
30, 48, 72, 189; Ellenborough's punitive expedition to, 32, 35, 50, 74;
Burnes' mission to, 53–4, 72; Stoletov's mission to, 176, 180; British
Agent accepted by Amir at, 179,
180, 191; British occupation of,
179; Abdur Rahman's return to
claim throne, 179, 181, 189; see also
Afghanistan
Kafiristan, 201, 202
Kamchatka, 94
Kandahar, xvi, 26, 30, 57, 72, 84, 103,
104, 109, 116, 178, 180, 182, 189, 190,
228, 231; Vitkevich mission to, 33;
Rawlinson appointed Political Agent
at, 30, 57; British occupation of, 179,
220; and relief of, 179, 181
Kansu province, China, xv, 152, 159
Karakoram, xvii, 151, 154, 158, 165
Kara Kum desert, xvii, 183
Kashgar, xviii, 42, 90, 118, 122, 131, 145,
151, 153, 158, 166, 170; Valikhanov's
mission to, 90–91; Forsyth's missions to, 91, 131, 154; Russian consulate established, 96; Shaw and
Hayward's visits to, 131, 151, 153,
154, 155, 160; Yakub Beg's control
of, 152, 153–5, 157; private gunrunning to, 153–4; Chinese recovery of,
160; Elias's missions to, 161, 166–7,
168, 202, 203; British trade relations
with, 166–8; Macartney posted to,
169, 210
Kashgaria, 90, 115, 122, 151, 152, 153–5,
157, 160, 162, 165
Kashmir, xvi, xvii, 16, 17, 42, 82, 107,
138, 154, 166, 201, 211
Kataghan, 205
Kazakh SSR, xv, xviii
Kazakh steppes, Kazakhstan, xv, xviii,
5, 8, 122; Russian expansion in, 7,

General Index (including Treaties)

Afghan Boundary Commission, 193, 194, 195, 197, 200, 201, 203, 205, 206, 208, 209
Afghan War, First (1838–42), 15, 16, 22, 29–31, 35–6, 45, 48, 50, 51, 57, 70, 85, 103, 110, 146, 178, 180
Afghan War, Second (1878–9), 14, 178–81, 182
Afghans *see* Afghanistan
Ambans, 90, 167, 168
Anglo-Afghan Agreement (1859), 174–5
Anglo-Persian Treaty, (1857), 105
Anglo-Persian War (1856–57), 102, 105, 109
Anglo-Russian Agreement (1873), 129, 143, 171, 176, 191, 198, 212, 213
Anglo-Russian Convention (1907), 1, 75, 143, 220
Anglo-Sind Treaty (1834), 23
Asian nationalism, 222
Aziatskaya Rossiya (Asiatic Russia: 1914), 38–9, 218

Bengal Past and Present, 66
Blackwood's Magazine, 69
British Army Intelligence (in India), 146, 149
Burma-Siam Boundary Commission, 208
Burma-Yunnan mission, 157

Calcutta Review, 68
Congress of Berlin, 96–7, 126, 149, 161, 164, 176
Congress of Vienna, 121
Congress Socialist Party, India, 220, 221
Corps of Guides, Punjab, 108
Cossacks, xviii, 3, 5, 44–5, 49
Crimean War (1853–6), 40, 50, 78, 82–4, 87, 88, 92, 94, 105
Cuneiform script, 57

Durand Agreement (1893), 212

East India Company, 10, 11–13, 16, 18–19; *cordons sanitaires* established, 12; indirect rule over Indian states, 12; Political Service, 15, 51–2, 140–41; Board of Control, 22, 23, 24; Secret Committee, 22, 31, 33; non-intervention policy, 23, 24; First Afghan War, 30, 31; 1839 Blue Books alleged to have been censored, 31–2; work of early members of Political Department, 51–69; Topographical Department, 52; casualties suffered by Political Officers, 69–70; and improvement in status, 70, 107; 'doctrine of lapse' and expansion of India, 79; Indian Mutiny ends rule of, 85; British espionage and, 135–6; *see also* Britain; India
Eastern Question, 40, 46, 82–4, 172–3
Espionage, 132, 133–50; use of word 'agent', 134; misconceptions fostered by *Kim*, 134–5; 'spies' named by Khalfin, 136–7; 'Pundits', 137, 145; Survey Department of Government of India, 137, 144–5; Davis's paper on, 139–40; Indian Political Service/Officers, 140–41, 142–3; newswriters, 141–2; Indian traders, 142; British Army Intelligence, 146; Russian activities, 146–9; leakages of secret information, 149–50

Foreign Office, 85, 101, 105, 116
Frontiers and Overseas Expeditions from India, 81

'The Great Game', 20, 51, 215, 218; origins of, 15–16; Anglo-Russian common factors influencing, 74–5; Davis's paper on, 139–40
Great Soviet Encyclopaedia, 217
Great Trigonometrical Survey of India, 137, 145